Still NO
FIXED
ADDRESS

Still No Fixed Address is dedicated to
Kate and Jai, and David along with his Kate
and Mia and Ellie. They encourage me to spend
their inheritance and to desert them for months,
but always welcome me back—poorer financially
maybe, but richer in experiences
to share with them.

Still NO FIXED ADDRESS

Jackie Hartnell

PIER
9

CONTENTS

PEOPLE YOU'LL MEET

While journeying with me you will encounter the following companions (and I don't want you to get confused).

My husband

Ian: who died in 1997, and whose death somehow started all this

The sisters

Naomi: the oldest sister and my constant travelling companion, who lives in Australia

Me: the second sister and I live in Australia

Carole: the third sister who lives in England

June: the fourth sister who lives in England

Stepha (or Stephanie): the fifth sister who lives in Australia

My family (now well matured)

Kate: my oldest daughter

Dave (or David): second-born and my only son

Kate: Dave's wife (just to perplex you)

Jai (or Jane): my youngest daughter

Mia and Ellie: my granddaughters (Dave and Kate's girls)

Exchange students (from an earlier life)

Christian: from Denmark, who lived with us for ten months through 1990–91

Alexandra: from Germany, who lived with us for ten months through 1991–92

Saana: from Finland, who lived with us for six months in 1992

In-laws and out-laws

Rod: once partner, now husband of June

James: Carole's son, hence my nephew

Leanne: James' fiancée, now wife

John Austin-Smith: James' dad and once husband of Carole

Monica: a good friend and the Norwegian connection

Assorted others whose paths crossed with mine in various ways and places.

ONE

NO FIXED ADDRESS:
MEETINGS AND FAREWELLS

'Most people live and die
with their music still unplayed.
They never dare to try.'

—Mary Kay Ash

T erry has only been a widower for three months and is doing it hard. Living in the house he and Jill had shared, and where he'd nursed her through her last months has been too distressing. Trying to deal with the sympathy of friends in his tiny country town in South Australia and managing alone becomes unbearable. It's easier to run away than to stay. So at the suggestion of his two adult daughters he's taken off in the caravan that he and Jill had holidayed in for many years, with his dogs Storm and Ci Ci for company—but they're not enough and it's too soon.

I'm in North Queensland heading south in my campervan Ski2 and choose the camping spot at St Lawrence because it looks close to water. It isn't, but serendipity takes me there though I don't yet know Terry or his story.

The camping book shows the $ symbol for payment but I cannot see where to pay. So I park Ski2 and approach my neighbour who is unhitching his caravan from his car. 'Excuse me. Can you tell me where I pay?' He explains that camping is free but hot showers are coin-in-the-slot. I thank him, stroll over to check out the amenities, and fill my kettle for the long-awaited cup of tea—my starting point when I arrive anywhere.

My neighbour wanders over as I'm enjoying my tea, we introduce ourselves properly and I make him a cuppa. This is Terry, and he's come over to say how much he admires women like me who take off on their own in campervans and caravans. Eventually I glean that what he really means is

3

widows who have the courage to go travelling alone and, more importantly, move forward in their lives.

I'm in the right place at the right time and as Terry's story unfolds I understand completely. Although my first solo journey eighteen months after Ian dies is an adventure and a chance to find out how much I like travelling, it is also an escape from the reality of an empty house. Terry hates being on his own in his van and when we meet he is going home—his daughters' idea may have been a good one, but not yet.

For the first time since Jill's death Terry starts talking about her dying and how he feels. I'm pretty sure he would have found it hard talking to just anyone—but once he discovers his first assumption is correct and that I am a widow, and particularly because Ian also died of cancer, he senses that I will understand what he has been through and the floodgates open.

He's trying to be tough. A woman can break down and cry in the face of sympathy but many men, particularly of our generation, don't believe they can. He hasn't realised that he needs to give himself time to accept his loss and allow the grief to heal. I can tell him this, strangers who meet briefly can say things that friends and family cannot.

Terry's two gorgeous dogs quickly find their way into my heart (and I could have kidnapped Storm, his Border collie), so when I return from my evening walk—looking for the inlet that isn't there—I ask him if he would like to walk the dogs with me in the morning. He would, and we have three walks together because we meet again at the free camping

4

spot by the Calliope River next evening. In retrospect I wonder if his healing began there as we shared a drink together, absorbing the tranquillity and beauty of a sunset over the water.

By the second morning Terry is talking about himself, his past and his working life, not just about Jill and his sadness. He's very down to earth—an ex-shearer/truckie/barley classer—and a good, kind bloke. Our relationship is one of kindred spirits despite being at opposite ends of almost every spectrum. And we don't even touch on religion or politics!

On our last walk he tells me he cannot understand 'what I see in him'. He says, 'You're an intelligent, educated lady, I'm rough as guts.' But as I write in my journal: 'Maybe he is, but he's sensitive for all that'. He describes us as ships that pass in the night and he's correct. But for him I am the right ship on the right night.

I tell Terry that it took me five years to let Ian go completely; to free myself of subconsciously needing his approval for everything I did; to believe that without him I, and my life, had value. But more importantly, it was a lot less than five years before I started enjoying myself again. As we say goodbye Terry says I've helped him though I'm not sure that the healing will continue. But it does. I've been in touch with him a few times since and he has found a lady friend and new happiness. Strange how chance plays such a large part in our lives; I often wonder what or who took me to that particular spot that evening to camp next to Terry.

Around thirty years ago I realised that almost everyone you meet has something in common with you. I have now taken numerous solo journeys and it surprises me how often travellers not only find things to discuss and agree upon (or otherwise), but also provide shoulders to cry on, laughter to lighten sadness, companionship, and tea and sympathy when needed—there are many ships that pass in the night.

I meet a young couple from the United Kingdom in a camping spot at the Barclay Homestead in the Northern Territory. When setting up and sitting with that first cup of tea I notice that there is an ant plague and move my chair many times—from dust to scant grass and back again—in the hope of escaping them. But to no avail and conclude that as long as I keep them out of my tea I'll survive.

Shortly afterwards a station wagon pulls in nearby, a young man gets out, opens the rear door and starts unloading. A few moments later a young woman joins him and they set up chairs and a gas stove, preparing for their evening. Suddenly she starts behaving as I had: slapping her legs, jumping around, doing the ant-avoidance dance. Finally she bursts into tears. My motherly instincts take over and I ask them if they'll join me for a cup of tea. They do and we spend the evening together, sharing a meal, sitting outside as the day eases into night, laughing as we fight the ants. They have been travelling for months; moving constantly, packing and unpacking, sleeping in the station wagon, and for her the ants were the final straw. It's hard yakka doing it that way and all it needed was a cup of tea, a sympathetic ear, and let's be honest a couple of glasses of red probably helped too. But spending the evening with someone else, talking about the things that

6

get lost in the mundaneness of every day, exchanging life stories and being open and honest, knowing that you'll probably never see that person again, helps put things back into perspective.

And it works both ways. When I'm feeling lonely, miserable or wondering why I'm on this road alone, sharing time with strangers also lifts my spirits, I don't only approach people when I sense they might need something, but also when I have a need. Often simply exchanging smiles with other travellers is all that's required for an invitation to chat. It's surprising how many times it leads to bottles of nectar being broached and enjoyed together, and evenings or meals shared around a camp fire.

This second book of my travel tales includes journeys spanning eight years. In these pages you will briefly discover some of the people I've met over those years who turned out to be more than ships in the night. I'm off to Europe next year before my joints get too creaky for those long flights, to visit at least four families I've shared camp fires or kitchens with.

After so much itinerant behaviour you'd think it would be out of my system; but I still have the travel bug, I still love leaving (and returning), I still have no fixed address. So join me as I become an 'exchange parent' to a young couple in Norway in 2005; in a crazy few days with all the sisters for a wedding; in my adventures with Jai in Cambodia early in 2006, and in Cambodia and Vietnam with Naomi at the end of that year. And in tales of earlier adventures like my first long solo trip in Ski2 to Darwin, and to assorted overseas destinations with my backpack and walking boots.

My journeys and my campervan are labelled 'Ski' because I'm 'Spending the Kids' Inheritance'. Ski10 will be my journey to write a book in Cambodia, that trip to Europe will be Ski11 and who knows where Ski12 will take me. But because I travel 'on a shoestring' I may be a centenarian before I spend it all. My kids (now in their thirties and forties) get as excited about my expeditions as I do. I suspect they see possibilities for *their* futures stretching ahead.

When I'm overseas on my own I stay in hostels, but when travelling with someone else we stay at hotels from the 'cheap' accommodation section of the relevant travel guide, and I always use public transport. If possible I cater for myself wherever I am. In Australia Ski2 and I stay in free camping spots, unpowered caravan sites and national and state parks. Even if I could afford to go luxury I wouldn't. I no longer travel this way just for economy—it's too much fun meeting other travellers and locals in hostel kitchens, by camp fires, and in buses and trains to do it any other way. I would be much more alone in three-star hotels and motels, or in a car.

Over the last few years, while travelling and writing, I have become more settled and content than ever before in my life, less needy of other people and their approval—just as well because writing is a solo activity, with no guarantee of praise from anyone. My contentment comes from meeting the challenges of the journeys and a new-found satisfaction in describing them in words. Six months of each of these activities a year seems pretty good to me—and travelling as cheaply as I do makes that possible.

But despite this contentment I have discovered recently that when I'm away I miss my family more than I used to. Since I started as a solo peripatetic person it's become no harder to leave, but the need to keep in touch with Kate, Dave and Jai and get back to them sooner puzzles me—am I starting to sense my mortality I wonder.

When I first retired I travelled for seven months and assumed that the miseries that struck were because I had been widowed a relatively short time, and was getting used to being on my own and jobless after forty years of paid employment and duty to others. But maybe I was just away from my kids for too long. Since then four months is the longest I've stayed away from home, but it is time to cut that string that holds me to them—unconscious and unwanted on their part, and fair to none of us. I have two longer journeys planned, each of at least six months. The first in late 2007, when I will live in Phnom Penh to write a book in Cambodia; the other when I take Ski2 to northern and western Australia where I want to be able to stay a while if I find somewhere I like. It will be interesting to see how I go.

My granddaughters are now becoming used to the idea that I'm not always around. When they say, 'No more long holidays Manny'—of course to them anything more than a fortnight is a long time—I say, 'Sorry kids, it's what I do.' They accept it, knowing most importantly that I love and miss them when I'm away. There will be many years after I've hung up my walking boots, passport and Ski2's keys that they can get their fill of me.

9

And whether you are alone or not, travelling isn't always on an even keel or a smooth sea and there are emotional roller coasters throughout any journey (how about a few mixed metaphors!). Be aware that this is normal. All travel, from the most luxurious to the shortest shoestring, will include emotional experiences triggered by your surroundings, your uncertainties, and your history and cultural background whatever they might be. If you have travelled without these soaring and plunging emotions, these moments of disquietude and times of tranquillity, maybe you have missed half the journey.

For me anxiety is part of my travel preparation. Going away for anything more than a few days brings pre-departure nerves, and no matter where I am I find myself getting anxious as I approach any new travel event. Whether it's a flight to Morocco, a bus to Scotland, a walk in New Zealand, or an upcoming trip with Ski2 to a new national park. It's that fear of moving from the known to the unknown. But the anxiety is replaced with excitement as soon as I'm walking towards the plane, sitting on the bus, driving out of my driveway, or pulling into a camp site. However mundane the experience sounds, if it's new it's exhilarating and frightening at the same time.

One of the tales in this book describes my first visit to Cambodia. Jai is to meet me at the airport in Phnom Penh as I will be spending most of my time with her; I don't have to worry about getting from the airport, finding somewhere to stay, how another foreign country 'works', or the language. And yet the same old anxiety is there to greet me as I wake each morning in the week before I leave. But it goes once it's too late to worry about whether I should have done any more preparation, whether I have enough US dollars, if I've had all the vaccinations ...

On my first overseas trip, I certainly felt more moments of misery than I have felt since or than you will probably experience on your journeys unless, like Terry, you take off on your own too soon after the loss of a partner. My unhappiness had a lot to do with a journey that was more than the places I visited—it was a journey of change and growth. When planning it, and even as I left home, I believed that it was a holiday and I was doing it for pleasure. Was I kidding myself or being incredibly naive? Looking back I wonder why I didn't realise how hard it would be. I must have been crazy, but I found strengths I was unaware of, and have never regretted it.

Thinking back to all of my travels over these few years, the positives far outweigh the negatives—pretty obvious I suppose, else why would I keep going. But it's important for you to know that the hard times can seem *so* hard when you are in the middle of them, but that they pass quickly, and the good times roll around again. And again. And again.

So let this book take you to places you haven't been and maybe some you have, or to share adventures you might not want to experience yourself. But most importantly, let it help you take a step into the unknown and take up the challenge of something you have always wanted to do but never quite had the courage to begin.

'I have wandered all my life, and I have
travelled; the difference between the two
is this: we wander for distraction,
but we travel for fulfillment.'

—Hillaire Belloc

TWO

SENTIMENTAL JOURNEYS FROM CORNWALL TO NEWCASTLE

CORNWALL, A PLACE OF MEMORIES
AND FIRST LOVE

As children we visited the village of St Agnes on Cornwall's north coast because our French grandmother had a cottage there. Every summer from 1951 to 1959 we spent two weeks of our school holidays with her; first with our father, then later just my three sisters and me travelling on our own by train to Truro (we didn't find June, our fifth sister, until after my mother died). We had marvellous holidays. Granny was wonderful and many things our mother wasn't—patient, tiny, loving, understanding—and St Agnes was one of the few English coastal villages with surf and a surf lifesaving club. Imagine it: four sisters growing into their teens, hormones on the run and these gorgeous tanned, fit boys in brief bathers and funny hats. We spent a lot of time in their clubhouse hoping to be noticed.

The year I was seventeen I sat on and broke my glasses in that clubhouse. It took a week for new ones to arrive from home, but what a week I had. Suddenly I wasn't the ugly one in glasses, I was as beautiful as my sisters and because I believed it I probably was. I couldn't see a thing—I recognised people by the blurred colours of their clothes and used my ears to cross the road—but it didn't matter. Naomi lent me a strapless dress: white with red roses and green leaves, a full skirt with one of those stiff petticoats and somehow I managed to keep it up—small breasts not withstanding.

One of the lifesavers was called Gerry. I can still picture him: shortish, chunky, curly dark hair and a lovely smile. His

14

dad owned the pub and he was home from his job in a mine in west Africa; I must have been a traveller at heart even then because it sounded so exotic that I suspect that is what I fell in love with. We 'went out' for the rest of my holiday, me refusing to wear my glasses even when they arrived. I was madly in love, and those hot moments in the back of his car were a revelation and a wonderful introduction to my sexuality—probably quite innocent by today's standards. We kept in touch by letter for a couple of years though we never met again.

Strange how events coincide. Three years later I was engaged to Robbie, an installation engineer at Marconi's where I was an apprentice electrical engineer. His job took him to foreign parts to install communications equipment. Just as exotic, and this time I definitely fell for the romance of foreign places not the man. I could see myself travelling the world—and I thought I could put up with him if that's what it took. What a schemer! Luckily before we tied the knot I realised that I didn't even like him, and breaking off that engagement was one of the catalysts in my emigrating to Australia, so I'm eternally grateful to him. And my final certainty that I should break off the engagement happened in Cornwall.

I had some South African friends who wanted to visit Cornwall but weren't allowed to drive on their South African licences—at least that's what they told me but I suspect I was better value than hiring a car. Robbie was in Aden and we planned a 'girls weekend' in Fowey on the south Cornwall coast over Easter. It's no big deal driving almost 500 kilometres for a four-day break in Australia, but it definitely was in England.

I drove a 1936 Austin 10, a fantastic first car but with a design fault—sometimes if the front and rear doors were opened at the same time their edges met. And they did that on a hill with my left hand gripping one door's edge, the engagement ring was crushed into my finger and its three diamonds fell out. You can imagine the disbelief as we scrabbled in the dirt and told interested passers-by we were looking for diamonds! We found them but this was definitely a sign that our marriage was not supposed to be. My finger recovered, I had the ring restored and returned it to Robbie.

So, not only do I love Cornwall's wildness but it has a special place in my heart. If I had to return to the United Kingdom to live I would be hard put to choose between Edinburgh (my favourite city) and a village in Cornwall.

WILD WALKS, GAMES AND CONVERSATIONS

When I arrive in England in September 1998 on my first journey after Ian dies, Carole rents a cottage for a week at Sennen Cove on the north Cornwall coast. She thinks it will be a great opportunity to relax and get to know each other. And she is absolutely right.

Sennen Cove is a beautiful spot like many on Cornwall's north coast and easy to enjoy; a tiny village, peaceful and sunny one day, wildly wind-blown the next, fishing nets and steep lanes dropping to the harbour. Carole, her husband

16

John and their children James and Kate spent their summer holidays here for years, but this time James and his girlfriend Leanne share it with us; John staying home to bring in the bacon, and Kate has bigger fish to fry than a holiday with mum and aunt.

It's a real 'holiday' week. Each morning waking to the sound of breaking waves, each evening playing games until late. But Carole and John are having marital problems so her brain is all over the place, as is mine—it's less than two years since Ian died and I think I'm reinventing myself. So James, a games fiend, is usually the winner; though word games are my thing and I Boggle them to death. One night we go nine-pin bowling (the forerunner of ten-pin) and I'm champion of that too, though I must have had a few glasses of red first.

We visit a few local towns whose names I've known forever but never got close to visiting. One morning it's Penzance—the flea market, the narrow and steep lanes, the fish shop. Another day it's St Ives. 'As I was going to St Ives I met a man with seven wives ...' is a still remembered puzzle from my childhood. We start at the Tate at St Ives where much of the collection is paintings by people who have made Cornwall their home and subject. The gallery, an interesting building on the cliffs above the beach, incorporates light and elegant curves in its design, and the stained-glass window at the entrance is as beautiful as any artwork.

We also visit Barbara Hepworth's studio that includes the workshop in which she sculpted, and a garden filled with her sculptures. I love her work: large outdoor pieces in stone

17

and metal, some softly rounded others straight-edged, many with holes through which glimpses of other sculptures can be seen.

Carole isn't yet a tramper like me but is prepared to follow my lead. We have a book of local walks and our first, on an overcast and windy day, is to Lands End—to see how we, and the weather, will go. Hard to believe I've never been to Lands End but Granny didn't drive and once we were in St Agnes that's where we stayed.

The whole walk is only about eight kilometres, a breeze even for Carole, and we are spoilt with magnificent views, wild scenery and winds—the iconic Cornish walk. I'm expecting an isolated headland, but that it isn't. Lands End is now a 'complex' with an old pub, to which a modern section and a 'conservatory' eating area have been added, an animal display and other outside attractions. But we feel like locals rather than tourists so walk past that lot. On the inland track home we unexpectedly find an art and glass sculpture gallery and tearoom where we admire the glasswork and enjoy teacakes and tea. It's in one of the villages whose name begins Tre...; unfortunately I've lost the rest in my brain somewhere, but there's an old saying 'By Tre, Pol and Pen ye shall know your Cornishmen' that applies also to place names.

At Mousehole (pronounced Mousel), perhaps one of the most beautiful Cornish villages, I find all my Christmas presents for Australia in one shop. The goods are perfect and the owner has a great sense of humour; probably helped by his first customer for the day spending £69. There are of

18

course other shops and galleries in which to wander, cafés for cappuccino and teacake, and I find a rain jacket for £15 that saves my life many times later on this journey. Carole's husband John has told us to have one meal on him, so we return one evening to an excellent restaurant where we both eat too much!

We pay for this over-indulgence next day with extra walking, starting by striding the beach before breakfast. Then to Lamorna Cove for a long, hard circuit walk—so badly described in the book of local walks that we get lost twice and I get attacked by stinging nettles while trying to find the track. In the end a helpful farmer's wife (who tells us she often rescues walkers using this particular book) leads us through their property to the coast path. We feel much better after tramping 15 kilometres.

Carole and I have the last day alone. Yet I wake early, slightly sad. Maybe because we talked for hours into the night about Ian, and the problems she and John are having. But also, even though I'm trying to cut the emotional cord that ties me to my kids, I am missing them—probably exacerbated by my pleasure in James and Leanne's company.

Getting up and at the day is how I deal with these periods of sadness, so Carole and I pack lunch and go tramping around St Just and Cape Cornwall. The view from the end of the Cape is fantastic: to the horizon and all we can see are rocky islets, a lighthouse and a single yacht. And we make it to a craggy outcrop for lunch; just us with another amazing view, a drop below and a three-masted sailing ship.

19

On our way back to Carole's home in Torquay we revisit St Agnes for the first time in forty years. We have many questions. Will it look the same? Will we find and recognise Polbreen Lane where Granny's cottage was? Will the cottage still be there?

St Agnes has exploded with caravan parks and modern estates around the edges but the village centre looks exactly the same—although I don't remember the video shop! Polbreen Lane, though now surfaced, looks unchanged and the cottage much as we remember. The present owner takes a photo of us in front of the flower-covered porch and insists we look through the cottage. It is so tiny that I wonder how on earth Granny fitted us all in. It hasn't changed much except that a small bathroom has been added—we used to wash in a basin of water and cross a small backyard to an outside loo.

We drive down to the beach, stopping on the way for Cornish pasties at the same pastie shop where, as children, we would order them on our way to the beach then walk up to collect them at lunchtime. It's now very up-market and has designer pasties, not just the traditional meat, potatoes and turnip but vegetarian, Asian and chicken; and perhaps they are no longer baked out the back, though they are as delicious as we remember. We sit on the beach—that looks smaller—and it's just as cold as it was in the 1950s. We've forgotten our thermos of cocoa so give swimming a miss!

After lunch we return to the village for a drink at the pub. The barman tells us that it has changed hands only twice in forty years and that many of those surf lifesavers still live locally. Above the bar is a photo of the St Agnes golf squad and some of those rotund older men are the golden heroes of our youth, including Gerry who came back from Africa and ran the pub. Oh, dear! Unfortunately they are all 'over to Perranporth' for a surf carnival so we can't catch up with them. Maybe just as well.

This week has been one of seesawing emotions, as I haven't spent much time with Carole since I left home at eighteen and we have a lot of catching up to do. We discover that as we have aged we have become more alike—in our outlook on life, our child-rearing philosophy, our sense of humour, and our sense of the ridiculous. It's on our wild walks and in the shared bedroom that Carole and I get to know each other again. We talk non-stop and long into the nights: analysing how our unhappy childhood affected our adult life; discussing menopause and masturbation, love and lust, widowhood and wonderful memories; hours of laughter, tears and hugs. And rueful grins exchanged as we squeeze our sagging bodies into our bathers.

LOOKING FOR CONNECTIONS AND WALKING THE WALL

My father was born in Newcastle-upon-Tyne and was brought up there until he was seventeen, by which time both his mother and father had died. I spent a couple of days 'interviewing' him earlier in this journey trying to find out what made him the man he is, and although my feelings about him are ambivalent I am looking for a connection with him and hoping to feel something special here in Newcastle.

Had I started genealogical research with tombstones to search out and city records to find, maybe it would bring me closer to him—but I haven't.

I'm also here because a lifelong dream is to walk on Hadrian's Wall. Coincidentally, at the start of this journey, I visit Alexandra in Stuttgart and we spend a day in the country northwest of the city. On our way back we explore part of the limes wall and towers that were built by the Romans to protect Germany against the Celtic invasion from the south. And although Hadrian's Wall was constructed to defend Roman Britain against Celts from the north, I love the congruity of these two constructions.

I have a quick exploration of Newcastle finding tourist information and then the hostel but note in my journal: '*Must* listen better to instructions', so I suspect I got well lost finding these two destinations.

Late November is *not* a good time to be a tourist in England and Vindolanda, the most popular and easily accessible section of the wall from Newcastle, is closed. Luckily Lawrence who runs the youth hostel is a great Hadrian's Wall enthusiast and lends me a book about it, gives me maps, recommends Housesteads as an alternative, and tells me which buses will get me there and back.

The Housesteads Roman Fort section of Hadrian's Wall is described as 'the most complete Roman Fort in Britain' and 'the best preserved of thirteen outposts along the wall'. I have the Wall to myself and walk about two kilometres of it, and though all that remains are ruins, the outline of the fort and civic settlement is still obvious; it is wonderful to wander among rooms divided by low wall remnants. Housesteads contains not only the last remaining visible example of a Roman hospital in Britain, but also well-preserved latrines that housed some of the earliest-known flushing toilets—designed and built almost 2000 years ago.

At one point, where the Wall rises vertically about four metres from the ground, I look north to panoramic views and imagine patrolling soldiers staring into the uninterrupted distance. And the Wall snaking east and west as far as I can see increases my wonder at the engineering feat it embodies. The Wall's narrow ridge backs onto an earthen embankment supported by a retaining wall, forming a platform on which the Romans fought attack from the north. I find it wonderful that I am possibly standing in the footprints left by a Roman soldier.

Like other ruins I've visited in the United Kingdom—including the Avebury circles in Wiltshire that are believed to be 4000 years old—much of the damage to the Wall is due to neglect rather than wars. Stones were constantly taken by local people for buildings—an early example of our modern practice of re-use. But it's good to see the history of places in 'living' walls rather than just in ruins.

The Geordies (people from the Tyne-Newcastle region) I meet are friendly and I love their accent, which I describe as 'unique but much Scots in burr and some words'. I am invited to chat to locals on all the buses I catch on my day at Hadrian's Wall and get wonderful village-life stories and local gossip; even a group of school kids at a bus stop invite me into their conversation.

23

Another benefit in travelling on local buses is that I can enjoy the countryside. Here it is a mixture of rolling dales and hills that remind me of the Lake District—without the lakes. The original houses are in beautiful gold-grey sandstone that reflects the surrounding carpets of red and gold autumn leaves. Sadly though, even in villages, new houses are built of brick—probably a reflection of availability of materials, cost and convenience.

I spend a morning in Newcastle, before catching the coach to York, and start at a gallery called Makers at Blackfriars that is housed in a restored thirteenth-century friary in Newcastle's centre. Blackfriars has been through assorted incarnations over more than 700 years and both the building and its current contents are absolutely beautiful. As well as housing an exhibition detailing the history and development of Newcastle, it is also a co-op of local artists: craft workshops, a gallery and a shop retailing their products. They have some of the loveliest items I've ever seen in wood, jewellery, pottery and textile and it takes me completely by surprise. I spend a happy few hours at this creative oasis in what had seemed an otherwise industrial desert, and for the first time on this journey I'm tempted to buy something for myself. Unfortunately (or maybe fortunately) neither my backpack nor wallet is bottomless.

24

Newcastle was built in 1080 and there are fragments of ancient parts—a wall, tower, turrets—but where I'm walking is industrialised and they seem incongruous. I'm sure there are attractive areas but they're somewhere else, and in my journal I describe it as 'old and rather nasty, and dirty new'. Sounds a bit harsh, doesn't it? Obviously I'd hoped for something 'nicer' and maybe it's an echo of my sadness in not finding a connection to my father. The Discovery Museum, supposed to be one of Britain's best displays of a city's history, also disappoints me. The exhibit showing 'Development of City' only refers to its development from the industrial revolution onwards; and I wonder if the designer of this display forgot Newcastle is at one end of Hadrian's Wall.

POOR YORK, SHE HAS TO COMPETE WITH EDINBURGH

York is a little disappointing but maybe because I'm still in the thrall of Edinburgh which I loved. But the people at tourist information don't help—curt, and grudgingly answering my questions. And when I reach the youth hostel I'm treated similarly, most unusual in my experience to date. This hostel was once a hotel and seems to think it still is— reflected in the cost and treatment of guests. There is a full-on reception desk, a restaurant instead of just a dining room with cheap meals for those who want them, and a very impoverished kitchen—and an attitude towards those who wish to self-cater. But no restaurant for me, thank you; I shop, cook dinner and enjoy the evening with a family from Torquay (in Victoria not Devon) and Vivienne from Mittagong south of Sydney. As often happens someone has stolen the matches from the kitchen and I have to pay for another box—normally I'm just given a new one. We Aussies

25

agree over dinner the 'meanness' here is definitely not the YHA attitude we're used to.

So next day I check out Micklehurst, a new backpackers hostel recommended to me in Edinburgh and for which I have a discount voucher. It is a marvellous Georgian house with large rooms—including a non-smoking TV lounge with comfortable chairs—and friendly and helpful young people running it; very different to the youth hostel. It is newly opened which may account for the friendly service and excellent condition, but maybe not—it could just be the attitude of the manager. It feels welcoming, is spacious, in the centre of everything *and* £5 a night cheaper. No thought required—I tell them I'll be back later.

I manage to trek around one-third of York's city wall before cold and hunger send me back to the hostel for lunch. As I'm checking out, a young man at reception helps reverse my bad impression. I mention that I want to get away from cities but am having trouble trying to coordinate buses, hostels and what I want to do; he suggests Sherwood Forest and is sure I can get there by bus. I picture something similar to the New Forest, in which I have tramped many miles, and happily agree to Sherwood Forest and Robin Hood. I cheekily use their book-a-bed-ahead system to book into the Sherwood hostel before leaving.

After moving into Micklehurst I finish walking the wall enjoying the contrasts within and without: inside are historic houses and elegant gardens of the old city; outside are parks, modern architecture, residential areas and constant noise of traffic. And as well as the bird's-eye view of York, like Hadrian's Wall, I also love the fact that I am walking where soldiers patrolled centuries before. And there's so much of it: York has more miles of intact city walls than anywhere else in England. I discover that some sections date back to Roman times, including a multi-angular tower from the third century that has ten sides, is almost ten metres high and is the only remaining Anglo-Saxon tower in England. But the majority of the wall dates from the twelfth to fourteenth centuries—quite new really! It's impossible not to feel its history as I tread the wall.

I explore the three main gateways that lead into the old city, enjoying the different pictures they offer of York's history. The 'Bar' in the gates' names refers to a simple bar that crossed the gate to stop traffic so that tolls could be collected. Micklegate Bar, the traditional entry point for kings and queens visiting York, is the main entrance to the city and was where traitors' heads were displayed—often for years—to deter rebellion. Yuck! Micklegate is four storeys high, and the living quarters on its upper floor are now a museum where I read up on the history of the Bar and York. I wish I could say I remember it all, but alas, no.

Bootham Bar still contains medieval stonework from the eleventh century, some of the earliest in the wall, and though Monk Bar is the most elaborate gate it is but a youngster, dating just from the early fourteenth century. Monk also has a four-storey gatehouse with an interactive museum where I attend a 'trial' to ascertain whether Richard III was an evil uncle or a maligned and courageous king. I cannot decide; too many preconceptions thanks to Shakespeare.

York Minster, originally built in the first century and said to be the largest Gothic cathedral of northern Europe, has been through numerous invasions, destructions and rebuilding. The result is a collection of architectural styles ranging from eleventh century reconstruction to a section that was rebuilt in 1984 after a fire. There are examples of whimsical gargoyles, stunning stained-glass windows, towering columns and carved pews, the usual paraphernalia of European cathedrals. But what makes this minster particularly beautiful are the 'Five Sisters' in the North Transept—delicately coloured and elegant lancet windows that stretch tall and slender to the arched roof.

I attend evensong in the minster—truly beautiful and it sounds wonderful in that space. Another evening I do a 'ghost' walk, something I always try to do if it's on offer. Most of these medieval towns in the United Kingdom have their ghosts of course so there's bound to be someone happy to walk the walk and tell the stories for a small donation. The guide is a natural actor and very dramatic and though I can't take it all seriously it's good fun. The most credible story is of a man who apparently saw Roman soldiers and horses— from knee height up—where later excavations found Roman ruins at about knee height below current ground level.

Beverley, near York, is supposed to be one of the most beautiful small towns in Britain and I go there for a day. Its minster, said to be one of the finest examples of a Gothic church of cathedral size in Europe, was founded early in the eighth century although the present building only dates back to 1220 due to damage during Viking invasions and the

Norman Conquest. The carvings are superb: beautiful, amusing and moving, and all display fine detail of facial expressions and clothing, and distinctly suggestive poses.

However I prefer Beverley's tiny St Mary's Church. Built in the twelfth century it has wonderful gargoyles, and carvings including a 'pilgrim' rabbit that is said to have inspired Lewis Carrol's white rabbit in *Alice in Wonderland* (his grandfather was a rector of St Mary's). More famous is a unique stone carving of five musicians that was donated by the Northern Guild of Musicians during the church's reconstruction in the 1520s. Nobody seems to know exactly who they were; they are simply referred to as Beverley's 'Minstrels' or 'Guild of Musicians'.

St Mary's is also famous for its Green Man carvings: depictions of a face surrounded by or made from leaves, branches or vines. Found in many cultures they are often associated with places of worship; and plenty of UK pubs are called The Green Man. Worship of a different sort!

I finally do a guided tour of York with a voluntary guide. Like many volunteers Geoff is so enthusiastic about his city that I cannot help but get caught up in his passion. He makes the history interesting, and as well as confirming details I've already unearthed I learn new facts. I hear about St Leonard's Hospital originating from an idea of welfare for the poor by King Athelstan in the tenth century; and further history of York's Anglo-Saxon era. During earlier explorations I had been touched by the stark beauty of the ruins of St Mary's Abbey and hope to learn more of this building. Unfortunately it isn't included in Geoff's tour but

29

he tells me it was founded by King William Rufus in 1088 and was a Benedictine abbey until the sixteenth century.

I hear of St Margaret of York and go to find her house. Margaret Clitherow who lived in the sixth century was quite a woman. She became a catholic on marriage then refused to deny it; hiding priests, allowing secret masses to be held at her house and, at the age of thirty, was crushed to death rather than renounce. Margaret's tiny house is now a shrine and in 1970 she was canonised by Pope Paul VI.

On my last morning I return to The Kings Manor, a place that weaves a continuous thread through the history of York. It has been a seat of government, a school, and residences that include the house where James VI of Scotland was accepted as James I of England. This square of beautiful architecture, now part of the University of York, gives me a superb medieval bite.

The Jorvik experience starts with a ride in a Viking longboat on a waterway where archaeologists discovered the remains of the Viking city of Jorvik beneath York. I journey through an apparently accurate re-creation of the city in Viking times—its smells, sounds and sights. I try to avoid 'tourist attractions' but the seeming authenticity of this one keeps me involved. Though I note in my journal: 'no more expensive touristy stuff!', so it wasn't super-interesting, and I enjoy the museum more. I felt the same about Richard III's trial in Monks Bar and conclude that I'm a reader and wanderer rather than a listener.

Even though York doesn't grab me like Edinburgh did, after five days I feel I could stay longer and I love the

30

atmosphere at the backpackers. But it's time to move on to Sherwood.

A SEARCH FOR ROBIN HOOD
AND ALL THAT

I spend two days in Sherwood Forest at Edwinstowe the newest youth hostel in the United Kingdom. It's only been open four months, is modern with Scandinavian-style furniture in timber and leather (or faux leather) but is warm and welcoming. It is environmentally friendly with sensors that somehow know when a room is empty and turn the heaters off, rainwater to flush the loos, and timed shower and taps—though I need to wash my hair and the timers are draconian. But some things never change: the matches have been stolen in the member's kitchen and the toaster is too narrow for muffins. Oh the hardships of hostelling!

At first I'm the only guest and that feels quite strange, particularly as one of the things I love about hostelling is meeting other travellers; this changes as families of two wardens from other hostels arrive to stay and a group of incredibly well-behaved primary school children arrive. I only see them at dinner—no noisy running up and down corridors or other behaviour I associate with kids on school camps—but enjoy chatting to their teachers before bed.

The village of Edwinstowe is named after King Edwin who ruled Northumbria in the seventh century. Edwin was killed in battle nearby and it is said that his friends secretly buried him in Sherwood Forest so his enemies would not steal his body. The friends later returned and built a small wooden church on his grave. By now his subjects called him Saint Edwin, so the village was named Edwinstowe—the holy place of Edwin. My exploration of it takes all of an hour and I find a cross on a pile of stones with a sign that says it marks where the church once stood.

Later while walking in Sherwood Forest I meet a local who has lived here for seventy years. His story of Edwinstowe's cross and cairn is that it's just a pile of stones left from King Edwin's chapel of the seventh century. I'm sure this must be the cross and pile of stones that I saw but don't argue with him; he's a local and I'm just an upstart colonial. And we all look the same I gather, because our conversation begins before I've even opened my mouth when he confuses me with an Australian woman he had met three months earlier who 'looked just like you'!

I'm here to walk in Sherwood Forest—romantic notions about Robin Hood, Maid Marion and their socialist ideals—and start early to walk as far as possible, but unfortunately it is small and depleted of oak trees. It's as I am wandering sadly through the conifers that I meet the local gentleman. He remembers it as it was and tells me that more than 90 per cent of the oaks were cut down for their timber during the Second World War and not replanted, replaced instead with the conifers that surround us. Robin Hood would not have approved, 'Meet me under the third pine tree from the left in row twenty-seven' doesn't have the ring of 'Meet me under the Great Oak in Little John's clearing'. It is hard to visualise Robin, Marion, Little John and their escapades in such meagre surroundings.

32

Let me digress for a moment. Later on this same journey Jai arrives to spend Christmas in England with me, and one of the places we both love is the new Globe Theatre in London. It has been rebuilt as close to the original as possible—including using oak for much of the theatre's timber. A small donation (£5 I seem to remember) pays for an oak to be planted in Sherwood Forest—so of course we pay for two. I think it will take a few centuries to replace them all and for them to reach the size they must have been in the 1940s, but it's a start.

There is peace among trees—even conifers—and plenty of birds to look for. And the local is interesting to listen to (even if he thinks I'm someone else) as he tells me what it was like seventy years earlier, and his take on the history of King Edwin.

Navigationally speaking, the walk is a disaster. I set off on what I think is the correct path—the hostel is well endowed with maps and I'm given directions. The path seems to follow the map (vaguely) but after an hour of uncertainty I make a decision never to move more than three turns away from an identifiable reference point so that I can retrace my steps and theoretically never get lost. Note that 'theoretically'—getting lost is one of my strong points. This forest reminds me of the Australian bush with numerous intersecting paths, so it's easy to get disoriented. Luckily I end up in Edwinstowe village, because I'm not back on the map until I reach the hostel.

In the afternoon I go to Ollerton mill with a water wheel that still turns occasionally, but unfortunately not

33

today. Though no longer in commercial use Ollerton, Nottinghamshire's last working water mill, now houses a teashop with views of the wheel; luckily the café *is* working today and I can assuage my disappointment with tea and cake.

Ollerton is pretty with attractive cottages and houses dating from the early 1700s. Local stone seems not to have been used but the old bricks are soft with round edges and muted colours. Occasionally my thought processes amuse me: there's an old butcher's shop with an original wooden sign 'M. J. Moloney. Licensed to deal in Game', and my first thought is that it's a betting shop—there's a vegetarian for you!

I have two hours to explore Nottingham though the bus station wants £2 for left luggage—talk about overcharge, give me Newcastle's 'leave it in the buffet kitchen for 50p' any day! But I've discovered the city is built over a series of caves and I'm a bit of a cave nut so there's no alternative; and my recent resolve not to spend any more cash on 'touristy' things goes out the window, too. Around 400 caves are chiselled out of the limestone and their earliest known use was in medieval times when, because of natural water, they were inhabited by people who would otherwise have lived in slums. But they have also been tanneries, storehouses and most recently air-raid shelters in the Second World War. They have been left just as they were when in use: the tanning pits still contain hides and chemicals; one cave has gas masks and other accoutrements of air-raid shelters; one habitation on multiple levels shows

34

how its inhabitants dug downwards for extra space; there are models of people in assorted historic costumes and one child is even sitting over a latrine hole. It is fascinating and I have no regret about doing this tourist thing.

Ironically as I travel south from Nottingham I pass the National Forest and subsequently find out it is 200 square miles of forest traversing three counties. It looks far more impressive and interesting than Sherwood and no conifers—from the road at least. But then I guess there would have been no Edwin's Cross, or Robin Hood and Maid Marion vibes either.

'Journeys, like artists, are born and
not made. A thousand differing
circumstances contribute to them,
few of them willed or determined by
the will—whatever we may think.'

—Lawrence Durrell

THREE

SPAIN: ART, ARCHITECTURE AND PASSION

After our adventures in Morocco in April 2001 and the fun of getting to Ceuta, Naomi and I reach the terminal for the ferry to Algeceiras in Spain at 2 pm—in plenty time for the 4.30 slow ferry and frustrated that there isn't one sooner. But that's travel for you. So we buy coffees, enjoy a picnic lunch and plan the next day—usual time-filling activities. We wonder why the woman from the ticket office is frantically signalling us, finally understanding that the ferry is now departing. Of course. We knew but forgot the two-hour time difference: an expensive memory lapse. We can wait for a 9 pm slow ferry and look for accommodation in Algeceiras in the dark, or extravagantly each pay an extra 1200ptas (A$1 is around 95 peseta) for the 5.30 fast one. No choice really. And there goes getting to Ronda on day one.

Hostal Levante in Algeceiras looks reasonable, though the man at reception doesn't instil confidence. His long hair is slicked over a shiny balding head (backwards not sideways); no English, which is fair enough, and he only removes his eyes from the television screen to take our money and give us towels. But we're tired and it's only for the night. My Spanish is put to the test almost immediately because when we try to wash (our clothes and ourselves) we discover the washbasin plug is too small. But the Spanish equivalent of 'Tough!' is all I get for my trouble, so I don't even bother to tell him about the leaks from the cold tap and the cistern, or that the cistern doesn't work!

Algeceiras improves when we find a local café where I am introduced to *patata* (Spanish potato omelette) and enjoy my first glass of wine in ten days—Morocco being a Muslim country and us not staying in high-class hotels.

In the morning we walk to the station and catch the 7 am train for the real start of our Spanish sojourn.

RONDA:
OUR INTRODUCTION TO SPAIN

Ronda, in Andalucia in Spain's southern mountains, is built on two edges of the deep El Tajo gorge and is *mucho frio*. I had thought 'Sunny Spain in May, bathers and sundresses—*Hola*!', but luckily have enough layers to survive. We stay in the new town (though 'new' is relative especially to an Australian) across the gorge from the old town with its combination of medieval and Moorish histories dating from well before 130 BC. It is here that I discover the many similarities between Spain and Morocco; not surprising because Islam was brought to Morocco from Andalucia and we are told at tourist information that this is the oldest Muslim town in existence.

At Hotel Purismo we have our own bathroom—an absolute luxury after our economy hotels in Morocco—and washing clothes and hair is a joy. Such simple pleasures, so easily attained. I can still visualise our washing-line arrangement, the most ingenious yet: hung from inside the wardrobe, across the shutters that are held open by my walking boots and our toilet bags, and weighed down with Naomi's backpack.

We enjoy getting to know the local area: its shops (*supermercado*, and *tabac* for stamps and telephone booth);

39

the beauty, atmosphere and stunning view from the top of El Tajo; experiencing hot chocolate and *churros* (a sort of donut) for the first time—a sweet and greasy Spanish breakfast specialty; and for me, the Plaza de Toros built in 1785 and considered the home of bullfighting, and its Museo Taurino. I hate bullfighting but find the history and costumes of the toreadors and matadors fascinating.

In the old town we wander amid Arabic and Spanish architecture: gateways, balconies with geraniums, ochre and white roofs, winding streets and alleyways, Arab baths, gardens and three old bridges crossing El Tajo with its winding river.

FERIA DE ABRIL AND OTHER FIESTAS

Sevilla

Unknowingly we arrive in Sevilla at the end of Feria de Abril, though we *do* wonder why we are met at the station by girls in flamenco costume giving out maps and kitsch pens. This fair is an unwinding after the solemnity and strictness of Easter: 'six days of music, dancing, horse-riding and traditional dress' (Lonely Planet guide). We are there in May, three weeks after Easter but it is definitely the April Fair.

We head off to the *feria* expecting public performances of flamenco, but discover that this festival is when families, friends and work associates get together for flamenco, eating and drinking. There are roped off *casatas* (literally little houses) and tents, which serve as bars mostly with

40

guards to keep people like us out. We innocently gate-crash two to watch the dancing before it is made clear that we are interlopers.

Many women, and children as young as two, dress in full flamenco gear and parade the streets. The men prefer to flaunt themselves on horseback, dressed immaculately, haughty in their showy hats, grey skin-tight jackets and even tighter black pants; riding erect, bareback with right hand on waist and left hand casually holding the reins on the saddle's pommel. And their horses, high stepping over the cobbles, are almost as immaculately decorated and groomed. Over a few days we see parades of horses, horse-drawn carriages transporting girls in their flamboyant flamenco gear, a few women on horseback just as upright and elegant as their male counterparts, and occasionally men on foot escorting women in bright flounces.

Córdoba

We are in Córdoba for its annual Fiesta de Patios—a competition for the best decorated patio. We visit different ones every night; beautifully decorated with fountains, trees growing in the most unlikely situations, and hundreds of pots filled with cascading plants wandering up whitewashed walls, scattered around or as part of a water feature.

The affluence of the area which we visit affects the 41 quality and quantity of patio decorations used, but not the enthusiasm or pride with which they are shown. And seeing them at night makes a difference; cleverly used light lifts mediocre decorations to something special.

One evening, as part of the patio fiesta, we find a performance by a flamenco dance school that reminds me of my daughter Kate's ballet concerts: the teacher, well past her youth, dancing the lead role with a young male student. And even my limited flamenco experience tells me these students are not particularly good.

Two days later on our way to visit more patios close to Iglesia San Augustin, we discover a stage, kids in costume and a street performance of flamenco at the other end of the spectrum. The dancers and musicians display fire and soul, and the choreography and standard of performance are excellent. The youngest dancers look about six years old, the oldest perhaps mid-twenties and they all have flair, enthusiasm, fantastic costumes and the art of flamenco.

Madrid

The fiesta of Sante Isidro is taking place in Madrid when we arrive; 'Is life in Spain a constant fiesta?' I wonder. Just around the corner from our *hostal* is Plaza Mayor, one of Madrid's main plazas, where something is always happening as part of the fiesta. One day it is painters, caricaturists and guitarists; another, a wonderful display of singers and dancers in highly decorative clothes (traditional Madrileños possibly). The women's dresses have double flounces and are tight, they wear two flowers on top of their heads, and the heavily embroidered scarves over their shoulders become part of their dance. The men wear black pants and grey jacket and cap. This dancing is a cross between ballroom and sedate flamenco.

42

And each evening we are entertained with live music from the plaza, not always to our taste but fun to hear in the distance.

SEVILLA'S MORE THAN JUST A FERIA

We want to stay in El Barrio de Santa Cruz, the Jewish quarter of old Sevilla, but finding accommodation is not easy because of the Feria de Abril. After a few 'no rooms' we find a small dark room at Hostal Santa Maria de La Blanca, a slightly expensive hotel with minimum facilities, a seemingly unfriendly landlord and a really bad bed. But each day we pass Calle Dos Hermanos (Two Sisters Street)—obviously we are meant to be here.

After one night I decide I must approach the manager, however unfriendly, to get the mattress changed.

'Es posible cambiarmi colchón, por favor? Mi espalda a mucho dolor y le colchón es roto.' ('Is it possible to change the mattress, please? My back is very sore and the mattress is broken.')

He apologises, assures us it's no problem and it's done by midday. Just goes to show first impressions can't always be trusted.

On our second day here my daypack is stolen. I take my eyes (and foot) off it for a moment as Naomi and I check a map and it's gone. Stupid, we'd been warned about Spain. Luckily it is a cheap bag containing nothing that requires reporting, but I'm sad to lose my journal, into which I've stuck tickets, notes and odd souvenirs. I replace most things cheaply and easily, although an inexpensive camera gives me

43

grief when it refuses to wind films on and doesn't tell me. I even manage to bring a new journal up-to-date before my memories flee.

Sevilla is a food lovers' delight. One night we dine deliciously at a tapas bar, one of the cheapest ways to eat in Spain and the gastronomic highlight is palm hearts in Roquefort. I note in my journal: 'Best meal yet and only 2050ptas between us', and that includes wine. On the way home we wander into a street of churches, which includes Inglesia de San Nicholas (that must be St Nicholas of Christmas fame) and celebrate him with chocolate and lemon tart. Another night we fill in a few hours before a flamenco performance with a tasty meal of patata and fried calamari washed down with a Spanish red, and dessert at our local ice-cream and yoghurt place. Come to think of it, I seem to find delicious food in most places I visit—just a natural foodie.

Naomi and I often go our separate ways. She to visit art galleries and take photographs, and me, of butterfly (or maybe grasshopper) mind, to flit to whatever is interesting me at that moment. I find another Plaza del Toros where a guided tour complements my visit in Ronda. I learn about trophies: a 'good' toreador must win three trophies in the day—either two ears and a tail, or three ears (gruesome, even though the bull is dead). Two mounted heads in the museum are 'Bulls of the Year' that gave a good fight but ended up dead anyway! The third head is the mother of the only bull to kill a famous bullfighter; she was slaughtered the following day so the 'accident' wouldn't be repeated. Seems to me the bulls can't win.

44

We explore the narrow walkways and plazas of El Barrio de Santa Cruz, and meander in the semicircular jumble of tiles, ceramics, statues and carvings that is Plaza de España. It is enormous, kitsch and beautiful. Quite over the top!

The Museo de Bel Arte is the only art gallery I visit in Sevilla and I've never seen so many religious paintings in such a small space. The highlights for me are an exhibition of Goya and El Greco, and the gallery building itself—an old convent where one salon's ceiling is decorated in gold and artworks, and columns are decorated with paintings.

El Mundo, a bar in Calle Siete Revueltas, offers genuine flamenco guitar and singing. It is still sleeping when we arrive at about 10.45 pm, and a local tells us it won't be open until 11.30 or 12.00. We wander the local streets window-gazing at an interesting mixture of shops then relax at the bar before the show starts at 12.30. We're the only foreigners there and are ready to leave when the first set ends at 1.30 am—sad to be old and tired. But I enjoy the atmosphere, the doleful sound of authentic flamenco, and its young local aficionados.

Sevilla's La Giralda and cathedral continually fascinate me as I wander; the silhouettes of their Gothic spires against the bluest of skies, and blue and white cupolas contrast with towering stone lightened by filigreed carvings and arches.

I have fantastic memories of Sevilla: narrow lanes and alleyways, clopping hooves and jangling bells, ochre, white and black facades; being gently laughed at as we struggle with Spanish; the arrogance of Spaniards who won't step out of the way; the differences between *España y Maroc* and feeling at home in our awful room.

45

ADAPTABILITY IS THE KEY
TO HAPPY TRAVEL

We are in the bus station in Granada because Naomi wants to see the Alhambra and gardens, and I'm following her Spanish fancies. As I mind the luggage while she uses the amenities I chat with an English family living in Córdoba. They also came to Granada for the Alhambra but are going home because there is a four-day wait for daytime tickets and, like Naomi, believe one must go in daytime as the gardens shouldn't be missed. Over lunch we decide we don't want four days in Granada and that Córdoba sounds a good alternative. We catch the next bus going there. Flexibility is a wonderful thing.

The youth hostel is in an interesting area but what a waste of time. There's no-one at reception, they charge extra for people over the age of twenty-six and eventually we are told they are *completo*.

But we find Hostal Rey Heredia which turns out to be the best hotel we discover anywhere and only 3000ptas a night. A double bed (but that's OK) on which we bounce before making a decision—and it is so comfortable that after a couple of days I wake pain free for the first time since the dreadful mattress in Sevilla. It's a small room, one of two in a courtyard sharing a good bathroom that we have to ourselves most of the time we are there. Absolute luxury. Again we are in the old Jewish quarter and within walking distance of everything we want to do. Also, there is a mosque down the road and the muezzin calling transports us back to Morocco.

We find what will become our regular restaurant, La Ribera, in the Plaza del Potro close to the river. On the first night I have delicious cod in tomato sauce while Naomi has roast vegetables. I've kept the bill from that night and we pay a total of 2400ptas for food and wine. We go back often and by our last evening are treated like locals.

Naomi is unwell on her birthday which seems unfair, but rests in our peaceful room while I wander happily for hours: losing myself in streets I haven't visited, finding shops for buying flamenco presents, enjoying coffee and croissants, discovering more old churches and a couple of patios we've missed, and exploring my own enthusiasms.

I find another Museo de Taurinos—what is it about the history of this cruel sport that fascinates me? Here are displays of famous matadors and toreadors, historic posters and paintings, exquisitely embroidered and beaded costumes and I wonder how men can fit into such tiny trousers, and more bulls' heads—the full catastrophe. Three famous bullfighters warrant a room each, and Manolete is the most revered. He died after being gored in the thigh in 1947 and the pelt of the bull responsible for his death is on the wall. I wonder if the bull's head I saw in Sevilla belonged to the mother of this killer. I continue to feel sorry for the bulls.

I love the paintings of Romero de Torres, an early twentieth-century Córdoban, and the Museo de Julio Romero de Torres features his portraits of sad-eyed but sensual Córdoban women. The Museo de Bellas Artes, which houses Spanish paintings from medieval to modern times, exhibits his landscapes and groups of people rather than his sensuous women; and this gallery is worth a visit for the building alone. It began as a fifteenth-century *caritas* (charity hospital), the ceiling looks original and there are remnants of early murals over the stairs. Details from religious artefacts and *retablos* (altar decorations) also appeal to me though I note: 'Religious paintings I've seen too many of'—bad English but you get my drift.

Postaca Plaza del Potro, a fourteenth-century inn, which the brochure tells us is very Córdoban, is a small whitewashed building with thick walls and a squat square tower. It is now a gallery exhibiting contemporary Spanish art: installations in black and red; ceramic pieces incorporating clay and acrylic that I like but not in *my* lounge room, thank you. My favourites are large outdoor sculpted ceramics combined with timber and metal, and beautiful black-and-white photographs of *baille flamenco* (flamenco dance) illustrating movement, emotions, shapes and form.

Córdoba is small and it's easy to find our way around— though we do get temporarily displaced almost every time we go anywhere. It's not as ornate as Sevilla but we feel at home. We are surrounded by the ringing of bells: telling the time, getting people to church and maybe just for the hell of it. We so enjoy staying in one place even for a short time that we decide to cut the Carcassonne out of our itinerary and extend our stays in Madrid and Barcelona.

48

THE FEAST THAT IS MADRID

The bus journey from Córdoba to Madrid is a delight. I enjoy rural Spain through the window: red poppies, people working in fields, Dutch-style windmills, churches becoming less Moorish. But as we come into Madrid it is kilometres of industry, suburbs, motorways with complex crossovers, and signs. Back in a big city. Ugh!

It seems convenient while we are at the bus station to plan our journey to Barcelona, especially as we are told that the train station is 'just up the road'. Naomi's turn, so she sets off to check it out and I stay with the luggage. After an hour I'm getting anxious, fifteen minutes later I'm planning what I'll say to the police, another fifteen and she's back, hot and weary but with good news. Our Eurail passes allow us to travel first class direct to Barcelona for 2125ptas. Wonderful! But suddenly it's 4.30 pm and finding accommodation becomes the priority.

We try hotels in the Puerta de Sol first, close to everything we want in Madrid. Naomi is weary after her trek to the train station so I leave her with the bags and go on my own. Finding a cheap hotel could be difficult because of the fiesta of Sante Isidro, but there are so many in this area I don't even start to panic. The first five have no room but Hostal Maria del Mar does, and it's the biggest, best-appointed hotel room yet—we even have a table and chairs. It is reasonably priced for Madrid at 3700ptas per night, though they charge extra for the shower—cheeky.

We manufacture another extraordinary washing line setup: from inside the wardrobe to the window, and back to the corner of the door. We worry that the landlady will object when she comes to make the beds, but she says nothing—maybe allowances are made for mature-aged travellers. We eat at the table, very civilised for a shoestring hotel—although we have to duck under the washing.

Puerta de Sol is interestingly commercial: shops sell myriad fabrics, buttons, ribbons; a print shop has an amiable shopkeeper; a gourmet food shop has a smooth talker who invites us in but his unctuousness does not persuade us to buy; and an up-market food area at El Corte Inglés that provides us with three days' breakfasts and lunches for less than 3000ptas.

When we stay in one place for a while we find a 'local' bar, restaurant or coffee shop. In Córdoba it was La Ribera, in Madrid it is Yenes café a pastry/coffee shop and bar (a not unusual combination in Spain) with a restaurant above. We spoil ourselves with coffee and cake here most days, and dine in the restaurant twice. It even has a resident drunk, holding up a corner of the bar and leering at us each time we visit.

Naomi is much more of an art aficionado than I, and visits many of Madrid's galleries while I wander and observe Madrid and the Madrileños. Museo de Lazaro Galdiano sounds interesting, but when I finally track down this obscure museum it is closed for renovations, surrounded by scaffolding, shouting workmen and dumpsters. But I discover Escultura al Air Libre with works by Pablo Gargallos, Carlos Sanchez and Manuel Gonzales who become my favourite modern sculptors in this Madrid moment.

For contrast I escape the rain in Salamanca a *very* expensive and superior shopping centre with expensive and superior clientele. But fun to window-shop and watch the shoppers.

I get some culture with Naomi at Museo de Arte de Reina Sopia's exhibition of development of art in Spain since the beginning of the twentieth century. The intensity of Picasso's *Guernica* engrosses me for an hour, but then I'm delighted to find more sculptures by Gonzales and Sanchez. On the way to the gallery we discover the Anton Martin area with 'local' shops: fishmonger, butcher, baker, a cheap shop for a new alarm clock, Koala Camping and Trekking (truly) where I buy 'maglite' batteries, and a cheap luggage shop to replace my daypack stolen in Sevilla.

There's a fascinating *Tesoro* (Treasures) exhibition at Palacio Real (Royal Palace) that includes historical documents, antiquities associated with Madrid's growth— bronze helmets, statues, lamps and pots; drawings and artefacts from an archaeological dig of 1861; and South and Central American, and Egyptian and African relics. But the highlight for me is Disco de Teodosia, an embossed silver disc about one metre in diameter made to celebrate a coronation in 393 AD.

I get well lost finding the palace, ending up in a courtyard surrounded by splendidly groomed and elegant horses, and men in black uniforms with red-and-gold trim and plastic soup bowls on their heads (true that *is* what their helmets look like). After twenty minutes I hear drumming: a military band in similar uniform and other people in green uniforms without soup bowls, arrive at a trot and break rank onto the footpath. I chat to a group of young men who think they are the cat's whiskers. Eventually the parade starts: marchers, band, jeeps, cars, bikes, horses and riders, and a fly-over of twelve helicopters. Very grand! Someone tells me it is to celebrate 130 years of the civil guard.

Naomi and I find peaceful sanctuaries in this teeming city. The garden of Parque del Buen Retiro; the *Real Jardín Botánico* (Royal Botanical Gardens) that are widespread and hilly; and the enormous gardens of Campo del Moro with tree-lined avenues, vistas across manicured lawns to the palace and a museum giving the history of the palace but which is closed for renovation (the story of Madrid for me). Here we are amused to overhear people arguing about whether dog droppings should be left on the paths—maybe we understand too much Spanish!

Among the original walls and tiles of the beautifully restored Attoch RENFE railway station is an indoor tropical garden. An oasis of water, palms and other tropical plants, sparrows resting and bathing, and turtles with red heads and yellowish striped legs cavorting in the water (as skilfully as turtles can cavort). A fine mist sprays from above and somehow humidity is generated.

One afternoon we discover a theatre close to our hotel with a poster for 'Pura Passion', part of Madrid's Danza 2001 festival. We get tickets for a song (by Melbourne standards) in the middle balcony of the small theatre. So drag out our glad rags and do the best we can to represent Australia's older shoestring travellers.

52

The superbly choreographed and beautifully costumed performance combines traditional flamenco with elements of contemporary dance. Women in brightly coloured dresses without the flounces we normally associate with flamenco, but used in the same way to emphasise leg movements. And like flamenco, sometimes the men have their own dance movements but at other times mirror the women's exactly. The dancers are accompanied by three singers, a violin, a guitar and two drums. It's exhilarating and the passion is never in doubt.

Our last evening in Madrid provides grist to the writer's mill. We've had a lovely day of wandering, lunching in a park, soaking up the atmosphere and are going to Yenes for a last treat before catching the train to Barcelona. As we cross Plaza de la Puerta del Sol with its crush of people my wallet gets lifted. The young woman, with her fake fur jacket and nimble fingers, is damn good because my wallet is at the bottom of the bag and I don't feel a thing. Luckily a very kind señor rushes up, tells us she stole something from me, and points to where she is making her getaway. Sure enough my bag is unzipped and my wallet gone. Like screaming banshees we pursue her, and with that conspicuous jacket and our determination she cannot escape. She acts the innocent until señor arrives with threats, when she reluctantly extracts my wallet from under a parked car where she's thrown it as we close in. The wallet is empty but I'm so enraged that I furiously wave it under her nose and her large offsider grudgingly throws me my plastic cards (rescued from the gutter) and 20,000ptas.

53

Thank God for our middle-aged and portly Madrileño saviour; we could not have managed on our own—fury would not have made up for lack of Spanish. I later conclude I must have left the zip in my small shoulder bag a little open after getting my glasses out to look at a map. I write: 'I'm not feeling paranoid, just a little hexed!'. But it's all part of the journey and my bad feelings disperse pretty quickly. Just as well with my recent history!

So what is Madrid to me? A mixture of people and emotions. Madrileños are elegant, the women particularly so: older women are often solidly built but still immaculate; middle-aged are a picture in grey brightened with apricot, lime or some such muted colour, or striking in black softened with white blouse and maybe a flower; the young are slim and elegant even in jeans and crop top. I feel positively scruffy particularly on rainy days as I wander in waterproof jacket, sloshy sandals and dripping hair, festooned with water bottle, daypack and securely anchored shoulder bag. I don't do much for the image of Australian women.

Driving and parking are a noisy hell. Cars park too close together or double park and if you need to get out you toot your horn until someone comes, and if you can't see why you are held up just toot your horn anyway. Parking is on corners, across pedestrian crossings, on cross-hatched areas on roads, anywhere really, and drivers only stop at zebra crossings if the alternative is to kill a pedestrian—a green walk light means taking your life in your hands.

It's a city in which to just wander and observe: shops and bars; galleries, museums and statues; impressive buildings with beautiful clean lines interspersed with domes, spires, statues and wrought iron in gold or black; poverty in the same street as the opulence of catholic churches and shops for the wealthy. And street performers on every corner.

BARCELONA IS GAUDI

Our overnight train journey to Barcelona isn't too bad. We don't have sleepers but with a carriage to ourselves have room to spread out and put our feet up. At 6.30 am we wash and freshen up and I somehow fit my feet back into my boots. Naomi finds these overnighters harder than I and feels nauseous, but recovers once we reach a café with mint tea for her and for me café mancharo; we agree to spoil ourselves with couchettes for our next overnight journey.

We get a taxi to La Rambla, the boulevarde that borders the *Barri Gòtic* (medieval quarter) where we want to stay. Naomi remains with the luggage as I search. The first four hotels are expensive, can't accommodate us for four nights or the beds are dreadful, but Hostal Fina is perfect. It's in an old, bustling, commercial area with street sounds very different to those we enjoyed in Fès in Morocco but just as much fun. The noise ends after midnight then starts again about 6 am with shutters opening, chatter of shopkeepers and street cleaners, rattle of doors, and squeak of trolley wheels. We have a small balcony overlooking the street and I'm out there watching by 6.30 every morning. It's in a great position, among the people who live and work in Barcelona, and minutes from La Rambla's pedestrian strip shaded by leafy trees, and filled with flower and bird stalls, cafés and a constant stream of people. And we can walk to Plaça de Cataluña, Barcelona's main square.

On our first food foray we ask in stumbling Spanish for a supermercado, and are directed to a produce market, Mercat de la Boqueria, where we buy cheap fruit and vegetables and extravagant dried fruit. Opposite the hostal we find a local café selling delicious salads that become part of our daily provisions. I am fascinated by the contrast on La Rambla between the exclusive shops of smart clothes and designer jewellery, and caged birds for sale—which I abhor.

Returning to our hostal one evening, we follow our ears and find a string quartet from the Youth Orchestra of Amsterdam, playing in a plaça in front of Iglesia San Maria del Pi to publicise a performance in the church that evening. So it's back into the glad rags and off to a concert. The music is enhanced by high arches, stained-glass windows and candlelight. I always try to find music in religious buildings but this is the first on this journey.

Our days in Barcelona are an Antoni Gaudi feast of Art Nouveau; each day finding another of his parks, mansions or churches, or a piece of architecture or sculpture influenced by his vision of art and design—which didn't include symmetry or straight lines.

Probably Gaudi's most famous building, and certainly the pinnacle for me, is La Sagrada Familia (sacred or holy family) church, the design of which he took over in around 1880 when the original architect, de Villar, fell out with church dignitaries. It was Gaudi's raison d'etre for his last forty years until he died in 1926—he was run over by a tram, which is irrelevant but interesting. La Sagrada was untouched for decades and is still less than half completed but workmen and architects are using his plan to complete his dream. Some people think it should be left unchanged as a monument to Gaudi.

La Sagrada is a combination of his ideas and traditional religious icons and architecture. The outside is covered in statues, gargoyles, depictions of scenes from religious texts, and curving and twisted pillars. Two facades in very different styles decorate opposite sides of the church: the northeast wall has the Façade of the Nativity completed under Gaudi's supervision—soft curved sculptures depicting the traditional nativity scene. While the contrasting southwest wall has Façade of the Passion, built more recently to Gaudi's design—jagged and hard-edged depicting desolation, pain, sacrifice and death. Inside the church pillars and columns are softer and divide as they rise, accentuating the high windows and soaring ceilings which seem to be formed of interlocking flowers.

Gaudi's plan has ten tall spires, the final one of which will be 180 metres high. They are set at unusual angles, highly decorated with sculptures and tiles, and with windows all the way up. The existing spires already tower over the church and Naomi and I climb two that are interconnected and a mere 90 metres high—nonetheless quite an achievement for this height-wary traveller. We circle on slim spiral staircases and cross narrow walkways between spires getting striking close-ups of decorations, heart-stopping glimpses of the city below and new perspectives on things already seen. Magnificent and movingly beautiful.

Gaudi was only thirty when he designed his first house, Palau Güell, for the family of his patron Eusebi Güell. It was very adventurous in the 1880s with asymmetrical arches; unusual ceilings, windows and latticed railings; and tiles used extensively. The vaulted brick stables, and a roof with wonderful patterns, bright tiles and ornate 'chimneys', were non-public areas where Gaudi was encouraged to try new techniques.

He designed Parc Güell as a 'model' village for Güell but it never came to fruition. Only two houses were built but the surroundings are a striking collection of more colours and designs in tiles than seem possible. Some are whole, others broken and rebuilt into curves or placed randomly on walls, chimneys and sculptures—radical designs for the time. The three-storey museum in the grounds of Parc Güell was originally Gaudi's house and is filled with his designs, paintings, furniture and plans for the Sagrada Familia, and drawings and furniture from friends and colleagues.

We wander streets of Barcelona rich with Gaudi and other Art Nouveau architecture. The Passeign de Gracia is pure Gaudi with striking facades, colours, decorations, roof adornments and lights. La Pedrera, the last residential building he designed, is now offices; an enormous and graceful symphony of curves, cream walls and balconies with subtle blue trim, and domes on the roof. Casa Battló is smaller, a fairytale castle with spired turret, balconies, tile-decorated outer walls and a roof of curving scales that reminds me of a dragon. It's hard to believe that these two buildings were designed by the same man.

We go up Montjuïc by funicular railway and admire a sculptural delight designed for the 1992 Olympics—tall, slim metal columns connected by fine wire, curving away from the eye wherever you look. But the day has its frustrations: the gardens of Montjuïc sound interesting but are closed; there are long escalators from the top to Plaça d'España at the base of the mount—a fun way to descend—but part is closed off for an automobile trade fair, so we have a long and boring traipse to reach the bottom; we hope to look inside a small domed Olympic stadium but cannot even breach its fence. We should visit the national art gallery of Cataluña in Palau Naçional, but when we get there the building is rundown and unattractive. Weariness wins, the philistine takes over, slothfully we return to the hostal!

To contrast Gaudi we visit more traditional religious edifices. The marvellous Barri Gòtic cathedral has a stone filigree spire through which the sun shines, gargoyles galore, massive arches and what seem like hundreds of statues. Inside are twenty-nine chapels, one for each guild of artisans that worked on the church, the most opulent for the most powerful guilds. The choir stall is intricately carved timber, the walls are decorated with more carvings and painted statuettes, and the cathedral's unpolished pillars stretch to the high ceilings. The cloister is sombre but lightened by thirteen resident geese and a few more chapels—including Santa Rita de Casa, which is filled with red roses because the previous day was St Rita's day.

Església de Santa Maria del Mar, described by the Lonely Planet guide as 'probably the most perfect of Barcelona's Gothic churches', is similarly stunning though understandably less ornate than the cathedral.

After bullfighting history, maritime museums are my favourite pastime. And Drassanes Reials de Barcelona (Royal shipyards of Barcelona) doesn't let me down. The waterfront museum is housed in a thirteenth-century structure used for centuries of shipbuilding, with high arches, old stone walls and original floors. I could have spent a day there among its superb displays of ships' history, shipbuilding particularly in Barcelona, maritime artefacts and sea-based exploration. The highlight for me is the restored Royal Galley of Juan d'Austria that took part in the battle of Lepanto in 1571. The waterfront is worth a visit even without the museum: the Rambla de Mar footbridge is edged with glass panels topped with curved metal beams (possibly depicting waves) and seems to float.

Barcelona is my favourite Spanish city—so far. Not just for the Gaudi architecture, but for her vibrancy, ambience and vitality. The excitement is helped by where we stay, however the city also has a casualness that is perfect for me. We relax and wander instead of taking advantage of all the city offers; hardly touching the surface of the art galleries and could have stayed twice as long. But I will return one day for the Picasso museum if nothing else.

60

ANCIENT ARCHITECTURE
—ROYALTY AND RELIGION

The Real Alcázar in Sevilla was constructed in the eleventh
century as a Moorish fortress and was a palace for Muslim
and Christian royalty for many centuries. Each room has
different tiles on walls, floors and ceilings; there are garden
courtyards with fountains, tiles and assorted trees some
perhaps hundreds of years old; decorations are of alabaster,
some a milky coffee colour others painted, reminding me of
Morocco. Part of the roof is called La Cupola de Media
Naranja (the cupola of a half orange)—I'm sure you can
imagine why. One room displays the oldest known painting
of Christopher Columbus with a model of his ship the
Santa Maria.

Córdoba's Mezquita is a must. Built by the Emir of
Córdoba in the eighth century, though many additions have
been made since. At one stage it was the largest mosque in
the Islamic world; in the thirteenth century it became a
church and in the sixteenth century a cathedral was built in
its centre. The Mezquita is still used for worship and the
opulence of the catholic cathedral overwhelms the simple
architecture of its Islamic origins. But these are evident in
the immaculate red-and-white-striped arches, the mihrab (a
slab indicating the direction of Mecca), pillar decorations
like those in the Roman ruins at Volubilis outside Fès in
Morocco, and in showcases of pieces of the old mosque and
other artefacts.

Next in our exploration of Córdoba's ancient buildings is
the Alcázar de los Reyes Cristianos (Castle of the Christian

61

Monarchs). Its beauty is unpretentious: old brick arches, curved ceilings and white-painted walls, and we are lucky enough to find two exhibitions. One is of old books and original documents in Ladino, an eleventh-century dialect of Sephardic Jews still spoken by about 200,000 Sephardim, descendants of those expelled from Spain in 1492. Ladino looks like a cross between Spanish and Yiddish; a fragment I read says: *'En komparasion kon las duras sufriensas ke pasaron los reskapados de los kampos de eksterminasion nazistas en Gresia'*, something about comparing the suffering of the Sephardim with the Nazi extermination camps in Greece.

The second is a display of enormous first-century mosaics attached to the walls and their designs also remind me of Volubilis. I'm awestruck that they were transported from archaeological sites and rebuilt on the walls here.

The gardens of the Alcázar are as impressive as the castle: water flowing or spouting everywhere; sculpted garden beds and topiarian trees; enormous rectangular pools edged with formal beds of purple flowers and small spraying fountains; brightly fruiting citrus trees; bits of antiquity stuck carelessly on walls (and in the cleaner's shed!); original murals showing faintly on outside walls; and walkways lined with old sculptures of kings and queens.

We locate the Sinagogia in Córdoba, a tiny ancient synagogue at the end of a narrow alleyway. There is one main room where the men worship and a first-floor balcony for women. Little of the original interior decoration remains, just some carved alabaster and a wall with Hebrew writing still visible. The majority of Sephardim were expelled in the fifteenth century, but the synagogue is still in use.

The Museo Arqueológico y Etnológico (Archaeology and Ethnology museum) houses an enormous collection of artefacts, mainly from Córdoban excavations. It covers periods from neolithic times onwards and includes intricately carved pillars of the first century, and massive pots, mosaics and sculptures. Even the building, a renaissance palace atop the ruins of a Roman theatre, has archaeological interest.

The 'Splendour of the Córdovan Umayyads' exhibition is at the tenth-century Madinat al-Zahra where only a fraction of the site has been exposed. The scant ruins of the mosque and village don't fascinate me as Volubilis did; I cannot sense what it was like to live here.

But displays of artefacts from the eleventh to eighteenth century seemingly in perfect condition make up for my disappointment in the site: artworks, jewellery, medallions, coins, tools of iron, lamps, and assorted vessels of pottery and bronze. Displays include capitals, some latticed like those at the Archaeology museum and others more like the Roman ones we saw at Volubilis; fretwork windows painstakingly restored; friezes and inscriptions from tombs; and ancient marvels in marble, plaster and stone. This exhibition from Al-Andalus, the earliest blend of Spanish and Muslim worlds, brings Spain and Morocco even closer together for me.

I have fantastic memories of my short visit to Spain. It's a place of intriguing history. The Spaniards are proud of

63

Spain and of being Spanish, yet they defile footpaths, dump rubbish in parks and seem to show little sense of responsibility for their cities which are graffiti galleries with too much traffic. Maps and signs leave a lot to be desired, footpaths are broken and littered with dog droppings, cigarette butts by the million, paper and bottles—but there are street cleaners galore so no-one seems to care. Although it's not perfect (and where is), Spain and its people call me back.

FOUR

A BIRTHDAY CELEBRATION
IN PRAGUE

'Travelling is not just seeing the new;
it is also leaving behind. Not just
opening doors; also closing them behind
you, never to return. But the place you
have left forever is always there for you
to see whenever you shut your eyes.'

—Jan Myrdal

Naomi, Carole and I are at a performance of *Carmen* at the State Opera house in Prague. None of us expected to be going to the opera but Carole has come reasonably well equipped with 'going out' clothes; Naomi and I scrabble in the bottom of our luggage for something halfway decent to wear—my versatile black and pink sarong becomes a long skirt again. Somehow we manage with aplomb, until the intervals when everyone parades, showing off their elegant best and checking out the opposition. We just try to blend into the wallpaper.

The production and performance are somewhat second-rate; though I enjoy the performance of Don José and Micaela his girlfriend, and my enjoyment is enhanced by Naomi knowing the story. But the company puts on a different opera every night so it's not surprising the standard isn't brilliant. And it's irrelevant, just to be here is enough.

The theatre is a plain brick building, nothing much to look at from the outside but the interior is stunning baroque: gold and white paint everywhere, bas-relief on ceilings in foyers and over staircases, with heavier sculpted ceilings in the auditorium. And bars, tables and chairs are scattered around for the intervals. The boxes are very ornate and it would have been lovely to spoil ourselves with one of those but unfortunately (or maybe fortunately for our purses) none was available. It hasn't turned us into opera buffs but it is a wonderful thing to have done.

I have been retired for over two years, Naomi just a few months and this, the first of many journeys of 'two sisters on a shoestring', has been a wonderful experience. By the time we reach Prague we have been travelling for six weeks, starting in Morocco. Sounds romantic, doesn't it; and I suppose it is.

Now we have four days in Prague with Carole, who is joining us from England for three of them, during which time we will help her celebrate her birthday in this historic city.

At the start of the birthday wanderings we pass the Prague State Opera house and suddenly taking Carole to the opera seems the perfect thing to do. It turns out that Carole has mentioned she will be here to a friend, who says the opera house should not be missed. None of us is a major opera enthusiast but *Carmen* is showing and we all know the music, so we book three seats up in the gods for the equivalent of A$20 a seat—mad extravagance!

After the day's explorations we rush back to our apartment, do the best we can with clothes, hairbrush and make-up and walk to the opera via a quick meal at Na mlatě (The barn), a wonderful local bar/restaurant we have found. I record my indulgence that night in my journal: 'Potato and cauliflower au gratin and a glass of wine'. And we return there on the way home to end the day with hot chocolate, fruit teas and slightly raunchy conversation.

THEY SAY THE JOURNEY IS MORE IMPORTANT THAN THE DESTINATION

Through Jarmila, a contact given to me by a friend Enid, I found a cheap apartment in Prague and booked it on the internet before leaving Australia. Despite thirty years in the computer industry this is a first for me, and so it is with some anxiety that Naomi and I wait for our contact to meet us when we leave the train.

But first is the journey to get here from Lausanne. Travelling on foreign public transport, especially if you don't speak the language, requires confidence in yourself and the system. We join a Czech train in Stuttgart but nothing causes unease until we reach Nuremburg where we are separated into different sections for different destinations, and we just hope we are in the Prague bit. But it was organised in Switzerland and the Swiss are very efficient (or so my uncle kept telling me) so it must be right.

I can't remember the price of the sleeper but our Eurail passes get us as far as the border; it costs less than a night's accommodation *and* we save a day of travelling—so a good deal all round. It's a fairly basic sleeper but we have the carriage to ourselves and can spread out. Though a carriage companion with whom to check that we are actually on our way to Prague would be a useful accessory. Unfortunately the attendant in our section speaks no English, and worse, he puffs a cigarette continually and the smoke filters into our compartment through the heating system.

I sleep very well, though I'm not sure whether that's because we've been travelling since 11 am and I'm weary, or that I have confidence we'll end up somewhere in the Czech Republic and if it's not Prague we can sort it out. The result is that when we stop for border control at 4 am I cannot wake. Naomi has her passport out and stamped while I am still surfacing; then I can't find my glasses and scrabble in

69

pack, under pillow, anywhere they might be hiding, while the border guard stamps my passport without even looking at me. I worry then that it might be a 'sight unseen' sort of stamp and I'll be kept in the Czech Republic forever.

We arrive in Prague in good time, in one piece and reasonably well rested—cheap couchette or not it beats sitting up all night—and Charles, who works with Jarmila and owns the apartment we are to stay in, *is* there to meet us. We are hustled into his car and as he drives he delivers a high-speed spiel about Prague, transport and Czech money. He leaves us at a coffee shop while he does some business with someone else, takes us to an ATM so we can pay for our accommodation in advance and finally drops us off at the flat in Movaska Street. He is exhausting and maybe this is why we make a basic mistake: for the first time we calculate the exchange rate the wrong way round and both end up with twice as much cash as we need. But let me say that Naomi does enjoy spending her leftovers on the last day.

The apartment building is an old house converted into maybe six apartments and ours is perfect; with a modern bathroom, functional kitchen and large light rooms. Not in the old town (too expensive) but only twenty minutes' walk or five minutes on a tram to Wenceslas Square.

BUT MAYBE NOT
WHEN IT'S THIS DESTINATION

The beauty of Prague's architecture greets us every time we turn a corner; each building is different but always with a gargoyle, painting or carving on a wall, decoration above or below a window; facades unlike anything I've seen before. It's a city of statues: large baroque ones on buildings; metal ones on roofs (I've never seen so many of these); and gentle ones in parks. And a city of beautiful and elegant buildings: houses and apartments, churches, cathedrals, municipal offices, and more theatres and concert halls than you could possibly visit in a month. Roof tops are wonderful, and not just the statues, I'm still fascinated by a photo I took of the slate roof on St Vitus' bell tower—rectangles in all shades of grey creating wonderful patterns.

Naomi and I arrive a couple of hours before Carole, so go searching for a tourist information office to get a map, find where we are in relation to the things we might want to do, and actually work out what those things are. Most information offices are only for booking tours but we find the most critical things: a map and information about using the trams.

Back at the apartment after Carole arrives we just relax into being here as we unpack (vaguely), chat, sort stuff out, chat, make loose plans, and chat. All that talking does wonders for the appetite so we go out into the cold and rain-threatening weather to find lunch; and discover Na mlatě around the corner from our apartment. It offers good food and excellent value, and suits the tastes of one vegetarian, one who teeters between vegetarian and the odd piece of chicken, and one determined carnivore. Our first meal, comprising assorted small dishes and salads, is ridiculously cheap and Na mlatě becomes our local haunt. It is run by mama, papa and two sons who, over the next few days, make

71

us feel like family. We are told we *must* go on our last night together because Mama always makes her special apple pie on Saturdays. We do, she does, and it is fantastic.

But we cannot eat every meal there—we should at least make breakfast and the odd cups of tea and coffee at home—so we need a supermarket and fruit shop. The supermarket we find is a maze of aisles with boxes, basic foods, piles of clothes, linen, toys and stationery. We are able to make ourselves understood and discover that the nearest fruit shop is quite a distance; but we are weary and we'll survive without for now. Instead we return to Movaska Street for cups of refreshing tea and boring supermarket pastries.

Carole has borrowed a book on walks around Prague that we combine with odd things that we know, to work out what we will do over the next three days. Eventually we decide that no fixed plan is best, just a lot of walking and wandering will be the go. Then we return to Na mlatĕ for dinner to check that our lunchtime judgment wasn't impaired—and it wasn't.

Carole's birthday is a beautiful day because we are all together and in Prague. Naomi and I bought her a card that I hid somewhere in my pack but now cannot remember where—luckily my determination (bloody-mindedness) pays off and I find it, but also I note in my journal: 'I seem to be forgetting lots; ear and antibiotics definitely making me odd!'. Though I don't know just how odd until I reach Bruges.

We have a slow start to the day with plenty of chatting and laughter, and no fruit! But birthday or not, chores must be attended to—Naomi and I need to book the train to

Bruges for three days hence. We amble to the station, though map difficulties have us finishing up on the wrong side of the tracks; staying on main roads may be navigationally safer but not nearly so much fun.

Booking the night train to Bruges is a breeze: the helpful young man knows his routes, speaks good English, is charming, and assures us that leaving our luggage at the station for the day before the train departs will be no problem. But I suspect he hasn't been an older, English-speaking woman wanting to leave luggage! More of that later ...

Wenceslas Square (Vaclavské Náměstí), a fascinating section of central Prague, is actually not a square but a boulevard—750 metres long and 60 metres wide—that was laid out during the reign of Charles IV. According to information I read it was originally Prague's main horse market but has always been the venue for meetings and demonstrations: where Czech's get together for anything from an anti-communist uprising to a celebration after winning the World Ice Hockey Championships. A statue of St Wenceslas on his horse—Good King Wenceslas of the popular Christmas song—stands at one end of the boulevard, and nearby plaques honour the memory of people killed during the Communist era.

After visiting the station we continue in relaxed birthday mode, starting with that visit to the opera house to book our tickets before finding a coffee in Wenceslas Square. We unknowingly go to the swishest hotel in the boulevard, not realising it until we visit the salubrious loos (and the bill

73

comes). These are the good old days when I can drink coffee and I note in my journal: 'lovely cappuccino'; I should damn well hope so, it costs as much as most of our meals at Na mlatě. But it's worth it for the loos alone and it *is* Carole's birthday.

We get to the Old Town Square on the hour, for the striking of the astronomical clock. Legend has it that the man who made this clock was blinded after he completed it and broke the mechanism out of spite—but apparently it is just legend. As far as one can believe written history it was designed by a professor of astronomy and maths at Charles University, and built by a highly skilled clockmaker in 1410; the original clock showed astronomical data. The mechanical figures surrounding the clock were added later and represent three of the seven cardinal sins and their destinies. Vanity admires her reflection in a hand-held mirror. Greed holds a bag of money. Sloth idles his life away with music and dance. Every hour Death pulls the bell and nods to tell the sinners their time is up but they shake their heads and stay put. And to add to the chaos the twelve Apostles arrive and run about. It's wonderful, and to me better than Berne's clock and that was striking enough.

During the afternoon the sun actually shines and we have tea in a café with outside tables and a lovely view of the Vltava River. I have a photograph of the three of us relaxed and smiling against a backdrop of the river and some of Prague's wonderful architecture. We are so relaxed we don't want to rush off and decide, unwisely though unwittingly, to leave Charles Bridge for the next day.

Walking back to the apartment we traverse a more modern commercial area—necessary even in historic cities—and I find an internet café to do a quick check of emails. In the pleasure of sharing Carole's birthday I've forgotten that it is also the anniversary of Ian's death four years earlier and there's a lovely email from my daughter Kate. The time difference means it's too late in Australia to call my kids and I'm cross with myself that I let this day slip past without doing that. But I'm not one to dwell on what cannot be changed and it's time to get into our 'best clothes' and spend the evening with *Carmen*.

Next day is the most 'touristy' one we have yet, visiting both the castle and Charles Bridge. But not until after Naomi and I have the frustration of trying to book into the youth hostel in Bruges. After three attempts we discover that the prefix we are dialling is incorrect; when we eventually get through, directory assistance has given us the number of the Europa Hotel in Bruges—tempting but we resist. The fifth call works, and we have beds for our first night.

Our castle expedition starts near the opera house—working out trams and tickets needed to get there is simpler than we expect; we find Prague an easy city in which to be visitors—mostly. Hradcany Castle is the largest medieval castle complex in Europe, comprising St Vitus Cathedral (said to be Prague's best known landmark), several palaces, towers, galleries, a monastery, a museum, Golden Lane and St George's Basilica. Hradcany has been the seat of Czech kings for centuries though wars, fires, repairs and renovations, and various political ideas have resulted in an interesting mixture of palaces, churches and fortifications. The first known building on the site was constructed in the ninth century and the last change was as late as the 1920s. Nowadays Hradcany is the seat of the President of the Czech Republic.

To do the palace justice requires probably a full day and more energy than we have but we manage four hours. The extensive courtyards and gardens, where we picnic in the rain, are worth browsing even in miserable weather. Climbing to the top of the spire and bell tower of St Vitus Cathedral warms us up again, and we are amused at three young Japanese women fast asleep on one of the seats that we assume are really for the more elderly (like us). For me St Vitus is memories of slender, elegant spires; wonderfully coloured windows; gargoyles; chiming bells and sleeping beauties.

St Wenceslas is supposed to be the most beautiful chapel at the palace, and it is certainly striking. While there we visit the highly decorated tomb of Wenceslas, and would love to see the crown jewels also housed here— unfortunately they are not for the proletariat and are held in a safe that apparently has seven locks, each key held by a different person.

Finally we leave by Golden Lane, a street originally lined with small cottages built into the castle wall. Now, most of them are tiny brightly painted shops to trap tourists, selling anything you might (or mightn't) want, though beautiful for all that. And of course we are tourists and cannot resist buying.

Then to Charles Bridge via side streets, and the architecture continues to stun us even in the rain. We cross the bridge both ways and the river is cold, grey and misty, but it doesn't matter; though I note in my journal: 'it is *so* cold'. Naomi buys a lithograph and earrings for herself, and I buy tiny prints both for myself and as presents. Mine are framed and on my wall and they take me back to cold, wet Prague whenever I look at them.

Even with its myriad stalls the bridge is stunning: long, wide, decorated with statues and black towers, and the odd busker ignoring the weather. Dave had been to Prague years before and bought me a cassette of a musician playing wine glasses—each tinkling to a different note—and I remember it was on Charles Bridge that he heard them.

We are so cold and wet that even though it's 6 pm we go into the first café we see for coffee and pastries before catching a tram back to the apartment, to relax briefly before our last dinner at Na mlatě. Here the sons tell us about their lives as they wait on us, and we talk almost as much to their parents who cook and serve at the bar. We are so lucky to have found such a warm-hearted family running our local restaurant. It's the last time the three of us will be relaxed together for a while and, helped by a variety of main courses, mama's delectable apple pie and a bottle of white wine, we talk late into the night of childhood memories, present lives and future dreams.

We would love to have a last lazy morning but there are things to see and do. The Jewish quarter, called Josefov after Emperor Josef II, is our first destination—Naomi and

I stayed in many Jewish areas in Spanish cities and the synagogues and other buildings are always interesting. We are sure we know how to get there but this time it is *not* easy. We end up on the eastern side of the city, nowhere near Josefov, so give up and return to Wenceslas Square where cups of assorted hot beverages and apple strudel are consumed. Having regained our strength we walk there, as we could have done in the first place. We wander the streets admiring the variety of styles of synagogues, some large and imposing, others older and smaller.

The history of the persecution of the Jews in Czechoslovakia is no worse than anywhere else, but it seems to appal me more because I'm aware that the streets I'm on were once a Jewish ghetto, but it was in the past and there's nothing I can do to change it. Incongruously close by is Pařižská, an exclusive shopping street that quickly brings us back to the present; here are shops selling Fabergé eggs, amber in many colours, pearls, gold, diamonds and amazing Bohemian glass.

We end up at the Vltava in the late morning for a river cruise, and I have an awful memory from that moment on the river's edge; nothing to do with Prague per se more to do with my insecurities. I'm walking behind Naomi and Carole who are chatting animatedly; suddenly I feel left out and the green-eyed monster strikes—it's irrational, unjustifiable, immature and unforgivable. In retrospect I'm tired and (though I don't know it) unwell, and I suspect something is coming from my teenage years when I had been jealous of my sisters, Carole in particular, even though I thought I'd

78

put all that behind me long ago. But for whatever reason I now speak out hurtfully—not saying why I'm upset of course. As Carole's life is not easy at this time my conduct is completely inexcusable. Of course she responds in kind—who can blame her—and we both end up in tears while poor Naomi can do nothing except wait for us to sort it out. But unfortunately once things are said, they can't be unsaid. I immediately apologise and we hug, later I write in my journal: 'Hope it's OK'.

We've had years of conditioning to hide our feelings and make the best of things, so though it's not a good way to start the boat trip I enjoy it at some level (I don't know about Carole). The hour's cruise, with a commentary in Czech, English, German and Spanish, tells us a little of Prague's history; shows us parts of Prague we have missed; and gives us insights into some of the buildings we've seen but know nothing about. And there is a man sleeping in the downstairs cabin—what is it about Prague that sends tourists to sleep when they should be enjoying its wonders? I love being on a ship's deck—to see as much as I can and to enjoy the fresh air—but today is too cold and I quickly join the others downstairs for hot chocolate.

When we leave the cruise we are still in the Jewish quarter and find a kosher restaurant for lunch where we sample an assortment of tasty vegetarian food, starting with delicious dips and Czech-style Lebanese bread. It is the most expensive meal we eat in Prague at 1200czk (Czech koruna)—about A$20 each—and we realise how much we are spoilt at Na mlatĕ. Judging by our enjoyment of lunch I conclude my earlier emotional outburst has done no permanent damage to either Carole's and my relationship or our appetites.

We wander back to the apartment via lovely streets and squares and a final tram ride. Then it's time for a last cuppa and hugs before Jarmila takes Carole to the airport. Naomi and I are to leave Prague on a train the next evening but we look at the information books in the apartment (a little late maybe?) and discover three monuments we'd like to see first.

Jarmila arrives next morning, checks we haven't destroyed the apartment then drops us off at the station. Finding left-luggage is easy, but from then on it's a circus. We are sent to four different windows for starters and when we eventually reach the correct one find two male 'helpers'—one a skinny, tattooed skinhead and the other a fattish Yul Brynner-style, shaven-headed gentleman with braces (on trousers not teeth). They share private jokes continually, falling about with laughter, and I suspect fun is being poked at non-Czech speakers. None of the signs is in English and, though I think the men could speak it if they wanted to, neither admits to anything except Czech. Finally everything is weighed and we pay 105czk (less than A$2) to leave it all. As the whole transaction has been performed with sign language (and hope) we wonder whether we'll get our luggage back. Prague is Praha in Czech and we rename this small microcosm of the city Praha-ha-ha.

My luggage has been getting heavier and heavier and it's now difficult to put my large pack on my back. It weighs in at the station at 25 kilograms (19 kilograms when I left home!) and I vow to travel more lightly in future. So being unwell is a good thing because I now rarely leave home with more than 15 kilograms regardless of how long I plan to be away.

Because of our incorrect currency conversion we have lots of cash left so set off for a last day's spending and sightseeing and, despite freezing cold wind and intermittent rain, we get to the three places we want to visit.

Tyn Church with its iconic double black spires is said to have the best example of a baroque church interior in Prague though unfortunately it is closed for restoration. But we manage to see a little through a door: heavy black and gold ornamentation and statues of saints. And even this restricted view shows great contrast between that heaviness and tall, slender, arched windows that produce the lightest church interior I think I've ever seen. White ceilings, walls and narrow-pillared arches intensify this light. It's lovely— and that's just from outside.

The Powder Tower is a 65-metre high arch over the road made of dark stone and highly decorated with carvings and sculptures; though I suspect its darkness is exaggerated by the dismal weather. Copied from a tower on the Charles Bridge, this is one of thirteen fortified gates to the Old Town and dates back to 1475; it was never finished because the king, Vladislav II Jagiello, moved to Hradcany castle in the 'new' town. Originally known as Mountain Tower it became the Powder Tower when it was used for storing gunpowder in the seventeenth century. The Gothic look didn't happen until the nineteenth century, and though I'm no great fan of

Gothic architecture I like the design and enormity of this tower gateway.

The cream of my day is Municipal House, said to be one of the most remarkable examples of Prague Art Nouveau. A picture of greens, golds and fawns; stucco decorations, statues, lead-lighting, curves and mosaics; and original furnishings and wallpaper. It opened in 1910 so is relatively modern, and all restoration has been kept as close to the original architecture as possible. The interior is decorated with works by leading Czech artists from that period, most notably Alfons Mucha; and although the style was criticised for being outdated when it was designed and built, it is now regarded as a striking piece of classic architecture.

My shopping spree is a delight; I don't often have money that I just *must* spend! I buy rings for me and my offspring: a tiny one—green amber set in gold—for my little finger; for Jai traditional yellow amber in gold; and for Kate a second-hand one of garnet in gold. None of this is planned but why not. Naomi goes a little mad—three rings for herself—green amber (larger than mine because she wears heavy rings with panache), a ruby and a lapis lazuli; and she also finds a garnet and gold ring for her daughter Juliette.

And of course we both do the grandmother thing at an Art Nouveau shop full of soft toys in fabulous fabrics. I love some of the large animals but must be practical—I have months of travel ahead—and find a dolphin in blue and green for an unborn grandchild and a tartan elephant for Mia. Strangely since she was two Ellie (the expected baby) has been elephant crazy and I'd be blamed if those presents had been the other way round! I'm not as extravagant on presents as I could be, instead using some of my koruna to purchase £30 for when we reach England, but Naomi doesn't stop until she has only 10czk left!

It has been lovely exploring Prague with my two sisters and it would not have been the same alone. We share wonderful light-hearted moments in the apartment, and the joys of discovering Prague's beauty. We try to work out how the Czech language is constructed as we shop—impossible despite phrase book and good intentions. We walk and wander together in the rain, constantly exclaiming and pointing to stunning architectural features, as well as find out how the trams work, discover many helpful and friendly people and explore the Charles Bridge with its art stalls.

Now it's time to collect luggage, organise food and water for the journey, and prepare ourselves mentally for another night of jerks, stops and starts. I'm highly relieved when we go through border control and whatever stamp I received when I arrived is fine and they let me leave.

83

'If you actually look like your passport photo, you aren't well enough to travel.'

—Sir Vivian Fuchs

FIVE

A SWISS BELGIAN CONNECTION: WHAT'S THAT ABOUT?

I have never before felt so ill; vomiting, covered in an itchy rash, temperature so high I'm afraid I'll set the bed alight. I seriously think I'm dying in a bottom bunk of a youth hostel in Belgium, and wondering what the hell to do.

Luckily this time I'm not travelling solo. This is a journey with Naomi my big sister, who won't let me die. But I wait, not wanting to wake her or the others in the four-bed dorm; every so often creeping quietly to the bathroom down the hall to throw up again. Even though there's really nothing to throw up. I have plenty of thinking time, and by the morning I'm pretty sure I know what's wrong. When everyone wakes I quietly tell Naomi that I'm feeling dreadful and what I think the problem is.

This is one of the youth hostels where you must vacate during the day. Not only the bedroom but the whole hostel and normally that wouldn't worry us—we have plenty of exploring to do. But there's no way I can do that, so ask Naomi to try and find a sympathetic person who'll leave me to die in peace. She does, they will, but even better they tell her there's a doctor nearby. She goes to check it out and he'll see me later that morning.

At the appointed time I stagger down the road, Naomi coming for moral (and physical) support, and my suspicions are confirmed—I'm horribly allergic to an antibiotic I have been taking. The doctor is wonderful: sympathetic, on the phone immediately to a colleague who is an allergy specialist, and I get strict instructions about stopping it right now and a prescription for an antidote to the allergy. Even contact phone numbers for an emergency hospital in case it doesn't

86

improve—see, I said I was dying. Further, he says they haven't used this antibiotic in Belgium for ten years. The worst thing about this one is that the allergic reaction takes over a week to become obvious by which time you are very ill. In Prague I had felt exhausted, my pack seemed heavy, I'd been grumpy and constantly nauseous, but had thought it was just weariness after five weeks of travelling on the cheap.

So here's the connection—that antibiotic was prescribed at a hospital in Switzerland. The country, my uncle (a serious Swissophile) had said, has the best medical system in the world!

FORTY YEARS:
A LONG TIME BETWEEN VISITS

Uncle Bryn must be in his eighties—I'm over sixty and he wasn't much younger than my father, Fred. Bryn's parents had 'taken in' my father and his younger sister Dorrie when their father died—their mother having died seven years earlier. Bryn's father, my father's uncle, gave them no choice: they had to move from the north of England to the outskirts of London. Dorrie was only nine so probably fair enough, but my father just out of school had an architectural career planned in Newcastle-on-Tyne and he never forgave his uncle for taking him away. That's all irrelevant in regard to meeting Bryn in Switzerland, but I think you need a little background.

So Bryn and Dorrie were brought up together, first cousins who fell in love—not a desirable marriage and in this case exacerbated because Dorrie and Fred's father had married his own niece, thinning the genetic pool even further (trying to work out Dorrie and Fred's blood relationship with their parents gives me a headache). And Bryn and Dorrie could only marry if she was sterilised. They were the 'rich relatives'; her part of her father's inheritance wisely invested, and he a successful barrister. My sisters and I said we felt sorry for them having no children, but I suspect we didn't mean it because they had everything else.

After being prevented from becoming an architect my father followed no career but had a wife and four daughters to support on the income from his inheritance (*not* well invested) and a meagre salary from a variety of jobs. When each of us turned eleven we had the big adventure of going up to London alone on a train, spending a week with Bryn and Dorrie in Kensington, being shown the sights and taken to the ballet, then being put on a train to go back to our impoverished childhood. Occasionally Dorrie and Bryn would drive down to visit us in Bedfordshire.

I lived in London for three years before emigrating to Australia and would visit Dorrie and Bryn, by now living in swish Hampstead. Dorrie would feed me a delicious meal but I'd find myself bored by their conversations then fall asleep as they showed me the slides from their latest holiday—what an ungrateful hussy. We had nothing in common, I always felt uncomfortable and rather like an unattractive elephant next to my tiny aunt. I compare this with the relationship I have with my nephews and nieces, and my kids have with their aunts and uncles and know we were a little short-changed. But they were who they were; it wasn't their fault they had little idea of how to relate to young people.

Let's roll forward forty years during which time Naomi and I exchanged Christmas cards with Bryn and Dorrie; then with he and Catherine, a French woman Bryn married after Dorrie died of cancer. Each year we'd tell them about our families, marriages, divorces, widowhood—anything we thought might interest distant relatives.

Catherine and Bryn divide their time between an estate in the south of France, their house in Chexbres in Switzerland and in visiting California. We are planning to go overland from Morocco to Prague and it might be fun to visit Bryn—now in his eighties; maybe he has become more interesting in later life and with a younger wife. We write jointly saying we would like to meet them and that we can make it to either France or Switzerland en route to Prague, how do they feel about it?

We get a positive response; they will be at Chexbres and would enjoy our company for a few days. Bryn tells us they will meet us at Lausanne, which is not too far from Chexbres.

We go as directly as possible from Barcelona, but having stayed in Spain instead of having a few days in France it's a long journey. It's not far to Cerbere on the border of France and Spain and the train is comfortable but crowded; in my journal I note: 'hundreds(!) of backpackers' and I think that exclamation mark is because I'm one of them. We have to change trains here, the onward train to Geneva departing at 10 pm, but the atmosphere of this desolate hub of a station makes it feel much later. The facilities are primitive with no food available and stairs must be negotiated to change trains and get to a distant loo that, when reached, is dire! We perch on our luggage playing Krunch—a dice game that gets exciting if the players take a few risks, and after a couple of hours in Cerbere we are ready for a little risk-taking. Trains come and go, and we entertain many transients as they try to work out the rules.

We eventually depart, in a carriage with reasonably comfortable sleepers, but unfortunately are disturbed by a young couple who get on about midnight and share compartment. I wake at 5.40 am as they leave feeling decidedly out of sorts; but watching the sun rise over France, enjoying a couple of villages we rush through and breakfasting on fruit all help improve my mood.

Naomi calls Bryn from Geneva and tells him we will catch the next train to Lausanne; sounds harmless enough but it isn't. Bryn says that he and Catherine will meet us, and that we should wait on the platform or the street when we reach Lausanne. Should be simple but it's a debacle. He doesn't tell us which street, we wait on platform three where the train deposits us, we wander to the surrounding streets, we wait in an underpass, then on the platform. Though we don't know what Catherine looks like, we definitely don't see Bryn. After an hour Naomi rings again; they'd waited on platform one for three-quarters of an hour before driving home and are not at all happy, but kindly agree to drive back and collect us.

We stand where we are told, they come back, they go to the wrong platform again. In the end Catherine finds us. We may not know what she looks like (elegant, blonde, youngish, lovely and smiling—where did Bryn find her I

90

wonder) but we are easy to spot. We are told we caught the 'wrong' train because the right one arrives at platform one—and of course we should have known that! We end up feeling guilty and it's a realistic re-introduction to this intransigent uncle of ours.

He's remarkably fit for his years, though as old in his head as I remember. Their house in Chexbres is very pleasant but we are booked into the local Hotel Bellevue because they have only two bedrooms and, according to Bryn, they sleep in separate rooms because of Catherine's health.

We have drinks at their house then a late lunch at a café on a pier overlooking the water—we always eat out and they explain it is because their cook is not with them. Just imagine the feeling of extravagance for these two shoestring travellers who have spent the last four weeks with the cheapest accommodation and food available in Morocco and Spain. It's a different universe.

The hotel is wonderful and it suits us fine to have time alone occasionally because, as I note in my journal: 'Bryn is not easy'. In my memory book I have a sepia-and-white photo postcard of the Bellevue in perhaps the 1930s or 1940s—less ostentatious, gardens rather than car park, but the building has hardly changed and the view not at all. The balcony overlooks vineyards flowing down the hill to Lake Geneva, and the Alps tease us across the water. The hotel staff, probably unused to shoestring travellers, don't even seem thrown by our smalls drying on yet another washing-line construction in the bathroom. Each day we breakfast in the dining room trying to behave as if this is

91

how we do it all the time. Each morning before meeting Bryn and Catherine we walk down towards the lake through vineyards that are tended by hand because of the steep slopes on which they sit. From the hotel balcony we watch a helicopter spraying fertiliser, so close we can almost see the whites of the pilot's eyes; it is like something from a James Bond film as he turns the helicopter on its nose to return along the vineyard, seeming to fly almost vertically.

On our first evening we eat at a restaurant in the hills behind Chexbres and suddenly I am struck with an excruciating pain in my ear that I assume is from the cold—it's only just warm enough to eat outside. It keeps me awake and I'm uneasy about the next day's plans to go up to Gstad in the mountains. I know Bryn will not want his plans changed but I need to see a doctor, and my aching ear doesn't want to be driving up and down mountains.

It is Sunday, no doctors on duty in Chexbres, so we go to the hospital in Vevy. Bryn lauds the quality of the Swiss medical system as I'm treated by a young man who diagnoses middle-ear infection and gives me a prescription for antibiotics, anti-inflammatories and ear drops. However, Bryn is not pleased at the delay and treats me like a naughty child—we are late for that journey up the mountain and he will not let me stay behind. My journal says it perfectly: 'Winding and steep, felt carsick and awful', and though the views are stunning and the countryside wonderful I cannot pretend it is a pleasant day.

We see traditional Swiss chalets in dark timber with high-peaked roofs, shutters, carved decorations and window boxes filled with geraniums, and walk alongside a river where Bryn surprises me with his knowledge of the flora. On the return journey we find a pharmacy that is open to fill the prescriptions and Bryn is again bad-tempered at the delay. Next day we are to drive to Mont Blanc and that worries me; he is not impressed when I say that if I'm no better they should take Naomi and leave me behind to sleep. His plan is the only plan.

I wake feeling a little improved though my appetite is not good, a bad sign for this food lover. It's a beautiful sunny morning as we breakfast on the terrace and the pain has eased a little; though I'm tempted to call and say that I'm still really unwell—I'd love to have the day at the hotel—but of course I don't.

In the end I quite enjoy the day, and Mont Blanc is stunning against the blue sky and with the soft, white and grey of glacier below. But there's an interesting optical illusion. Mont Blanc doesn't look like the highest peak and though logic tells me that it's to do with distances, angles and elevation, I want the highest peak to look higher than the others! We lunch at Chamonix alongside L'Arve River that is fed by glacial run-off, its rushing flow accompanying our meal. Later we drive close to the largest vertical glacier in Europe, my first glacial sighting ever and I'd never conceived just how large they are.

On the way down we stop for afternoon tea; I'm beginning to enjoy eating again and food with Bryn and Catherine is plentiful and delicious. Then we walk alongside *bisses*—man-made channels for water and irrigation—this type being dug out of the ground and lined with rocks. The air is clear and cool in the sunshine and the walk is a wonder of yellow and purple wildflowers.

We visit Bern, of the bear pits which I know about and really don't want to see but Bryn insists. It's as awful as I imagined. Bears have been kept as pets by the city fathers ever since Bern's founder killed a huge bear there, and apparently the ones in the pit are direct descendants of tame ones fed in the fifteenth century. But bears at the bottom of a deep pit and for what? To entertain visitors. Sorry, exploitation of animals for human entertainment is another of my soapbox topics.

But the rest of Bern is a wonderful maze of cobbled streets leading into elegant squares dotted with sculptures; medieval buildings overhanging the footpaths; a striking sixteenth-century clock tower (I couldn't resist that) with revolving figures that tell the hours, and a market and expensive shops where we find a glass paperweight as a present for Bryn and Catherine. Bern was destroyed by fire in 1405, rebuilt during the fifteenth and sixteenth centuries and little of its architecture seems to have changed since then.

Bryn and Catherine are well known in many of the restaurants we visit, and treated like family friends in those close to Chexbres. At one the chef joins us and he and Bryn hold intense conversations about politics and the 'Companions', an exclusive group that has a similarity to our Freemasons but who run a program to train talented young people as chefs, carpenters, scientists and engineers. Over three years from the age of about sixteen these apprentices travel on foot through France, Switzerland and Germany finding a 'Companion' who will take them in and teach them.

94

The most delicious foods I eat—obviously my appetite is improving—are a speciality of the Perigord region; a crisp apple 'dumpling' made with filo-type pastry; and a truffle omelette, my first (and possibly last) taste of truffles.

During this truffle evening Bryn acts quite strangely; about halfway through the meal he starts sulking, says he's 'had enough of us all' and refuses to speak to us. So Catherine, Naomi and I chat in our Franglish uninterrupted, no doubt rubbing salt into the wound. Maybe it's also because I have made a joke of them arguing over whether Mr Chip (their little dog) is allowed truffle, and we three women have probably monopolised more than he is used to. Finally I suspect the truth emerges when he asks, 'Are all Australian women as assertive as you two?'—talk about a 'damned if you do, damned if you don't' question!

On my return visit to the hospital, though my ear is really no better, I'm told to complete the course of medication as there's nothing else to be done. Ah well! At this stage I expect it to clear up. I refuse to let Bryn pay for these hospital visits— food and hotel is one thing, but this is my responsibility, though it will be hard to get him to accept money. But he cannot withstand that 'Australian assertiveness' especially as I thrust an envelope at him as we get on the train to begin our journey to Prague. He has no time to refuse.

The train journey is long but has its moments of interest, especially an amusing peek into Swiss culture. Between Lausanne and Zurich we unknowingly book a 'silent' compartment. A smartly dressed and coiffed Swiss woman of uncertain age tells us quite firmly that we are not allowed to talk, that this is a carriage for people who wish to travel in silence. Definitely not Naomi's and my style! Then even more strangely the carriage for the next leg is also classed as silent, but this time nobody takes any notice of that injunction. I have to say I haven't struck this particular railway idiosyncrasy before.

Travelling on public transport always offers challenges, and if I've learnt anything it is that there's a Murphy's Law that's to do with placement of carriages, station facilities and the station entrance one chooses. Luckily we have a spare hour and a half at Zurich, because we need to buy food for the journey, the loos are at the other end of the station to us, the train is not on the departures board and when we find the platform it is up and down many flights of steps— fine for me with a backpack, but not brilliant for small-wheeled suitcases.

It all works out of course and I have a note in my journal that 'I ate very smelly cheese and enjoyed it with dried apricots and apple'. Reading this I feel sympathy for the others sharing the carriage. I love a cheese called esrom that smells rather like disgusting socks—and I seem to remember the cheese from Zurich was of that variety.

So we say farewell to Switzerland and our touchy uncle. I feel disloyal criticising Bryn and unfair in the difficulty I have liking him: he and Catherine are very generous, paying for the hotel, and taking us to cafés and restaurants that we could not afford. All we can do is to give them their presents from Spain, the paperweight from Bern and indoor plants and pots for the house that we buy before we leave.

It's forty years since I last spent time with Bryn but I won't be rushing to repeat the exercise. I suspect he likes Naomi better than me. She is gorgeous looking and dresses smartly, quieter, calmer and not as argumentative—all significant attributes in his eyes. But he and Catherine enjoy showing us the Switzerland they love: Lake Geneva with the views across its water to the Swiss and French Alps; villages nestled on the hillsides with their vineyards clutching the sides of the slopes; the neighbouring towns, and the restaurants that just happen to be their 'locals' when they are in Switzerland.

Switzerland is clean, safe, pristine and beautiful; the weather is hot and the skies and water blue, but for me it has no soul or excitement. Though I suppose after the tourist brigands in Morocco, and wallet and bag snatchers in Spain, excitement might have been hard to find.

There's an irony in the ear story. It continues to bother me over the next three months of this journey so I eventually get it checked after I return home. It confirms what I know—that we have excellent medical people in Australia. The Ear, Nose and Throat specialist I visit takes five minutes to diagnose that I have a jaw problem; only my brain thinks my ear is at fault!

GETTING BETTER IN BELGIUM 97

By the time we reach Bruges in Belgium I'm bone weary. We've spent a few days in Prague—a fascinating city though my ear problem stops me enjoying it as much as I should—before catching another night train to Bruges. I've never been to Belgium and should be excited about another new place to explore, but it all seems too hard. Mind you, we've had three overnight train journeys in ten days—perhaps more than enough for age-challenged travellers!

When we arrive at the station we are both ready to stop but I'm younger than Naomi (not a lot but I try to look after her), so I leave her with the luggage and wander into town to obtain some Belgian francs. It's a lovely old town, fragments of medieval buildings, a winding road into the city, interesting shops, and I pass a small hotel that is an attractive old house with geraniums in window boxes—all very European. But getting money is the priority and working out where we'll stay if we don't like the youth hostel can happen later.

I don't anticipate a problem getting cash, but how often do expectations and reality not coincide? There is only one Cirrus automatic teller machine in Bruges and it's broken; but I carry a few traveller's cheques for just this contingency—and I find a money change bureau that is open. Lucky that!

When we planned this journey we were not sure whether we would stop in Belgium, so have no guide book—it feels strange; we've come to rely on these wonderful helping hands. We have the address of the hostel that we booked from Prague and though it's quite a trek it is also an opportunity to look at more beautiful architecture, plenty of trees and gardens, and shops specialising in chocolate, dolls and lace and, unexpectedly, amazing shoes—strappy numbers with heels to the sky, glitzy and brightly coloured.

The hostel is in an old house; very comfortable and we don't mind sharing a room with strangers. We meet two girls travelling together, one from Tokyo the other from Argentina, who are both living in Köln and studying at the university—not German language, but law and commerce in German. Makes what we are doing seem most unadventurous.

We book in, claim our bunks and go exploring, though again I'm surprised at how tired I feel. By the evening it is obvious there is something wrong but it's not until I wake in the night that I realise what it is. Once the magic antidote cuts in, Naomi and I enjoy the four days of my recovery.

Although there's no kitchen at the hostel there is a room with tables and chairs so we can buy food that doesn't need cooking and eat cheaply. And after a day I'm getting hungry again—I think the only thing that would stop me eating for more than a couple of days would be death! During her solo exploration Naomi finds Tous Paris, a wonderful delicatessen, where each day we buy salads, cheeses, bread and fruit. We have Swiss army knives and Moroccan plastic plates—minimalist self-catering at its best. Luckily we have similar tastes in food; fruit for breakfast and do-it-yourself lunches make travelling on a shoestring a pleasure however badly the Aussie dollar is doing. If it is expensive to eat in cafés in a particular country we cobble together reasonable dinners even without cooking facilities, but where it's cheap we treat ourselves to evening meals.

Bruges is a pretty city with winding and narrow cobbled streets; small houses, archways between alleys, interesting facades, and houses with gargoyles and statues on their

99

corners reminding me of Spain—except that they are not all religious. Nothing seems ostentatious or too large; I describe it in my journal as 'everything at people size'. And although there are plenty of visitors in town, it doesn't seem to be heavily into kitsch tourist dross.

Bruges calls itself 'The Venice of Northern Europe', and maybe it is, with canals and natural waterways everywhere. There are guides in boats inside the city, and people living in boats of all shapes and sizes. Outside the city we see barges, and small and large power boats, but no yachts, though possibly we're looking in the wrong place! We walk alongside canals and rivers, and discover four Dutch-style windmills: one being used for its proper purpose, one residential, and who knows what the other two are for. I have never been this close to a windmill before—they are ENORMOUS.

I remember my first meal in Bruges, on our second full day there and I'm well on the mend. It is cold, damp and blowy but we find a café next to one of the canals where they serve a creamy vegetable soup—and it is wonderful.

One day we spend six hours wandering and exploring— and it is lovely to have that energy again. We visit a museum in an historic infirmary in the Potterei district, possibly dating back to the twelfth century. It now houses a large and varied collection of furniture from Gothic to baroque, Bruges tapestries, a major collection of silverware, and paintings and sculptures—many of which are religious.

As we explore Bruges the bells in the tower often serenade us, more than just telling the hours it seems, and we willingly climb 366 steps up a narrow and steep staircase

100

to the top of the 83-metre high belfry. Apparently this bell tower has a slight lean to it but it isn't obvious to me—probably just as well with my fear of falling—and not only does it provide lovely views of this medieval city, the building itself is fascinating.

The belfry is also known as the Halletoren (tower of the halls), because three sides are enclosed by the former market hall. The belfry was added to the market tower in the thirteenth century but was destroyed by fire and rebuilt many times before the city fathers saw sense in the mid-eighteenth century and gave up on timber. A Gothic-style open parapet was added in 1822 and it is to this that we climb.

We time our ascent to hear the carillon and it's as if we are inside a massive music box; a large rotating drum triggers hammers to strike the outside of a selection of forty-seven bells—wonderful and worth the climb.

The 118-metre high spire of Church of Our Lady (Onze Lieve Vrouwekerk) is visible from many points around Bruges. It began life in the ninth century as a small chapel, but since the thirteenth century additions made include Romanesque, French Gothic and contemporary eighteenth century; recent renovations, though, have reverted to medieval design. The church is now an exhibition space and its brilliant white-painted walls, vaulted ceilings and timber arches are a stunning backdrop to religious and secular paintings and sculptures. I circle a Madonna and child sculpture in Carrara marble entranced by its beauty—one of the few works of Michelangelo found outside Italy.

In my solo wanderings I find Saint Walburga Church in a not-so-popular part of Bruges. It is locked, but has large glass doors through which I see much of the interior. More importantly there is a concert of light music that evening, so another chance to see a performance in a religious edifice. Although it is not performed by live musicians we enjoy the concert: light religious music in beautiful surroundings with good acoustics. And of course we can see the detail of what I glimpsed through the doors earlier—its baroque-style interior comprises a striking black-and-white-tiled floor, and works of various seventeenth and eighteenth century artists featuring magnificent marble surfaces and beautifully crafted altar, pulpit and communion bench.

Next morning we must leave Bruges, though I could easily have wandered for a few more days. And as I've been writing this I have revisited my photographs of Bruges— and realise how beautiful it is, and how much I'd like to go back. Maybe one day.

SIX

AN EXCHANGE PARENT
IN NORWAY

'Of journeying the benefits are many:
the freshness it bringeth to the heart,
the seeing and hearing of marvellous
things, the delight of beholding new
cities, the meeting of unknown friends,
and the learning of high manners.'

—Sadi Gulistan

I t's 2 June 2005 and I'm both excited and anxious as the train approaches Stavanger in Norway. It takes me back fifteen years to when Christian our first exchange student arrived in Australia to live with us for a year. Ian, Jai and I were at Melbourne airport awaiting the unfamiliar—we'd never been host parents before and Christian was an unknown entity. OK, we'd read his self-assessment and that of the exchange organisation, but what could they tell us about his hopes and fears, his loves and hates? He must have felt far worse anxieties than I'm experiencing as I approach Stavanger; he was only sixteen, alone in a foreign country and going to people he knew nothing about. We later discovered that his greatest fear was that he would find himself in a family with whom he had nothing in common, or worse. Now I'm on my way to live with strangers for a couple of months as a sort of exchange 'parent' and am feeling decidedly apprehensive.

At least I can have a Plan B, Christian couldn't; if it doesn't work out I can leave, go to the youth hostel and try to find another family. But I'm pretty easy to get along with, pretty flexible in my needs and understanding of what it's like to have a stranger descend on your household and become part of the family. It should be a terrific experience, but it's a new one for my hosts and they are probably feeling as anxious as me.

Janette and Pål (pronounced Paul) had answered my advertisement in a Stavanger newspaper for a family to board with for June and July. We had many communications by email—them finding out why I want to stay in Stavanger, me trying to assess whether someone older than their parents could fit into their lives, both parties trying to establish whether we might be able to live together for two months.

Deciding where to go on my travels is never an academic exercise, it's usually an impulsive response to something I see, hear or read. My journey to Stavanger in 2005 is the result of just such an impulse. When I landed there off a ferry four years earlier—after three months of living out of a backpack, in and out of countries, cities, villages and hostels—I had already decided that next time I would go somewhere to settle for a few weeks. To explore from a base, get to know people for more than an intense few hours on a bus or train, become part of a small community and start to speak another language. I had thought it would be Italy, visited so briefly in 1998. Then I landed in Stavanger and it was 'Goodbye Italy. Hello Norway' and I'd learn Norwegian.

I wrote in an email that 'somehow this small coastal town on the edge of a fjord has grabbed a bit of my heart'. I was really only there by chance: I'd wanted to go north to see the midnight sun but had run out of time; I'd wanted a 'proper' ferry ride having just done the tourist special through a fjord that is part of the Flåm railway experience— awe-inspiring but not a Norwegian in sight just lots of tourists like me. Finally, there were sentimental reasons too, as Ian had been there on ships in the Second World War and Jai had visited during her exchange student days in Denmark. So instead of returning to Oslo I caught the coastal ferry to Stavanger, walked out of the terminal, fell in

106

love with what I thought was a delightful little fishing town and decided to return some day. Although I had no idea how I could live in Norway, writing in my journal: 'Dream on, Jackie', because it had to be the MOST expensive country I'd yet visited.

HOW ON EARTH
DO I FIND A HOME?

In December 2004 I decide it's time, I'll go to Stavanger next year. I find a reasonably cheap flight to Copenhagen because there's no Melbourne to Oslo special deal, but that'll do. I can visit Christian and his family and Jai's host family from her year in Denmark before taking the train and ferry to Stavanger. In March I think I'd better do something about finding a family to board with as I'm flying out at the end of May. I Google for B&Bs but get only hotels. I register on a 'home-stay' website but all I get is a dubious offer from a gent in South America. Finally I find the Stavanger Tourist Information office on the internet and email them asking for help. Nina replies suggesting I compose an advertisement to go into local newspapers for a family to board with.

'A good idea,' I email back, 'but I don't speak Norwegian'. No problem; using wondrous electronic communication Nina happily translates what I write. Then my Swedish friend Monica checks to ensure that they aren't advertising something completely different to what I intend!

It reads: *Overnatting önskes i Stavanger av Australiensk dame i privathjem i Juni og Juli 2005. Önsker Bed & Breakfast og fritt bruk av kjökken til andre måltider.Vill betale, men kan også*

gi privat-timer I Engelsk konversasjon. Vennligst ta kontakt for
svar på spörsmål og mer detaljer; ... .

Which translates roughly as: Accommodation required in
Stavanger for Australian woman in a private home for June
and July 2005. Requires bed and breakfast and use of the
kitchen to cook evening meals. Will pay, and is willing to
give help with English conversation. Please contact with
questions or for more details; ... .

The first response comes from Pål and Janette. After a
few email exchanges we think this has a good chance of
working, but I haven't yet given them the bad news—my
age and vegetarian habits. There's deathly silence for two
weeks and I wonder if it's too much for a couple of
carnivores in their early thirties. I am so used to the idea
that I will live with them that I'm devastated and fire off a
quick, 'Please let me know if you have changed your mind'
to Pål. They haven't; he has been ill and not checking his
emails. Whew! Our communications continue, our
electronic relationship thrives, though attempts to send
photos so we can recognise each other fail. Pål and I
discuss practicalities and life philosophies, Janette and I
practicalities and recipes.

Despite discovering that Gausel where Pål and Janette
live is seven kilometres out of the city centre and I'd dreamt
of living in a cottage in the 'old' town, I'm very excited
about going back. Now it is to be put to the test. I am ten
minutes out of Stavanger, nervous as Christian must have
been, but excited that my dream of four years ago has come
to fruition.

GETTING TO KNOW
MY NORWEGIAN FAMILY

I travel to Stavanger on my Scanrail pass by a convoluted route. But thirty hours after leaving the warm embraces of Jai's host parents Per and Jutta in Espergærde, northeast Denmark, I'm there. Per is concerned for my safety with people I don't know and insists I email him once I arrive to let him know all is well, otherwise he will hotfoot to my rescue. I guess correctly that the young woman with curly auburn hair scanning the faces of the few passengers left on the platform is Janette, and the young man whose face expresses the same concerns that I feel must be Pål. I've only seen his name written and can't pronounce these vowels so call him Pal but he is kind enough to ignore it, and we greet each other with warmth and trepidation.

They express wonder that I have only a medium-sized backpack and small daypack, but happily take them over. I am longing to see their house, my home for the next two months, but they want to show me Stavanger. So we do a guided tour of the city that takes all of half an hour—the detail of which I forget in even less time—before the fifteen-minute drive to Gausel.

Their house is pretty: white painted with black trim, on three floors with the lowest one tenanted. It's very Scandinavian with polished timber floors, furniture in black leather, stainless steel and glass, and elegant blinds. Minimalist and uncluttered, the opposite of mine; but they *have* only lived in it for a few months. My bedroom is under the eaves overlooking Gandsfjorden one of Stavanger's boundaries, and from my window I see the mountains across the water. Over two months I watch them in all their moods; sometimes hazy mist rises from the fjord and shrouds their feet, on days of brilliant sunlight their grey height divides the water and sky, and in the rain they are bleakly sombrous.

It is more than a B&B. I am treated as one of the family and after four days I feel quite at home. Janette and I quickly agree we'll shop together and share cooking duties, a great way to exchange cultures. She is a morning person so we chat over breakfast before she goes to work. Pål is a person of the night, completely unsociable in the morning, and after Janette goes to bed we spend hours discussing philosophy and politics, Norway and Australia, and everything in between. We are surprised at how many similarities we discover between ourselves and our two countries, despite the Norwegian reserve with strangers that is so unlike Australian openness. Once I discover how strong this reserve is I realise just how lucky I am to have found a family to take me in.

After a week Pål asks me, 'What would you have done if you didn't like it with us?' I tell him that I would have gone to the youth hostel and looked for another family.

'But,' I ask, 'what would you have done? I have a door key and maybe I wouldn't want to go.' He laughs and says he knew it would be OK.

Food is not as different as I expect, though one dish is worth describing: *Ris Grøt* (rice porridge) a traditional Saturday lunch. It is somewhat like our rice pudding but

110

salty, and there is a 'proper' way to eat it: pile the porridge in your bowl, make a well in the centre into which you put a lump of butter, sprinkle liberally around the edges with sugar and cinnamon (and much discussion ensues between Pål, Janette and anyone else at lunch regarding the order in which these are sprinkled), take a spoonful of rice and spice and dip into the now melted butter, then eat. I manage a small serve the first Saturday, am more enthusiastic the second, and my final serve at Janette's parent's house tastes positively delicious. Otherwise dishes are similar, though with more cream and cheese than I am used to. I love *rekesalat*, a low-cholesterol deal with shrimps, hard-boiled eggs and mayonnaise—I'm joking about the low cholesterol. In exchange for these delicacies I introduce Pål and Janette to vegetarian cuisine.

When I set off for Scandinavia I left the completed manuscript of my first book with the publishers—if it wasn't up-to-scratch they could decide not to publish. During my third week in Gausel I get an email telling me it has been accepted—great excitement. No cheap alcohol in Norway but to hell with it, I blow much of the second part of my advance on a bottle of champagne that Pål, Janette and I knock off after they get home from work.

Both Janette's nephews come to stay for a weekend from Farsund, a small town on the bottom tip of Norway's southwest coast where most of Pål's and Janette's families still live. Ole (pronounced Ooler) who is seven comes first and Erik, almost twelve, the next weekend. Norwegian children are encouraged to be independent and they each

111

make the three-hour bus journey alone. I often notice the confidence of young children alone on buses and in shops, minding younger siblings, and generally doing things I think we would not encourage.

It takes a while for Ole to relax with me but I enjoy communicating with him in Norwegian. All children learn English at primary school but Ole's is pretty basic and he won't try. The ice is broken on Sunday morning when I teach him Fish, a card game. Good for my Norwegian, too.

'*Har du en tre takk?*' ('Have you a three, please?') Then '*Fiske*', when there is no three. We become real friends later that day when we climb to the top of the mountain that I see from my bedroom window, and I lend Ole my binoculars. I even get a hug when he leaves.

Erik is less shy and once he gets used to me is prepared to exercise his English a little. We get to know each other over games of Rummy and while participating in 'Siddisdager', a festival for Siddis, the people who are at least second-generation Stavanger born. We all enjoy the city's festive atmosphere and free breakfast, though none of us are Siddis.

As the cold, wet summer progresses I become more and more part of Pål and Janette's household. I am with them on 7 June 2005, the centenary of Norway's independence after centuries of wars and occupation, and am thrilled to be included in their pleasure as we watch the Norway-wide celebrations on television. At weekends we do things as a family: wandering on local beaches; clambering up pristine sand dunes (only pristine let me say because footprints last

112

just minutes in the wind); climbing a mountain or exploring pine forests close to Stavanger; and when the weather is reasonable we share the summer chores of house-painting and gardening—I even dig a veggie patch and plant a crop of rocket.

Weekend lunchtimes are often lengthy. Sometimes friends join us, sometimes it's just we three, a great time for communication between us. Over lunch one Saturday a few weeks before I leave, they ask me why Ian and I got married—they know we had lived together for eight years before doing so. I explain that both of us almost died—separately—and one day I just decided I would like to make the final commitment and marry him. I'd rung a friend who is a civil marriage celebrant, booked his first available Saturday afternoon, and told Ian that we were getting married on 24 May. Typically Ian, his response had been 'Good idea'.

This story amuses them, but reminds Janette that she had asked Pål to marry her in 2004, a leap year. He had said 'Yes', and they were supposed to get married in 2005, their tenth year together; it's now July and it still isn't happening. I ask where they want to get married and it's in Farsund close to both sets of parents.

'We'll be there in two weeks,' I say. 'If you get married then, I can be at your wedding.'

'Be quiet, Jackie,' says Pål. 'I don't want to talk about it.'

Janette and I try to persuade him to consider it but he won't budge. Two weeks later we are in Farsund where Janette's mother Patricia works at the courthouse where

113

people can get married. They decide they do want to get wed, immediately and can't understand why it's not possible—damned bureaucracy! They do get married, in 2006, but unfortunately I cannot be there.

In Norway marriage is not seen as important by society or government, but family and parenthood are. Norway (and Finland I learn in talking to Saana) has a very liberal attitude towards gender equality to time off from work to care for children. Legislation ensures that the mother and/or father gets paid leave to look after a baby for its first twelve months; and I'm in Norway during summer holidays and it's obvious that dads take their fair share of responsibility for child care.

STRUGGLING WITH NORWEGIAN

I know that Scandinavian languages are difficult. I've stayed in Denmark a couple of times, I've heard Jai speak Danish, and I've visited Sweden and Norway briefly. I have a phrase book covering all the Scandinavian languages, which is *most* confusing: how can countries divided by just a line on a map, spell words the same but pronounce them so differently? And some words look like English and even mean something similar, but that's where the similarity ends. However, I'm determined to give it a shot.

I purchase the *Lonely Planet Guide to Norway* a month before leaving Australia but forget about a dictionary. With only a few days left I ring the local bookshop that has only a phrase book. That will have to do; it will help with

114

pronunciation, and my first purchase in Stavanger must be a Norwegian–English dictionary.

Pål and Janette both speak reasonable English, so my Norwegian doesn't get as much exercise as I'd like. But English conversation is part of the deal so that's fair enough and they want to practise, particularly Pål who needs it in his job. I buy a small dictionary that becomes my bible, and spend at least half an hour a day with the *Stavanger Aftenblad* (a daily newspaper) trying to translate a news item that I later check with Pål or Janette. I read about two boys catching a 2.5-kilogram trout; a teacher of sixty-seven who is still teaching; a reporter trying to discover why local football teams have the names they do; and a break-in at a gun club's premises with the theft of sixteen guns from a safe made of eight-millimetre thick steel and weighing 1200 kilograms. I could be almost anywhere in the world.

After a month my pronunciation isn't bad. I'm automatically saying the final 'e' on words, and getting those 'æ, ø and å' vowels correct, I can say and almost understand the numbers from one to a hundred, and can remember odd phrases. Many written words make sense but spoken Norwegian is incomprehensible. There is a lilting modulation—a kind of sing-song intonation—in their speech that is wonderful to listen to, but difficult to understand. Pål has an Oslo accent while Janette's comes from the Farsund region, and they add to my confusion by disagreeing on pronunciation. I really admire Jai who was bilingual after five months in Denmark.

I try to speak Norwegian in shops, on buses, with people I meet but it's difficult because cruise liners often call in to Stavanger so shopkeepers reply in English when they hear my Norwegian. At the fish market, my favourite place in Stavanger, I always use Norwegian but we often finish up poring over my dictionary as these wonderful older men, who were once fishermen I'm sure, try to explain that these particular fish cakes include onion. Towards the end of my stay I manage to perform the transaction of buying a phone card with no word of English from either party—a great thrill.

OOPS, STAVANGER ISN'T A SMALL TOWN AFTER ALL

Typical me, I only start researching a month or so before I'm due to leave Australia; after my flights are booked, I've found my hosts, and am definitely beyond the point of no return. I discover Stavanger is hardly a little fishing town—it is the fourth largest city and the oil capital of Norway. But to put it in perspective, in 2005 the population is only 124,000.

I spend about six weeks in Stavanger, and get to know it well despite the weather, which is as great a challenge as the language; Norway's southwest is having an almost record cold and wet June and July. My explorations are definitely challenged but as I keep telling myself I'm not here for the weather. My dreams of daily latte at a café by the harbour are foiled, but the money I save buys me a new rain jacket.

Gausel is an easy bus ride from Stavanger Sentrum (centre) and with a special summer bus pass I can go everywhere I want on foot or bus. While Pål and Janette are

116

at work I wander for hours, becoming familiar with what it was that drew me back. The city still feels like the small fishing town I fell in love with: its harbour, its quayside market of fruits, flowers and fish, and its cobbled streets winding up and down between the shops in the new town— because cobbles can withstand the ice of Stavanger's winter, I'm told.

I constantly return to the old town or *gamle by* (pronounced bue with the lips pouted) dating back hundreds of years. I love how its narrow cobbled streets pour down the hillside to the harbour meandering between white-painted cottages and old factories. The fish market has been moved under cover (good for cleanliness, bad for ambience), but the old fishermen still treat me with humour as I struggle to ask for *reke* (shrimps), *fiske keke* (fish cakes) or *røyket makrell* (smoked mackerel). And the produce is still as delicious at the *jordbær* (strawberry) and *morell* (cherry) stalls.

Stavanger has been destroyed by fire many times, little of its origins still remain and even the 173 white-painted timber houses in the old town, now protected by the equivalent of our National Trust, date back only to the late eighteenth century. In the inner suburbs many houses are 150 to 200 years old: timber, painted wonderful colours, invariably two or three storeys high with attic rooms and steep roofs with ladder or steps attached so chimneys can be swept.

117

I have to do something in this cold, wet summer so join the library where I find a small cache of English language whodunits and classics. A real treat after my struggles with *Aftenblad* translations, but the children's picture books I borrow to help my Norwegian are not as interesting as the newspaper articles.

Soon after my arrival I go to the tourist information office to meet Nina and thank her for her help, and to collect maps and brochures. I discover that I can explore five museums on a one-day ticket and cannot resist that sort of bargain. But it's impossible in a single day—particularly as museums are scattered around the city and only open between 10 am and 4 pm. I spread them over two days and hang the expense!

I begin at the Maritime Museum on the edge of the old town where Stavanger's development is described as going from 'Fish to Oil'. From its beginnings to present day everything has been sea-based: transport, fishing, trade, ships for wars and emigration to today's oil rigs and tankers—a fascinating history for a water nut like me.

A smooth segue takes me to the Canning Museum, also in the old town at a factory that has been around since the 1800s. Its exhibits describe Stavanger's fishing industry, which began with herrings, salted for preservation but not very tasty I'm told. They disappeared in the early twentieth century but luckily sardines hung around, and thousands are still smoked and tinned each year though no longer at this factory. But I visit on a day when they smoke sardines for visitors to try—when else would a shoestring gastronome visit?

The fish are hung by their heads on long wooden skewers, suspended in enormous ovens over open wood fires and smoked for an hour. I have the smoking room with

118

its tantalising aromas to myself except for a large man in a massive apron who takes a skewer out, suspends it in a frame, and shows me how to eat the fish: pull the sardine off leaving the head behind, press gently, twist the tail and the spine and ribs pull out, resulting in a delicious almost bone-free sardine running with natural oil and ready to pop in the mouth. He hands me paper towels and says, 'Have as many as you want', then leaves. What an invitation. Who says there's no such thing as a free lunch?

If I had enough lives I would be an archaeologist in one of them so Stavanger, one of the richest areas in Norway for Bronze and Iron Age finds, is perfect. Even suburban Gausel has its Viking graves. The Archaeological Museum fascinates me. Its glass cases contain artefacts—jewellery, weapons, farm implements, household wares and skeletons—from Stone Age through Bronze and Iron to the Middle Ages, and all found close to Stavanger.

If I go to Jernaldergården (Iron Age farm) on the same day as the Archaeological Museum I can get in free—so of course I do. Some time last century a farmer found burial mounds on his property close to the city. There was one Stone Age, one Bronze Age and two Iron Age mounds as well as the remains of four long houses from the Iron Age. Three of these have been restored and this is Jernaldegården. Archaeologists worked out the construction, where posts were placed, that the houses were built on a slope, and the floors were made of dirt packed with animal blood with drains underneath to allow effluent to run off. Animals were kept inside on winter nights, on the high side of the house

119

so their waste ran away through these drains. It feels quite surreal to walk on the floor of a house that may have been built three thousand years ago.

My young guide tells me that if a landowner finds remains of habitation earlier than sixteenth century, the authorities must be notified, and all interference with the site must stop immediately. Worse the landowner must pay the cost of excavation. Understandably not many are reported.

And here's a fascinating detail about ancient wool dye: blue (*woad*), made from fermented leaves, was improved with the addition of aged urine and pots of it would be left in houses for this purpose. I'll stick with the ageing of wine in today's households, thank you!

Two historic houses are included in the museum ticket and they are quite different. Ledaal is imposing, rectangular and three storeys' high—painted a peach colour with dark trim when I am there—and surrounded by manicured gardens. It was built at the end of the eighteenth century for Gabriel Kielland a wealthy ship owner and a great uncle of Alexander Kielland, one of Stavanger's favourite sons, who wrote novels highlighting the social injustices of nineteenth-century Norway. Ledaal is currently the royal family's summer residence but memorabilia in the attic includes the Kielland family tree. I am particularly interested because Monica's adoptive mother was a Kielland descendant.

Breidablikk Manor was also constructed for a ship owner, Lars Berensten, and it displays opulent decoration and furnishings of the late nineteenth century. I find it less imposing than Ledaal but more beautiful. With dormer windows peeping out of the slate slopes of high-peaked roofs, bay windows on the ground floor, timber-painted ochre with dark highlights, and less formal gardens.

The Oil Museum absorbs me. I spend half a day wandering in and out of interactive displays traversing the geological events that resulted in the North Sea oil fields, and through the development of the industry in Norway; reading about terrible oil-rig disasters and enjoying models of rigs and all aspects of life on them. For me, the sort of tourist who goes into information overload very quickly, this is quite an achievement.

At the Stavanger Museum that covers everything the others don't, only the Alexander Kielland room engages me. The displays of stones and bones, geological information and Stavanger's recent history leave me cold. But as I walk back to the harbour for smoked mackerel and cherries the Domkirke (Cathedral) organ is being played.

The Domkirke, on a rise above the harbour and an icon of Stavanger, was built in the time of St Svithun a ninth-century bishop; apparently Stavanger is an adaptation of his name. Made of large blocks of rough grey stone with simple stone arches inside, and metal domes and spires green with verdigris outside, it combines Medieval, Gothic and Norman styles. Originally built in 1125, and extensively renovated after a fire in 1272, it is small for a European cathedral, friendly and welcoming rather than awe-inspiring and I often sit inside just to enjoy its ambience. Hearing the organ

121

is a bonus and I experience the Domkirke's fine acoustics for the first time; on another day its ringing bells attract and delight me.

Though Stavanger is not the small fishing town I expected, I thoroughly enjoy participating in its life.

EXPLORING STAVANGER'S SURROUNDINGS

Buses are my most common mode of transport in Stavanger, though dealing with the idiosyncrasies of the drivers can be challenging. I'm usually on the right bus, and I have a timetable and map to help me, but don't always finish up at the right stop. Drivers seem to think service means not admitting they don't know. My Norwegian may contribute to the problem, however, one driver doesn't know where the botanic gardens are, another the art gallery—both of which I say in reasonable Norwegian. But Stavanger administrators in their wisdom have sent half the bus drivers on holiday and cut services so perhaps these are temporary drivers who don't know the routes. Male drivers flirt with passengers and talk on their mobile phones, but the classic is one who misses a turn, then asks passengers to watch out of the rear window as he reverses because he can't see what is behind the bus. Luckily I see the funny side of these incidents.

122

It is almost impossible to get away from Stavanger without going over or under the surrounding sounds and fjords. I go to Haugesund with Janette and Pål and en route we drive under a fjord through a tunnel that drops to a depth of 223 metres. It's an odd feeling, particularly as I get a phone call from Kate in Australia on Pål's mobile phone at the deepest point. It makes Melbourne's tunnel under the Yarra with its odd leak seem quite mundane.

With Janette and Pål I put on my hiking boots and climb Preikestolen (the Pulpit) an extraordinary granite rock formation that towers 605 metres above Lysefjorden. Once at the top, for those brave enough to go to the brink there are wonderful views down into and along the fjord. I surprise even myself with my courage, but all I see from the edge are clouds, rain and mist. Disappointingly no indication that we are so high above the fjord, but it's an achievement just to be there. Two days later when a few sunny hours seem possible, I take a ferry trip to the end of the fjord, craning to see a tiny Preikestolen, about one centimetre across, way above my head. At the fjord's end we climb 600 metres in a bus, a mind-boggling half hour, with the road unwinding below.

There is always water to be enjoyed. Stavanger has three harbours and three lakes: Breiavatnet in the city centre, Store Stokkvatn, and Mostvatnet close to the city and with the art gallery on its edge. The latter two encircled by walking tracks that I enjoy at least once. On these walks I'm really aware of a major difference between Australians and Norwegians: we Aussies always exchange the time of day when meeting on a walk, even stopping for a brief chat; young Norwegians might exchange a '*god dag*' (good day), while older people generally avoid eye contact with a stranger altogether.

123

BERGEN:
A CULTURAL (AND WET) CITY

I take *Polarlys* a Hurtigruten (fast route) ferry up the west coast. I want to see the fjords and sounds from the water and go north of the Arctic Circle in the hope that the sun will shine long enough for me to see it at midnight. *Polarlys* departs from Bergen, Norway's cultural city so I'm told, and also the second largest, and the wettest—rumour has it that it rains 360 days a year.

I enjoy a calm, sunny ferry ride from Stavanger to Bergen and arrive in beautiful sunshine hoping this bodes well for the next few days. I find a youth hostel close to the harbour, the open-air market and the 'old' area, leave my pack and go off to explore while the sun is shining—having already experienced eighteen days of rain in my first three weeks in Norway.

On my earlier visit to Norway I spent a night in Bergen and remember it as a beautiful unspoiled city, so give myself a day and a half there. But three cruise ships are in dock and it's noisy, chaotic and crowded with every man and his troll out exploring the boutiques on the waterfront, 'ooing' and 'aahing' over wonderful Norwegian woollens, investigating the fish market and admiring the galleries in the old warehouses—too many people for me. So I take off to locate the wharf where the Hurtigruten ferry departs, and to find a supermarket. I'm a deck passenger on *Polarlys* and though I don't know how it all works I *do* know I'm not going to spend my rapidly disappearing dollars in the dining room. It's a beautiful evening, and I'm happy wandering Bergen's back streets.

124

Next morning the rain is absolutely sheeting but I have a day to explore and am not going to waste it bemoaning the weather. Luckily I replaced my rain jacket a few days earlier suspecting I might need it, and I even have waterproof over-pants. My journal says: 'A very wet day— understatement', and though I don't know it, I'm being prepared for my five days on *Polarlys*.

I meet an Aussie at the hostel who has worked all over the world but doesn't enjoy the retirement golf-latte-wine life, so travels continually. I note that he is an 'interesting bloke', but not interested in me, I think. Damn it! What the heck, I'm off to investigate Bergen.

I catch a bus to Gamle Bergen (Old Bergen), a reconstructed village of houses from the eighteenth and nineteenth centuries. People realised that these would be historically valuable, so at the end of the nineteenth century they were stored for the future and the village opened in 1945. Five houses are set up as if people still live there: a doctor/dentist (and am I glad I wasn't around then), a ship's master with a study full of charts and navigation aids, a private house belonging to a wealthy townsman and a couple of shops. An excellent insight into how people lived.

It is incredibly wet but I plod around the whole village (wishing I had Wellington boots) admiring the exteriors of the other houses and finally walking back to town. The Bryggen Archaeological Museum offers shelter and a wonderful display of artefacts that were discovered during its excavation: the original foundations from the twelfth and fourteenth centuries and the hull of a boat, sections of which are still intact. I also find information about the fire of 1955 that almost destroyed the Bryggen area, and details of the controversy over whether to bulldoze or rebuild. Most buildings were reconstructed and are now workshops, studios, galleries and shops, and Monica's maternal grandfather was involved in the project.

Bryggen, or wharf, with its brightly painted warehouses, is a successful tourist magnet. A few original buildings still stand with open first-floor areas, bare timber beams and walls, and original wooden steps between levels. I admired these on my first visit, as photographs on my wall attest, and enjoy them just as much the second time.

OSLO:
CITY OF HISTORY AND CHARM

I remember Oslo with pleasure from my first brief visit to Norway; an attractive city with its centre nestled around a large harbour. I spend two weekends there on this journey— the first on my way back to Stavanger after my Hurtigruten ferry trip. And not only is it a good excuse to return to the capital but Monica's friend, Carol, has invited me to visit.

As I am getting money from an automatic teller machine at Oslo station I place my fabric bag by my feet and someone takes it. Disappointing for them—all it contains is my Lonely Planet guide, my map of Norway, a novel and a cotton shirt. Frustrating for me—these are critical to my wellbeing.

It seems ridiculous to report it, but a police report is required for me to claim a new Lonely Planet guide and map

126

on my travel insurance. It is easy—especially compared to my subsequent experience trying to get a similar piece of paper in Cambodia. But two days later, I'm back at the railway station and there it is in lost property with my belongings intact!

On my return to Australia I find a letter from the police station that Monica translates for me: the police assure me they are doing everything in their power to find my stolen property and apprehend the criminals. I write back thanking them for their hard work. But I hope it is just a pro-forma letter, I'd rather they catch real criminals.

Carol, originally American but living in Norway for decades, had been a friend of Monica's mother, Wencke. She is seventy-six, a little incapacitated by a stroke but full of energy and suggestions for my day in Oslo. When she learns I am to visit the island of Skatøy on the southeast coast she draws me a map of Otterøy (where Wencke and her family had their hut), marking the headland where it was located in case I can get there.

We visit the Viking ship museum—Vikingskiphuset, Viking Ship House, isn't that delightful. The Vikings buried people of significance in beautifully decorated long boats, and those in the museum were discovered in burial mounds in the 1800s, remarkably well preserved by the blue peat which surrounded them. At some point the mounds had been plundered of valuables, but their archaeological value is incalculable. One boat has been completely rebuilt using original techniques and treatment of the timber, one partially restored and one preserved as it was found. There are also other artefacts on display: carts, sleds, pottery, tools, jewellery and remnants of fabric. This museum was built specifically to display the boats and artefacts and it is marvellous, with stark white-painted walls emphasising the simple lines of the black-tarred boats.

My next Norwegian history fix is at the Kon Tiki Museum: a different historical picture but, for someone who loves maritime history, just as fascinating. The Kon Tiki, the balsa wood raft on which Thor Heyerdahl sailed from Peru to Polynesia, is displayed with details of its manufacture and a map showing its journey in 1947. There are also replicas of the two reed boats Heyerdahl had constructed to sail from Africa to the Americas. The ropes holding the reed bundles of RA1 broke down more quickly than expected and it sank before completing the journey. But RA2, Heyerdahl's second boat, used a different design and type of reed, and he completed the journey successfully in 1970.

I spend a delightful afternoon with Gustav Vigeland's sculptures in Frogner-parken. He portrays wonderful aspects of humanity's love and warmth with his figures of people in stone, bronze and iron. They are the flabby bodies and wrinkled faces of grandparents, the delicate bodies of babies, the budding sensuality of puberty, and always the joy and sadness of the human condition. And so lifelike that I cannot help smiling at the father giving his young son a shoulder ride, the toddlers clambering over their grandmother's back, and children at play. I use thirty-six shots of film and still it isn't enough.

128

A few weeks later I have another weekend in Oslo, with Saana. We get a self-contained flatette at the Haraldsheim youth hostel where I've stayed before and spend time talking, eating, catching up on the seven years since we last met, and I happily wander around Vigeland's sculptures again.

We also explore the Norsk Folkemuseum for a day: a collection of small settlements from different periods of history comprising over 140 buildings, mainly from the seventeenth and eighteenth centuries. However there are reconstructions of earlier structures, the cream of which is a Stave Church from the thirteenth century: a timber construction using staves (wooden posts) and with finely carved decorations, a shingle roof and unique architectural style. There are also indoor displays of traditional costumes showing immense variation between regions, and clothes and dwellings of the Sami (indigenous people from Norway, Sweden, Finland and Russia).

On my own I enjoy Oslo's town hall, the harbour and its shrimp boats to which I give my custom, and reacquainting myself with this city that had charmed me on my last sojourn in Norway.

A COASTAL FINALE AND
FARVEL TO NORGE

I spend my last few days in Norway meeting Pål and Janette's parents: a lovely end to my Norwegian adventure. Pål's parents, Anneki and Halve, live in Farsund in a house that has been in the family for four generations. His parents are at their *hytter* on Skatøy so we stay in this rambling but luxuriously appointed house, and Pål and I explore the town on foot as he shows me where he spent his childhood.

Janette's parents live at Vaness, an even smaller town outside Farsund. Arne is Norwegian and Patricia is originally from the United States but has lived in Norway for thirty years. Arne takes us in his boat to picnic on a local island and I conclude that the ratio of boats to people in Norway matches sheep to people in New Zealand. The cost of alcohol guarantees a thriving moonshine culture and I learned at the folk museum in Oslo that not so long ago your host would be insulted if you went home without becoming falling-down drunk on his moonshine, so I cannot possibly say 'No' to Arne when he suggests I try his home brew—and it is quite drinkable when combined with apple juice! Janette's brother and sister-in-law live nearby so I catch up with Ole and Erik and meet their parents.

After Farsund we continue round the coast to spend a few days on Skatøy, and Halve and Anneki make me very welcome. This is the beginning of Pål and Janette's summer holiday, and the end of mine. Everyone I meet from Pål's and Janette's families is friendly, welcoming and warm, but maybe it's not just by chance; if Pål and Janette had not had these traits they might not have invited me to share their lives.

130   Anneki cooks her traditional 'welcome to the hytter' meal: waffler, a sweet waffle, traditionally eaten with either strawberry jam and cream, or strong brown Norwegian cheese made from goat's milk. A cheese I have found impossible to eat but am determined to try again. With

waffler it is quite palatable, enjoyable even. Maybe their sweetness softens its bite.

Kragerø is a tiny town on the coast, the gateway to hundreds of islands off Norway's southeast corner, from which ferries or water taxis will take you to the islands. I go from Skatøy to Kragerø alone one afternoon and return with a puzzle that I still haven't solved concerning a *frisør* (hairdresser) called Rosa Luxemburg. My mother had a second cousin called Rosa Luxemburg who was a Polish revolutionary killed in Germany in 1918 and it is such an unusual name there must be a connection. Unfortunately it is Saturday afternoon and the salon is closed, but I will find out one day.

Monica has often talked to me about her childhood summers on Otterøy and of Wencke building the hytter after the war, and Pål, Janette and I take Halve's boat to try and find it. It requires precise navigation and seamanship (in the cold wind and rain of course), but we eventually locate the headland and a man is there pulling in his boat. We explain what we are looking for and he tells us his family bought the property from Wencke a couple of years before she died and points out the original hytter. It is exciting to have found it and I photograph madly for Monica.

We have a lovely few days on Skatøy though the weather is not warm enough to tempt me into the water. We walk, talk, sit in the sun, eat and drink, and share a hot spa in the garden one midnight with Eilat (Pål's brother), his girlfriend Tine, and a couple of bottles of bubbly; it's 39°C in the water and about 5°C outside. Wonderful!

I could happily spend a week among these islands but unfortunately my plane ticket says otherwise. So Pål and Janette drive me to Larvic to catch the ferry to Denmark, and although it's a sad *farvel* to my Norwegian kids we'll meet again. Especially now that I have a Norwegian granddaughter!

Although everyone says Norway is the most expensive country in the world, how I travel and because of my time as an exchange parent, I don't find it so. I have a wonderful two months and could not have been luckier with my Norwegian hosts. My welcome was better than expected and our similarities were amazing considering I was an Australian in my mid-sixties and they were Norwegians in their early thirties. Stavanger was delightful, the weather atrocious, the language a nightmare; but I'm so delighted with the experience of being an exchange parent that I'm seriously considering repeating the exercise somewhere else.

SEVEN

NORWAY'S WEST COAST: RAIN AND FJORDS

'Being in a ship is being in a jail,
with the chance of being drowned.'

—Samuel Johnson

Maran and I sit on the ferry going across to Moskenes in the Lofoten islands, soaking up the all too rare sunshine and enjoying hot chocolate as we pretend the weather is warmer than it is. We want to get to Å (or Å i Lofoten), a small village on the southern end of the islands. We're prepared to walk from Moskenes to Å if we have to although we'd rather not, as Maran has a large backpack and a heavy suitcase.

The timetables show that the buses only run every three hours, which will give us no time in Å if we wait for one of those, so hitching a lift is the only option. We look harmless and clean, why wouldn't someone offer us a ride. Neither of us thinks that *we* might be in danger, of course. Is this because of the law-abiding nature of most Norwegians I wonder—at least when they are not under the influence of alcohol.

I'm slightly in front of Maran as we leave the ferry and see a couple with a dog unlocking a campervan. Cheek might do it, so I approach.

'Excuse me, do you speak English?'

'Oui' is the monsieur's response, which is rather nice.

I ask if they are going to Å—they are; and whether they can fit another two into their magnificent vehicle—they can. He is a hydrology expert working in third-world countries and along with his dog has joined his daughter, a student in Trondheim, for a few weeks' holiday. We have a wonderful journey: the hydrologist and I enthusing about campervans and France (I was an au pair there back in my dark ages); Maran and his daughter talking about being

135

foreign students in Norway; and *le chien* wagging his tail, smiling widely and licking the two extra pairs of hands fussing him.

We get to Å in fifteen minutes, thank our chauffeur, and leave Maran's luggage at the tourist information office until 4 pm, giving us three hours to explore the village.

I had cruised through the Lofotens on *Polarlys* (Polar light) and after talking to other travellers, reading the Lonely Planet guide's description, and seeing their towering grey splendour, I was determined to get there somehow. Bodø is the only place on my route south from which I can do it and my time line has only one spare day. So though it may be crazy to take a day trip involving two long boat rides, I'll do it.

I pick up ferry and bus timetables as soon as I arrive in Bodø and work out how to get to Å, even considering a five-kilometre hike. Then I meet Maran in the youth hostel kitchen; she's in Bodø to do her PhD and is going to the Lofotens to stay with friends, so if she can leave her luggage somewhere she'll join me in the Å adventure. If not, I'll go it alone.

Originally the Lofoten islands were only used for cod fishing in the spring, and although many of the other islands possess working fishing villages, most of the nineteenth-century buildings in Å are now museums.

Maran and I explore everything, even attaching ourselves to a couple of guided tours to get free information. The cod liver oil factory sells its oil to tourists (and it tastes no better than when I was forced to swallow it as a child), while the other buildings—houses, huts, stables, boat sheds—are for exploration and information. Except the Bakeri, about which Maran has heard good things, so we try a *bolle* (sweet roll) just to check it out. And after exploring the last museum building we have a quick bite in the café where Maran introduces me to *Verdensbeste* (literally 'world's best') cake—meringue-topped, cream-filled, with a slightly chewy base. Delicious! We walk to the very tip of the island and down to a beach hopefully using up some calories, before getting a bus back to Moskenes where I catch the ferry to Bodø and Maran awaits her friends.

The atmosphere is idyllic, the sea calm silvery-blue pewter, streaked with ripples, and from the ferry the snow-capped sharp peaks and rounded tops of the Lofotens stretch as far as the eye can see. A teasing taste. If I'd known of their beauty I would have jumped ship earlier and spent a couple of weeks walking the Lofotens from north to south. The ferries and buses are infrequent but getting to Å would have been possible and the youth hostel spread between some of the old buildings would have been fun.

THE *POLARLYS* JOURNEY

Getting organised

One reason for being in Norway in June is to explore the west coast by ferry and see the midnight sun. Having done a trip from Bergen to Stavanger on a coastal ferry four years earlier I naively think I can get north of the Arctic Circle in the same way. Unfortunately coordinating buses and local ferries requires more days than I have, but it was my choice to live in Stavanger so I'm not grumbling—there are just too many things to do in this life!

The Hurtigruten line is the only one that runs ferries all the way up the coast. They are like cruise ships, but take freight as well as passengers from Bergen in the southwest to Kirkenes in the northeast, stopping at thirty-three ports on the way. They cruise through sounds, fjords and the narrowest of channels between islands. Despite the liner-like look of the Hurtigruten ferries, it is that or nothing.

I check timetables, the ports of call, how to get back and what it will cost. No way can I afford the time or money to do the whole journey to Kirkenes, and much as I like the sound of Nord Cap (north cape) it isn't worth two more days just to visit it. So five days and four nights on *Polarlys* going as far as Tromsø, 500 kilometres above the Arctic Circle, will have to do. Hopefully there will be plenty of opportunity to see the midnight sun, and plenty of Norway to experience before settling back home in Stavanger.

I find out from my Lonely Planet guide that I can travel 'deck class' on the Hurtigruten ferry, saving the cost of a cabin. I guess they expect these passengers to sleep on the deck—excellent idea if the weather permits. But whatever the weather there's no choice for a solo shoestring traveller: single cabins don't exist, no dormitories are provided, no single supplement and by the time I check, only three-berth cabins are left and I'm not paying for one of those. So a deck passenger I'll be.

138

Booking *Polarlys* is a challenge in itself. I'm not too enthused about paying by credit card on the internet, particularly 4000Nok (around A$890). I like a person to deal with and a good old-fashioned receipt. Surely I should be able to find a travel agent to do this—Stavanger is a city for goodness sake. Someone at the local ferry terminal knows of an agent who might help, but it would cost me an extra 10 per cent to do it through them. So thanks, but no thanks. I return to the internet and of course it's OK.

Life as a deck passenger

The evening before I depart from Bergen I find the Hurtigruten terminal and the ferry leaving that night. The pictures on their website haven't prepared me for just how large she is, and I suspect *Polarlys* will be similar. If I hadn't already booked (and paid) I think I would be cancelling the idea and doing it on buses and small ferries no matter how difficult, but by the time I leave the next day my enthusiasm has returned.

Passengers without a cabin must be a rarity, at least out of Bergen. 'I don't know about deck passengers, go to deck three and ask the purser,' I am told politely but firmly when I reach the front of the queue of immaculately dressed couples with their luggage.

So I pick up my pack, tramp the length of the walkway alongside this ferry that looks like a luxury liner, and assisted by assorted crew members find the purser. He isn't thrown: he points me to an adjoining small room with racks where I can leave my luggage, tells me where I will find a shower, and which areas I'm 'allowed' to use. I ask him if it's correct that I can sleep in one of the lounges. 'Certainly. Once all the passengers go to their cabins, just sleep on a couch.' How sensible.

I deposit my pack and go off to explore. There are seven levels: the lowest one inaccessible—probably for freight; the second seems to be crew accommodation and where I shower. Levels three, four and seven have public areas: gangway, purser, information desks, lounges, dining room, café, a library and a couple of bars; plenty of places for me to hang about. Five and seven have access to deck areas where a deck passenger can spend her days (and nights) enjoying the scenery, lounging on a lounge, and partaking of the odd beverage. Little knowing what the weather god has in mind, I write in my journal: 'Large outside deck on seven, I'll probably spend time there'. But despite *Polarlys*' size it's exciting to be here, although sunshine would have been nice that first evening.

I'll be sleeping round a curve as the couches are narrow and banana-shaped, but it's free so I'm not complaining. I find a table by a window on level four close to the café where I will buy cups of tea to accompany my self-catering, and decide this will be my daytime possie.

I have shopped well; tonight it's two rolls, smoked mackerel and avocado, with fruit and yoghurt for dessert and breakfast. I anticipate that I may have to eat in the café and dining room, until I discover that lunches are 275Nok! I check the schedule and am relieved to see there's at least one stop each day long enough for me to shop. I'll be able to self-cater, with an occasional treat from the café perhaps.

Most of *Polarlys*' passengers are tourists like me (though they have cabins), but some people embark for short hauls between one or two ports. The majority of those doing the full journey from Bergen to Kirkenes are my age or older, with a few families and a handful of young singles; they are mainly from the United States and Europe with just a *soupçon* of Australians.

At an information session I hear about a cruise card for purchases on board. It'll be easier than cash or credit card no matter how little I plan to spend so I go to the café where they are dispensed—but only to people with a cabin number. I'll see about that!

I return to the purser and ask if I can have a cruise card. 'No problem,' he says and starts pecking at his keyboard.

'Name?' That's fine I have one of those. He next requests cabin number. I remind him I'm a deck passenger. 'Sorry the computer wants a cabin number.'

'I have a credit card, surely that's good enough?' I ask.

But no way will the system let him issue me with a card. I was a computer programmer in an earlier incarnation and know it could be done, and there's a principle here. But I'm not about to spoil my five days for a principle.

On the first night I find it hard to get to sleep, dropping off eventually at 12.30 am after the band in a nearby bar stops playing and some night-owl cabin passengers in the Panorama lounge leave (don't they know it's my bedroom?). At 3.30 am I am woken by three chatty Norwegians who got on sometime during the night. They are the reason for the deck passenger option of course.

My 'bedroom' has wonderful floor-to-ceiling windows and I sleep facing them so that I wake to waves and islands rushing past, or to look down on a dock as we load or unload early morning cargo and people. I get up early each day, the pattern being set on my first morning when cleaners arrive at 4.30 am, have a wake-up shower then relax and doze at *my* table (nobody arrives to beat me to it that early), enjoying the peace and gentle movement of *Polarlys* and buying my first cup of tea when the café opens at 6.30.

From this spot I watch the snow-capped mountains fly by as the day (invariably) degenerates into wet and cold. Outside the windows, so close you can almost touch them, islands dotted with tiny settlements jut like rocky mountains from the sea, surrounding us as we wend our way through the fjords. The sides of fjords are high vertical cliffs with small patches of clinging foliage, clouds softening the tops, and water cascading down in single falls or sheets, cutting paths through the green and grey.

On the first morning over my breakfast of fruit and yoghurt I see a young woman eating at an adjacent table. Debra is going to a conference in Trondheim and has a cabin but is otherwise travelling as cheaply as she can, and we share breakfast and the rest of the day.

I became known to other passengers as that slightly eccentric woman travelling alone without a cabin. But thanks to that eccentricity people stop to chat. Their conversations invariably start, 'Are you the one who ...' a little

142

too embarrassed to finish I do it for them, '… doesn't have a cabin? Yes.' Then the questions follow. Where do you sleep? How do you shower? Why do you travel like this? I explain that I wouldn't do it any other way and how much I gain from journeying as I do. A few interlocutors become friends for the duration of the journey and beyond.

I wash my undies in the shower each day (a quirk of lightweight travellers) and drape them over my pack in the baggage room to dry. I had been embarrassed at the thought of wandering the ship in my thermals (aka pyjamas) but I get undressed in a loo on the seventh level next to my 'bedroom' and dressed in the shower room next morning. At 5 am only the cleaners are around, and we exchange grins.

I'm used to being active and go stir crazy stuck inside because of the weather. So in arctic gear of scarf, rain jacket and over-pants I tramp around decks five and seven; sometimes so blowy it takes my breath away. Expecting sunshine I left my woolly hat in Stavanger, didn't I! Whatever the weather I get off wherever we stop during the day: to stretch my legs, marvel at more mountains and beautifully painted timber houses, and of course to stock up on provisions. This self-catering works well and I feed myself ridiculously cheaply.

Five stunning days in the wet   143

The 20-kilometre long Geirangerfjord is supposed to be the most beautiful in Norway. Quite a statement. It certainly has breathtaking waterfalls: De Syv Søstre (Seven Sisters), Friaren (the Suitor) and Brudesløret (Bridal Veil) cascade down the walls, swelled by the quantity of rain that has fallen since I've been in Norway. Some passengers go on an excursion to Geiranger, the small settlement at the end of the fjord, while I enjoy the scenery from *Polarlys'* deck: the falls, filtered through pine trees, rush from the top of the fjord walls and frame the village; the opaque greeny-grey water which would be stunningly green in sunshine. We are surrounded by beauty despite misty views, clouds and constant rain.

We have twenty minutes for our first stop at Ålesund and Debra and I rush up Aksla, a high tor overlooking the town, meeting Kieran and Carol from Emerald in Victoria on the way. At the top we do the 'So you come from Victoria, do you know …?' routine, and discover in astonishment that they and I have friends in common in the small town where I live.

Later in the day we return to Ålesund to collect those who visited Geiranger and I have an hour to get to the supermarket. I come out of the 'wrong' shopping centre exit and am well lost, but using my basic Norwegian get directions from locals. During my dash around the harbour I plan that if I reach the wharf and *Polarlys* has gone I will somehow get to her next port of call. I gave up worrying long ago, now I plan instead. But neither worry nor planning is necessary, the crew waste twenty minutes loading cargo and I could have ambled back.

144

We have a few hours in Trondheim but because I'm coming back on my way south don't need to do the tourist trail. Instead I accompany Debra until she turns towards the university then set off to find the youth hostel so it will be easy when I return. It's at the top of a hill, as they often are, but the twenty-minute walk with my pack will be perfectly manageable.

I get caught up in the start of an annual bike race from Trondheim to Oslo. Talking to an official I discover that it's 550 kilometres, the serious riders do it in thirty hours while the 'slow' ones take up to thirty-five. Oh, dear! When I did the Queensland bike ride in 2004 I took eight days to ride 560 kilometres.

Assuming this weather is here to stay I go into a second-hand clothes shop to look for a hat. But at 98Nok for one that's not very attractive, my woollen scarf will do fine, thank you. Not expecting such dreadful weather I also left my boots behind (a light pack's a good pack), my sandals are definitely unsuitable so I'm doing all my tramping in the casual leather shoes I have with me to meet royalty. Soft and comfortable they may be, but these shoes are not made for walking and they let in the rain. So my feet are the greatest sufferers.

We cross the Arctic Circle into the Land of the Midnight Sun (aka Land of the Midnight Rain) at 7.10 am. The skipper blows the horn loudly and often—nobody is to sleep through this momentous event—and we crowd to the port side of the deck watching the tiny island and filigree globe on its stand appear through the morning murk. No clap of thunder, magic sunshine, or other sign; just a lot of drizzle getting heavier.

145

I'm a sucker for glaciers and apparently Svartisen is the second largest in Norway so I extravagantly go on an excursion. I also like the idea of a small boat in the fjords instead of Polarlys' vastness, and hold a ridiculous hope that the sun might shine. My waterproof jacket and over-pants save me again; it doesn't stop raining the whole six hours—my wettest excursion ever. All that is visible are the blue-white foot of the glacier and misty mountain tops covered in clouds—the picturesque nature of which is definitely beginning to pall. Our guide is a German woman who speaks incomprehensible English with Norwegian 'sing-song'. But we soggy sightseers, crowded together for warmth, work out that we are being shown a salmon farm, a salmon-processing factory and sea eagles.

A bus takes us from the boat to meet *Polarlys* at Bodø and we stop at Saltstraumen where, at each tide change, 372 million cubic metres of water are forced through a 150-metre wide sound creating a maelstrom. It is impressive even in the rain. Herring gulls know when the fish will be eating the plankton that is pushed to the swirling surface; and alight and take off on a spinning merry-go-round of whirlpools. Fisher people huddle coldly under umbrellas patiently hoping for their share.

The bus driver provides us with information and statistics about fishing, weather, the countryside and northern Norway's industrialisation, most of which I forget immediately. But I do remember that puffins nest near Bodø each year, arriving at 2 pm on 10 April—or so he says. It seems an odd freak of instinct; and I wonder how they deal with leap years. Despite the wet greyness I really enjoy this day away from *Polarlys*.

That evening we cruise into the Lofotens—a stark wall towering out of the sea with cloud haloes and small settlements nestling at its feet. We squeeze into Trollfjord, the scene of fights between traditional hand-line fishermen and people using automated fishing methods (true), but also a Viking versus troll battle (fable). The sides of the fjord are so close that you can almost touch them and though the rain feels like sleet I am out there in waterproofs, grimly clinging to a stanchion to record the event—and have rain-spotted photos to prove it. We are treated to Troll Soup in celebration; though whether of the battles, the weather or the majesty of the place I'm not sure—and definitely unfair to trolls.

I spoil myself on my last morning with *frokorst* (breakfast) in the dining room with Kieran and Carol, and Rob and Moira from Canberra; the Aussies with whom I have spent many hours—wet ones on shore and dry ones over glasses of nectar. Frokorst is excellent value as we chat, eat and laugh for ninety minutes, particularly as I can find no-one to take my money.

My final treat is a traditional 'crossing the Arctic Circle' ceremony. Few people volunteer but I'm foolish enough to have a go at anything. I kneel in front of Neptune who, with a great deal of pleasure and some Norwegian imprecation (or blessing), deposits a ladle of ice and water inside my rain jacket and jumper, and a glass of port in my hand. In such weather I would have appreciated more port and less ice. 147

I repair to the Ladies' loo, strip off my wet clothes and dry them under the hot-air hand dryer, a trick I learned one night after a very wet walk—an appropriate farewell ritual for a deck passenger.

TRAVELLING SOUTH AND WEST

My feet on the ground in Tromsø

I leave *Polarlys* at 2.30 pm, saying goodbye to the Aussies who are continuing to Kirkenes, and walk into Tromsø centre. After the crowded ship it is lovely to be on my own again, with my pack on my back and ready to explore somewhere new. I get a bus pass, maps, and brochures about Tromsø, then catch a bus to the hostel that is actually a university hall of residence—not unusual in summer months. I cannot book in until 4 pm, so take the opportunity to walk to the local supermarket to buy provisions for the next few days. I always enjoy food shopping in new places; the ordinariness of it grounds me. And it will be a joy to cook again.

After settling into a light and airy dorm and inspecting the clean kitchen and bathrooms I know I will enjoy this hostel. I can travel on my pass as often as I like, so after a quick cup of tea I catch a bus back into the city and just wander to get a feel for Tromsø. Later at the hostel I cook dinner revelling in the fact that I can: fishcakes, salad, bread, yoghurt and melon (easy, delicious and cheap).

A Danish family—Mum, Dad and two teenage sons—are playing a card game as I eat and invite me to join them, and we play cards and talk until 11.30 pm. The whole evening reminds me why I enjoy hostels so much.

The botanic gardens are on my 'must-do' list and even better than I'd imagined. The most northerly in the world, they cling to a hillside and tumble towards the fjord on which

148

Tromsø sits. The flowerbeds are built atop mounds and crisscrossed by stone walkways so you can get close to everything, and the species and colours are myriad. There are also wonderful arctic plants from many places: Norway, of course, but also Africa, China, Patagonia, the Himalayas, New Zealand, and Kirovakan in Mongolia which was the most northerly botanical garden before this one opened. There is a fascinating selection of plants from old Norwegian gardens as botanists try to preserve historical species; and gardens of herbs for cooking, medicine and witchcraft!

On the bus back into the city I get a stunning view of the Arctic Cathedral backed by dark snow-capped mountains. This cathedral with its towering white triangular roofs reminds me of the Sydney Opera House, although the cathedral's peaks are steeply pointed. But most striking is the east wall, an enormous triangular stained-glass window in glowing colours that complement the stark whiteness and modern architecture. I think you'd either love it or hate it, and I love it. It is just as dazzling inside and my experience is heightened by six children singing, their soprano soaring into the towering peaks.

I visit other churches too. The Protestant Domkirke (the old cathedral) is small for a cathedral, no towering peaks or ceilings here, just a single finely pointed spire. The outside painted immaculately in dark cream with pale-blue trim; inside the dark wooden walls give the church a sombre feel but its tiny organ is beautiful. Apparently this is the most important cathedral in north Norway and one of the country's largest wooden churches. The Vår Frue kirke

149

(catholic church) is tiny and quite plain outside, but inside is a delight of blues, creams and gold and even the organ mounts have delicate highlights. The two churches were built in 1861, and according to the Lonely Planet guide both claim to be the 'world's northern-most bishopric'.

The Kunstmuseum's (art gallery's) collection is a mixture of design, sculpture, textiles and paintings many of which are scenes of the Lofotens: its islands and fishermen. And a special exhibition shows 150 years of Danish art with some very interesting works. I move on to the contrast of a small glassblowing studio run by three young artists and I've never before been so close to the glassmaking process. They are making chunky wine glasses; not to my taste but I can appreciate their skill.

My day of Tromsø tourism ends at the Polar museum with its fascinating exhibitions of the treks to both poles by assorted Norwegians with Roald Amundsen being the best known, and a section about Svalbard (literally 'cold coast' in old Norwegian) and its history of settlement and development since the Middle Ages.

By the time I get back to the hostel I've walked miles in those wrong shoes, and have sore feet, and I'm *very* cold—I washed my jumper and didn't put on thermals because the forecast was for improvement. Well I suppose the fact that it didn't rain—much—was an improvement.

But all that changes. I wake at 1.30 am and get my first glimpse of that elusive midnight sun shining between the dispersing clouds. It is like daylight, with glowing sun and shadows on the ground.

Industrial Narvik in the midnight sun

On the bus from Tromsø to Narvik I enjoy land-based views of the mountains, lakes and fjords for a change, and in Narvik I stay at Breidablikk guesthouse. I have the cheapest bed I can get, in a dorm that is in the depths of the house with no breakfast, tea-making facilities or fridge. I have bought food for dinner, breakfast and lunch so hope the newly arrived sunshine won't be *too* hot.

At the war museum I discover how badly Norway fared in the Second World War: it was occupied from June 1940 to the end of the war, and photographs of a completely destroyed Narvik are an eye-opener. The city was a major target because of its iron-ore loading facility, developed because the Gulf Stream stops Narvik harbour from freezing in winter. Many people were killed—civilians and military, Germans and Allies, and the harbour was filled with sunken ships. After the war Narvik continued to be used for transportation of ore so the port was rebuilt, but it is big and industrial; no picturesque fishing harbour here.

The summer has definitely arrived by the end of the day and I'm glad to have a window because I wake at 1.15 am, open the curtains and there is the midnight sun again, reflected on mountain tops and sparkling through trees.

By morning the sky is cloudless, and though probably only about 23°C it's a joy after the cold and rain. The guesthouse is close to all I want to do so I walk, relishing the sunshine. First to find a Stone-Age rock carving but I assume it's the antiquity that makes this important not the carving itself, because it has been detailed in red paint so it can be seen.

151

I go to the war cemetery and adjacent Peace Church. Built after the war, the church is quite plain outside but beautifully decorated inside. The cemetery is solemn, tranquil and well maintained; the greatest number of war graves is for Germans who in death have been shown as much respect as Narvik's defenders from the United Kingdom, Russia, Poland, France and Norway. Looking at the ruins of Narvik after 1940 this respect says a lot about the local people.

At the city museum I learn about Narvik's beginnings (and that red-painted carving is one of eight around Narvik, all thought to be about 5000 years old), its growth, death and rebirth. I also learn that thousands of captured Russians were brought to Norway to help with wartime building projects and imprisoned in the most dreadful conditions, few surviving. I wonder sadly whether the human race will ever learn humanity.

The day's highlight is the Fjellheisen cable car that climbs to 656 metres. I should wait until midnight and watch the sun drop to the horizon from the top but am too weary. However it is fantastic even at 8 pm with the sun at sixty degrees. The cable car ride is wonderful, and I explore the summit and enjoy the peace before meandering down six kilometres of walking track; meeting evening walkers, joggers, and a cyclist going up. And around every bend I see water, mountains, cable cars, and always the silver birches.

I describe my impressions in my journal: 'Sparkling pewter of the water with ripples from a tiny boat and the wind. The path of the sun is pale gold, silver and white'.

152

At 10 pm it is still mild and I sit on the guesthouse terrace in a light top and sarong until midnight. It's like daylight and I can see the harbour—attractive from this distance—and across the fjord are snowy mountains behind which the sun dips and rises again.

Bodø—gateway to the Lofotens

Another bus, this time to Bodø, and I'm becoming so blasé about the scenery. But we are now blessed with sunshine and there are wonderful reflections of mountains and clouds in the water. I had noticed a young man when he arrived to catch the bus. He dismounted from his bike, took it to pieces and put the bits into a bag, which he then chucked into the luggage compartment, and I had wondered 'What if he drops a small piece into the grass?'.

Part of this journey is by ferry and he and I meet on the deck, each enjoying the sun, water and views. I ask him whether he's ever lost a small but critical piece of his bike while packing it up. He tells me he has done it so many times he's quite confident. He's from Switzerland, finished school the year before and is travelling in Europe by bike, bus, train and ferry wherever the wind takes him, before going back to university. He's never done anything like it before, and having a wonderful time. What a great way to fill in a year.

I have booked into what I consider a *very* expensive guesthouse in Bodø, at least compared to hostels, but breakfast and linen are included and it's part of the youth hostel complex so I can use their kitchen. This is where I meet Maran, my companion for that day in Å.

153

I have only one day left to explore Bodø. I begin by walking to Bodin kirke and the bells call me from about two kilometres away. This is the oldest, unchanged medieval stone church in Norway dating from 1240, with a baroque pulpit and sculpture behind the altar. It is Sunday and I time it perfectly for a 10 am service. Out of respect I don't photograph inside, but do so outside and am lucky because about a quarter of the female congregation is in traditional costume. Pål and Janette later say it had to be a christening or another significant service for them to be in traditional clothes, but as I saw no babies or children I don't know what the ceremony was. Foolishly I had not thought of attending the service and am dressed completely inappropriately—I could kick myself, it would have been wonderful.

I visit the museum and an exhibit shows that the Germans used the same scorched earth policy in Bodø as in Narvik, though not why. And, thanks to German bombs and the US Navy 'rescuing' Norway, these cities sadly lost most of their medieval buildings; the majority of architecture is from the 1950s to 1970s.

Before catching the train to Trondheim I treat myself to a light meal at a fish restaurant in the centre of Storgat, a street filled with tourists and traffic that passes either side of this island eatery. I have an entrée-size bowl of delicious *fiske zuppe* (fish soup), similar to Janette's with less fish but the same flavour. Then I get a free coffee, decaffeinated and freshly made. At 42Nok it's definitely my best value meal in Norway.

154

Falling in love with Trondheim

The overnight train journey from Bodø to Trondheim (or Trondhyem as the Norwegians say) is easy. I choose a window seat and with the constant sunlight I have views to spoil me whenever I wake.

My earlier recce pays off, I know exactly how to get to the hostel, and there is a bonus: it is early morning and I get a free breakfast even though I haven't stayed the night. The noise in the dining room is incredible, mainly generated by a group of Americans here to compete in Norwegian folk-dance competitions. Most of the dancers are my sort of age and very enthusiastic about folk dancing.

Trondheim has a large student population so is filled with life (and bicycles). On the steep hill that runs up to Kristiansten Fort is a conveyor belt at ground level to which you attach your bike, stand on a pedal and let it pull you to the top— clever, but rumour has it that it doesn't work. The Trondheim council, keen to get cyclists into the city, also provided free green-bikes to be picked up and left at points around the city as needed. I see many empty green-bike points because the temptation to steal free bikes (even green and not particularly good quality) was too much for the law-abiding Norwegians! Apparently Oslo tried the same system with the same result.

Trondheim has the most wonderful atmosphere and ambience and I love the areas of Mollenberg and Bakklandet with their old timber houses and the warehouses from the eighteenth and nineteenth centuries on the edge of the Nidelva River. If (when) I come back to Norway to live I will look for a family in Trondheim.

155

But Trondheim is perhaps best known for Nidarosdomen, the largest cathedral in Norway and also Scandinavia's largest medieval building. After hours of tramping around it I don't doubt it being the 'largest'. Nidarosdomen reminds me of Salisbury Cathedral, and is believed to have been designed by an Englishman because of its similarity to many cathedrals in the United Kingdom. Over the centuries much has been destroyed by fire, the only original parts being the Chapter house, one of the chapels and the transept. As far as possible all restoration has been true to its Gothic style, even to the details of carved statues and gargoyles. But as restorations weren't officially completed until 2001, can it be truly medieval?

There is a lunchtime recital on the original organ, wonderful in this enormous religious edifice with its atmospheric and acoustic perfection. I repay that pleasure by climbing up narrow winding steps to the top of the tower where the view over the city and the sloping roofs of the domen make the climb insignificant.

I stay in medieval mode by checking out church ruins that were found during excavation for the library and a bank. The remains of the twelfth-century Olavskirken (St Olav's church) were found at the library; St O was a despotic king who was sanctified after death. There is a bonus here too, a couple of skeletons with an extra skull! The ruins beneath the bank are of the medieval Gregorious Kirke, which is better presented but no skeletons to add that extra frisson.

All the people I spoke to on *Polarlys* who had explored Trondheim said I must go to the Ringve Music Museum—

156

and they were right. I'm fascinated to find instruments I've never heard of: examples are bagpipes from countries other than Scotland and Ireland; and a Norwegian fiddle, a highly decorated violin used for folk music that has a second row of strings that vibrate when the top ones are played.

The collection was built up by Victoria, a Russian-born woman who married Christian Bachke, a music-lover, who owned Ringve Manor. Before Christian died, he asked Victoria to use their house to exhibit old musical instruments for the people of Trondheim to enjoy. Victoria did better than that, collecting all manner of memorabilia and insisting that the instruments be played. There are six rooms, each decorated in the era of, and with memorials to, a particular musician. For example, the Chopin room features one of his death masks, and a chaise longue that belonged to him decorated with tapestry cushions made by George Sands (one of his lovers). The guides, mainly students from the conservatorium, play each composer's music on the antique keyboards, and though I understand why a guide is necessary I would have loved to wander on my own.

My second day in Trondheim is completely different. At an early breakfast I sit with Colin whom I had met the night before. We chat about life, death and everything in between (as one does with strangers). Then discover that we are both ready to abandon cities and Kultur and go walking in the woods. I have already checked out what is close by and discovered Bymarka, a woodland area easy to get to. We take the Gråkalbanen tram and a scenic ride through

Trondheim's suburbs, and I'm chuffed at how easily I can ask for a Pensioniste ticket in Norwegian.

We have no map but foolishly I trust Colin when he says, 'I'm a geography teacher, you can't get lost with me.' We had expected to find a map on a board, trail markers or something helpful at Lian where we plan to start walking, but no. Instead we ask for help (in Norwegian–English) from other walkers who also get off the tram. They offer suggestions and I start negotiations with a woman who has a map she doesn't need, but Colin says we'll be able to manage—which I trust no more than the 'I'm a geography teacher' comment, but I shrug OK. They invite us to join them but the four hours they've allowed for their planned walk will be too slow—we both feel in need of a good tramp.

We labour up a hill to a restaurant where the walkers said we could buy a map, but it is closed for renovation. I should have persevered with my private map buying transaction because though the owners are there they have no maps and not much English. Finally one of them offers to drive us to Granåsen where, he assures us, we can get into the forest with its trails for Nordic skiing in the winter and hiking in the summer. We accept, having no real idea of where we are, but hoping we will be able to get back to somewhere we recognise at the end. We find ourselves in a school camp of Norwegian 'red Indians' who ignore us completely, but one of the tribal chiefs luckily has some English and assures us we are on the right track—sorry about the pun—and points us to the start.

158

It is a wonderful day if unnecessarily long: a circuit via Rønningen, Marken and Grønlia that luckily returns us to Lian. We hike an extra six kilometres or so because a signpost has been turned around by some clown and we take off west instead of north; possibly proving that walkers should use a compass—or concentrate! As we drop steeply down towards fjords instead of around a lake we are alerted to the error of our ways—another bad pun—and it's a steep haul back to the misleading signpost where we use the sun as a compass to find the correct trail. Colin is good company and a good walker and we hike about 20 kilometres. The extra kilometres (particularly those up) are great justification for two glasses of very expensive ale on our return to Trondheim.

Thus ends my explorations in search of the midnight sun. Next morning I farewell the folk dancers and catch the now familiar bus to the city for the train to Oslo.

'A journey is like marriage.
The certain way to be wrong
is to think you control it.'

—John Steinbeck

EIGHT

A FLYING WEDDING TRIP

I t's October 2005 and I'm at my nephew James' wedding in the tiny thirteenth-century parish church at Mawnan Smith outside Falmouth on the south coast of Cornwall. The vicar, a woman who brings to mind a slightly scruffy but slimmer 'Vicar of Dibley', allows her sense of humour to appear occasionally—like when she winks at Leanne when nobody responds to the mandatory question about 'just cause why this marriage cannot proceed'.

It will take more than the pouring rain and cold to dampen this wedding. James and Leanne are happy and giggly reminding me of my son Dave's wedding to Kate six years earlier. And I remember thinking at *that* wedding it was a marriage with a chance of lasting. I feel the same about James and Leanne. Their love and joy fill the church with radiance.

Although taking place in this old church it is hardly a conventional wedding. The words spoken are a combination of the traditional service and James and Leanne's own contributions, again like Dave and Kate's. There are three 'best men' because James has three best mates so how could he choose just one (and between them they manage *not* to lose the rings). Leanne is a member of the Phoenix Ladies Barbershop Chorus who sing while the register is being signed; and the young daughter of one of these women sings 'I watched the sunrise', her soprano filling the church.

This is a description of a wedding, so there must be a paragraph about the clothes. It's a 'pink' wedding with some chocolate brown thrown in. James, the best men and the three ushers have brown suits, very pale pink shirts, and the

162

pièces de résistance are kipper ties made of the fabric they'd used for the invitations—hot pink background, with large flowers and paisley patterns in other pinks and brown. Rod, John, Jim (Leanne's dad) and Morley (the dog) all have bow ties of the same fabric—Elaine, Leanne's mum, made all the ties and deserves an award. Leanne's dress is not pink but ivory, slim, a drape across one hip and floral lace decorating the top—my description doesn't do it justice, it is gorgeous. The four bridesmaids' dresses are just as dazzling: two are in brown, floaty, strapless with longish, tiered skirts; and two in paler mushroom, shorter, fluffier and sparkling; and all in wonderful high-heeled pinkish strappy sandals. The bridal bouquets are palettes of pinks and dark browns.

James and Leanne invited 150 guests and it's just as well no more of the Australian contingent crossed the world to be here. As it is the church is too small and though extra seats are brought in, some people are stuck behind pillars though I'm lucky and I can see the altar. My journal says: 'It is a beautiful day. Sitting in the lovely little church I feel joy at being able to be here'.

The church's main door is an arch framed with flowers, something the local parish women do for every wedding, and it's a wonderful way to enter. After the wedding people leave through a side door that takes them into the small cemetery, with its ancient tombstones and a cliff-top view over the sea below. The surroundings and view should be spectacular additions to any wedding photos, but not today. It is so wet and blowy that gallant friends and family hold onto wedding finery and hats, and umbrellas are

163

dropped at the last moment as the photographer shoots against the sombre surrounds. But joy and laughter are neither drowned nor blown away.

Those of us not involved in the photographs thankfully shelter inside the church until we are unceremoniously booted out so the vicar can prepare for the next wedding. James and Leanne depart for the reception in James' trusty Robin Reliant (a small three-wheeled car of certain age), and we are handed instructions for finding The Riv, a cliff-top pub at Mawgan Porth on north Cornwall's surfing coast, the venue for the celebratory shindig. Confusing for those who don't know the area and for some who do. I'm with Carole, the bridegroom's mother who's done this trip before, but following the navigation instructions definitely doesn't get us to The Riv. It doesn't matter though, it's lovely countryside to be lost in and we get there in the end.

First priority on arrival is a drink, and then it's time to catch up with people I know; to meet Carole's ex in-laws about whom I have heard much over the years; and to chat with others who are neither of the above. James and Leanne had thought that guests might walk down to the beach but it is a steep descent, we are dressed in wedding finery (though for me finery is an overstatement) and the weather is definitely not walker-friendly. Only a few foolhardy young people take up the suggestion.

164

The party is fun. With interesting guests, enough food to feed two armies but definitely not conventional wedding nosh—I remember miles of pizza and bowls of sweets. The electronic music is a little loud but who cares; it's a party for the young and I feel lucky to be there. I've never seen a wedding cake like this before, though my daughter-in-law caterer later tells me it's not unusual. Made by Elaine it is tiers of cupcakes iced with flowers, which were digitally scanned from the invitation fabric and printed onto sheets of very fine icing—I naively thought Elaine and Leanne had hand painted each one! Plates of these are balanced on cake decoration pillars, and topped with a small traditional cake on which the 'bridegroom' is a karate man doll and that they cut with a martial arts machete—James is a martial arts enthusiast. Just to keep the whacky atmosphere going the best men deliver individual 'best man' speeches—three different perspectives on James and Leanne.

Then it's time for dancing, with live musicians and James and Leanne leading off with the bridal waltz, as they should, before the rest of us are invited to join in. And of course I do.

AN UNEXPECTED JOURNEY

Carole and I had gone to Falmouth in August following my Norway sojourn, and spent time with James and Leanne who live there. I heard about their wedding plans, visited the church at Mawnan Smith, the bright blue-painted Riv at Mawgan Porth, even the luxurious hotel where they would spend their wedding night—part of their honeymoon, a present from Carole and John. I wondered at the bridesmaids' outrageous sandals, had the kipper ties described and admired the bridesmaids' dresses; and had

165

been involved in their excitement. But lovely as the idea might be, going back to England for the wedding would be ridiculous, impractical, impossible.

By 2005 Naomi and I have been trying to get to Vietnam for two years. Unfortunately she has a shoulder injury that makes carting even shoestring traveller's luggage impossible. But after successful surgery early in the year it looks like we'll make Vietnam in October.

The first half of the year I write obsessively (the writer has replaced the traveller) to complete the manuscript of *No Fixed Address* before I take off for Norway. I chain myself to my desk, escaping occasionally to look at the *Lonely Planet Guide to Vietnam* and talk to a travel agent who specialises in southeast Asia. It looks possible: I will return from Norway and have six weeks hard editing with the publisher before we can go; I operate well under pressure so it seems perfectly reasonable. But when I get home and look at the work my opus needs it can't be done, and of course the book and publisher have priority. So Vietnam goes on the backburner. Again! I feel bad messing Naomi about but she understands and we promise ourselves come hell or high water we will go to Vietnam in 2006.

A few days later I'm thinking about the disappointment of abandoning Vietnam, and subconsciously reflecting on James and Leanne's wedding. All we Australian family members have those pink-and-brown invitations on our fridges with no real expectation of accepting, except Stepha who has Frequent Flyer points. I've never had enough of these with any airline because when I decide to go somewhere I just find the cheapest flight—loyalty to an airline, you've got to be joking.

Normally this would be crazy, an extravagance I couldn't afford. But I've had an unexpected windfall, an advance from my publishers. Me, an unknown writer, what confidence! But isn't that lucky?

Why don't I use it (at least what is left after the Norwegian champagne extravagance) to take Naomi and me to a wedding, to *be* crazy and go to England for a week. I'm worried she'll feel it's too profligate, but I want her to see how much I need her company on this trip so plan a visit. After the usual exchange of family news, films seen and books read I bite the bullet explaining that I want to go to James and Leanne's wedding and want her company on the long flights—I've only just got back from one of those twenty-two-hour marathons so it is said with feeling.

But she doesn't say, 'No'. Not then. Instead, 'I'd love to, but it's a lot of money.'

I say, 'We'll only go if I can find a cheap flight.' And incredibly I do. Emirates—never flown with them but they were the first to have individual TV screens for economy passengers so they must be OK. And Dubai airport is supposed to be fantastic. We can go.

Some days later she rings. 'It's too much, you can't pay for me.'

'I can. I want to and I have an advance just waiting to be spent.' Once I've decided something I'm pretty immovable.

We'll have to pay for a few days at a B&B for the wedding

in Cornwall, but we'll do that as cheaply as we can and the rest of the time we'll stay with Carole in Devon.

In addition to the wedding one of the special things about Naomi and I going is that for the first time in our lives all five sisters will be together, even if only for a couple of days—and maybe that's just as well. June is a half-sister we discovered after my mother died and, although individually we have spent time with her—Naomi, Carole and I even shared a barge trip with her in 2001— with three of us living in Australia and family commitments over the intervening twenty years, we have never all been in one place at one time. June and Rod are as excited about it as the rest of us. Though he should be worrying, he'll be spending two nights at a B&B with five assertive sisters. What a man!

Wedding outfits need to be found, begged, borrowed or stolen but there's nothing else to do. Excited emails fly between sisters, and aunts and nephew. We extravagantly plan two weeks in total to allow a few days for flight and wedding recovery.

Everything works as planned and while helping Jai with a pre-Cambodia-departure garage sale she sells me a snazzy black dress for A$1, originally purchased in Denmark she tells me. But it fits, is more elegant than anything else in my wardrobe, and I can tart it up with pink tights and pashmina-type shawl (they did say a pink wedding) and high-heeled black shoes I wore in my incarnation as a computer consultant. Naomi does elegance better than me and has clothes in her wardrobe to grace a wedding. It all comes together and we're ready to go.

168

HOWEVER YOU GO
IT'S A LONG WAY

The day before our departure it looks like I might be doing it alone. Naomi rings with a flu-like infection not confident that she'll be able to go—a long flight when you're feeling poorly is decidedly unpleasant. She sees a doctor who gives her antibiotics and the advice that she should stay home, but she doses herself on everything imaginable and at almost the last minute bravely decides to come.

The flexibility that is a prerequisite for travellers comes into play; instead of doing it all by public transport from home (the shoestring approach and quite fun) I drive to her house so we can go to the airport together.

The flight from Melbourne to Dubai is harder than it need be. We spend two hours sitting on the tarmac while technicians search for, find and fix a hydraulic fluid problem. It doesn't worry me; it's preferable to a 'she'll be right' approach. But we're cooped up for an extra two hours and the half-hour changeover time we had in Dubai goes negative, however we are assured by the attendants that the onward flight will wait. We can but hope.

Sure enough it does, but it is a mad dash through the airport that fleetingly looks most impressive, onto the next plane hoping that our luggage will also make the transition. The little we see of Dubai as we land and take off, and the smell and feel of it on the bus from the plane to the terminal reminds us of Morocco, telling us it's time for another exotic journey.

The second leg of the flight is shorter but something is exuded by the air-conditioning system that aggravates Naomi's cough. Also the video system is broken so no individual film choice—and this was an Emirates initiative!

But flying northwest from Dubai the views of the Middle East land mass are spectacular: pale sandy-coloured mountains and valleys; large lakes; and areas of habitation with rivers and dams providing enough water to support small settlements. The mountains and valleys are stunningly beautiful, and they must be enormous because we can see the geological formation in detail from the plane: craters, folded pleats, circular knife-sharp ridges, eroded 'cliffs', rounded edges and taller ones behind, all highlighted by the sun. Mountains powdered with icing sugar stretch all the way to Turkey, and one of the attendants is able to confirm that a towering snow-covered peak is Mount Ararat.

When we reach Heathrow Naomi is still holding herself together—just. Unfortunately it's a three-hour wait for the bus and Heathrow is pretty ordinary: it's a long way to push trolleys between terminals, almost nowhere to buy food or drink, and waiting areas are grim. Maybe we're spoilt by more modern airports but Heathrow is England's gateway to everywhere for goodness sake. The National Express bus terminal is dismal: a tiny waiting room with minimal seating, and my backpack doubles as a seat yet again. By the time we reach Carole's haven in Torquay after a four-hour bus journey I suspect Naomi is wishing she'd stayed at home.

170

SISTERS TOGETHER

Stepha who has been staying with a friend in Dorset, joins Carole, Naomi and me in Torquay for two days before we all go to Cornwall.

We inspect and approve each other's outfits. But the weather is chucking everything at us and we realise that although it will be cold in the church, when the party at The Riv really gets going and we start dancing we will need something lighter and more party-like. So we shop for a cooler top for Stepha, Naomi looks for dressier pants than those she has brought from Australia, and I want to find some large glitzy earrings to brighten up for the party. Carole has to collect a coat that's been altered and find a hat—mother of the groom and all that. We Aussies left our Akubras at home.

We spend a lot of time talking, laughing and trying not to annoy each other—the four of us thrown together to share jetlag and pre-wedding nerves. Hardest for Carole, and Naomi who gets worse and has to visit the local doctor; but with more antibiotics, acidophilus, friars balsam to inhale and two days rest, maybe she'll be OK by Saturday.

I'm using James' old room, often shared with Leanne over the eight years since they met, and sleeping in his old bed that I call the 'bonking bed' for reasons I'm sure I don't have to explain. I often stayed with Carole on earlier journeys while James either still lived at home or came back with Leanne for the odd weekend, so I know what I'm talking about. Its wire base is decidedly saggy and not too good for my back. But nobody ever dies from a dubious bed and I have fun teasing them about it when we meet up before the wedding.

171

Carole and Stepha leave early to get to Falmouth for a rehearsal where Stepha, the actor in the family, is to take John Austin-Smith's part. June and Rod will collect Naomi and me so the four of us can have a little extra time together. And besides, Carole's car is absolutely loaded with wedding gear. The plan is that June and Rod will leave their place by midday, reach us by 2 pm and have a quick sandwich before we go southwest. But it is close to 5 pm by the time they arrive, and we've been getting puzzled and a little irate.

We had expected to go out and find somewhere to eat on reaching Molesworth Manor on the north Cornish coast but by the time we all arrive, and Carole and Stepha are even later having got lost in north Cornwall's lanes, none of us feels like going out again. But we discover why June and Rod were late collecting us. They decided that five sisters being together for the first time deserve something more peaceful, private and memorable than the local (dubious) pub. So June has prepared food and organised use of the B&B's dining room. She is a great cook and we enjoy a delicious meal, enhanced by wine from their wedding in 2004. Despite weariness it is a delightful evening and patient Rod, the sole male and brother-in-law of four of us, deserves a commendation.

Molesworth Manor, an old manor house in rambling gardens, is sumptuous: wide-sweeping staircases, thick walls, opulent living rooms and large, high-ceilinged bedrooms. It's the sort of place that deserves a few days for the sheer pleasure of luxuriating in its surroundings, not the sort of place to rush in and out for a wedding. June and Rod have the honeymoon suite (they arranged it so why not), Carole and Stepha are sharing a twin room and Naomi and I get the 'family room', the cheap option we requested. Crowded with narrow bunks, a single bed and a dressing table, no wardrobe but wooden hooks on the wall that are designed to chuck our clothes on the floor, and not even tea-making facilities; we think it's actually for kids. A third person could use the bottom bunk, but they'd need to be small and not suffer from claustrophobia. But there's a wonderful view over fields and woods that we admire next morning and the breakfasts are as sumptuous as the manor house. Fruit, cereals, as much tea, coffee and toast as you want and, for most people, a different cooked selection every day. It's a shame I don't really do the 'full English breakfast', I could feed myself for a month.

We travel in different configurations to Mawnan Smith, Carole and I going via James and Leanne's house to help the 'girls' get ready. The prospective bridegroom has been taken off to the north coast by some of the best men and ushers for his last surf as a free man. They have been threatened with the direst of calamities if they don't get James to the church on time and it would be brave men who would risk Carole's wrath on that.

POST-WEDDING RECOVERY   173

Naomi, Stepha and I—not the oldest maybe, but the weariest—leave the wedding party earlier than Carole, or June and Rod and enjoy a quiet cup of tea and analyse the day before bed. Next day we all have a much needed lazy start. A taxi has taken James and Leanne to the local airport to begin their journey to Morocco (more of the wedding present from Carole and John) so nobody has to rush, not even June and Rod who are off to the Lake District. We meet for breakfast about 9.30 am, the food is as good as the day before but this time we are relaxed and it tastes even better.

I haven't seen Kate, James' twin sister and one of the gorgeous bridesmaids, for a couple of years so we catch up in one of the sumptuous lounges before we return to Falmouth. Carole takes Kate to catch her train to London while Naomi, Stepha and I clean James and Leanne's house as a surprise for their return. It's not as bad as we anticipate considering the bride and four bridesmaids beautified themselves here; but we *do* collect six bags of rubbish; and I discover a few computer-generated sheets of bright pink flower-decorated icing.

We have a night at a B&B where Carole and I stayed in August. I'm spoilt with a double bed to myself—a real treat after James' bed in Torquay and the bunk at Molesworth Manor. Then it's back to Carole's place in pouring rain, to the 'bonking bed' and an aching back. But normalcy is good; though Naomi and I only have two more days before we fly home.

174   The last day of this very rushed trip is to Winkleigh, a tiny village deep in Devon countryside, to lunch with John Austin-Smith at his 'local' that does a tasty pub meal. This is followed by a muddy walk in the woods, though to our great relief it's not actually raining.

Next day it's a bus to Heathrow and back to Australia. We have an hour in Dubai, time to explore the airport a little and it *is* impressive. I buy miniature camels for Mia and Ellie (I never return from one of my trips without something for my granddaughters). I write in my journal: 'Very swish; murals, textured pillars and lovely colours. What a contrast to Heathrow! That's oil money for you'.

Naomi is feeling a little better by the time we reach Melbourne so we use the Skybus and public transport option to her house. It is quite disorienting hauling suitcase (Naomi) and backpack (me) up the suburban streets of Blackburn after thirty hours from Devon via Dubai. Travel is a strange warper of time and experiences. I note: 'A subdued and mundane ending to a crazy trip'. Crazy maybe, but I wouldn't have missed it for quids.

175

'It is not because things are difficult that we do not dare, it is because we do not dare that they are difficult.'

—Seneca

NINE

CAMBODIA:
COUNTRY OF SMILES

When my daughter Jai was about eight years old we rode a tandem bicycle together. She wanted to be in front controlling the machine and, as I believe everyone should try new experiences, I let her do so. I was petrified. Not because she was a bad rider, but because I like to be in control. Twenty-two years later she's working on an Arts Aid project in Cambodia and I'm on my way to visit her. Along with my backpack and bag of Australian goodies for her I have borrowed a motorbike helmet. Jai has a moto and plans for us to explore Phnom Penh together—me as a pillion passenger. It's only a 125cc motorbike, but even so ... I imagine the tandem experience repeated—only faster.

All that anxiety is for nothing. She's an excellent motorbike rider and has had four months to get used to Phnom Penh's crazy traffic. Two hours after my arrival we are on her bike and off to the Lucky supermarket for basic groceries. Next day it's back on the pillion for a leisurely breakfast and mother/daughter catch-up at one of her favourite cafés, before a visit to the Russian market where they sell produce and food, clothes, jewellery, stationery, electrical goods, hardware and anything else you might want. Then it's Khmer (Cambodian) noodle soup to take back to her house, with me riding hands-free holding two plastic bags of soup, noodles, vegetables and spices (soup in a bag—believe me it is how it's done) as we moto home.

Over the next few days as I explore the streets of Phnom Penh from the back of Jai's bike, or try hard to respect the cultural sensitivity of *moto-dob* (motorbike taxi) drivers by

178

not touching them, I become very relaxed about not being in control of the machine or the city's mad traffic. At first I wonder how anyone survives, but once you are part of it you realise that everyone looks out for everyone else, the one in front is given right of way, and almost anything goes. For example, to get across traffic to the correct side of the road, you either go in front of oncoming traffic or drive up the 'wrong' side until you can cross.

I love the excitement of being among hundreds of other motorbikes with their fascinating loads: unimaginably perilous mountains of firewood, guttering, building timber; chickens hanging upside down on poles, or held down with mesh; pigs in an enormous basket—lots of little ones or one large one; and assorted foods in baskets, on panniers, on heads of passengers (no OH&S concerns here). Everything is precariously balanced through Phnom Penh's chaotic traffic or on broken potholed dirt roads. Families travel with up to two parents and three kids on a single motorbike, often with a little one asleep in front of the driver with head on the handlebars. And they exchange smiles with these *barangs* (foreigners) who respect their customs by riding side-saddle.

Helmets are rarely seen and moto drivers, my daughter included, often wear the flimsiest footwear. I am 'sensible' and bring protective clothing—jeans and even a denim jacket—but the temperature is in the high thirties all day, with humidity probably over 70 per cent. No way can I wear them; they go into the bottom of my bag and I ride, like everyone else, in shirt and skirt (side-saddle) or shirt and pants (astride). Just occasionally I imagine the pain of grazes if I come off, but mostly I just relax into it, lean with the bike, and enjoy the experience.

Twice I go without helmet. Once when Jai and I go out to dinner and want to be elegant (helmets are hell on the hairdo), and on my last night as I'm going home from a nightclub I realise I am enjoying the feel of the breeze through my hair!

JANUARY 2006

Cambodia through Jai's eyes

I am utterly spoilt by having Jai in Cambodia to show me what she has come to love (and struggle with) in this country of contrasts. She shares her fondness of the Cambodian people, her insights into Phnom Penh, her passion for the food, her friends, acquaintances and activities. I return to Australia with a head full of images, enthusiasm for the organisation for which she is working, and a determination to do something for Cambodia.

Jai meets me at the airport and my initiation begins into how you do things with a little language and know-how. She jokes with four moto-dob drivers, two of whom insist that they can carry us and my luggage, but she is so relaxed and friendly that one of them even finds us a tuk-tuk—we have decided that this will allow Jai to tell me a little about Phnom Penh en route. She bargains with the driver for the cheapest possible trip quite confident in how to do it. Though I can't understand a word it is obvious she is saying

180

something like, 'Seven dollars, you've got to be joking'—
drivers enjoy barangs doing this, especially a young female
with a ring in her lip.

In one of her early emails from Cambodia Jai wrote: 'The
people still smile smiles wider than the Mekong and are
quick to laugh and giggle and whisper about my lip ring, and
stare unashamedly, all of which brings me much joy'. And
she's right. No matter how little they have—and unless you
have been to a third-world country devastated by war,
corruption, poverty or all three, you cannot begin to
imagine how little that might be—the people are gentle and
loving, and always smile when you make eye contact. The
children greet you with the biggest smiles of all and, if they
know enough English, ask your name, where you come from
and how old you are. Often those as young as twelve run the
stalls in the markets, and they can bargain with the best,
then when you beat them down they still treat you like their
greatest friend.

I am hardly ever alone on this journey. I spend eight days
as a delegate with Cambodian Living Arts (CLA), the
organisation with whom Jai is working, the rest of the time
we have together. I enjoy being with my daughter and her
friends, but also enjoy exploring Phnom Penh on my own
when she has work to do.

I am dwarfed by the Independence Monument, and filled
with wonder at the opulence of the Royal Palace which I
admire from outside on my wanderings. Jai still hasn't been
to the Palace or Wat Phnom so we plan to do them together
in my last week. Unfortunately she is unwell, and we lose a

181

day in the hassles of my stolen bag (more of this later). So it will be next time. I spend hours at the National Museum with its rooms of pre-Ankorean statuary and gods, pottery and bronzes; post-Ankorean artefacts with fascinating exhibits, but my favourite is an old loom on which traditional silk fabric is threaded as if the weaver has just left for a moment.

The main streets in Phnom Penh are wide, sealed and in good condition so walking is easy. But away from the tourist area dirt roads, potholes, dust and piles of rubbish make it a challenge. I quickly learn to dodge the holes, wear a *kramer* (cotton scarf, pronounced kramar) over my mouth and always have a bottle of water.

In London in 1999 I christened Jai 'Imelda' (after Imelda Marcos who abandoned hundreds of pairs of shoes at her palace in Manila) because her greatest joy was a shoe market in Camden Town. She is still shoe crazy and anywhere that makes shoes for US$12 to $18—in your design or theirs, in beautiful soft leather and in one of over a hundred colours—is bound to be Jai's second home. This is Beautiful Shoes in Phnom Penh. We visit there on my third day in Cambodia, taking a pair of sandals she had made in Vietnam a couple of years earlier and which I have yearned for ever since. A young man draws Jai's sandals and the shape of my sole, measures the dimensions of my feet, and hands me swatches of leather. I choose a brownish burgundy and he says, 'Come back in a week.' Jai orders a pair of white slender-strapped sandals from one of their catalogues— elegant, impractical and *sooo* feminine. When I collect my sandals they are perfect: comfortable, casual and smart—perhaps the best US$12 I've ever spent.

I will digress for a moment. When we arrive at Beautiful Shoes Jai burns her arm on the exhaust pipe of her moto; the man who runs the shop sees the burn and, as caring as all the Cambodians I meet, slathers it with a white cream. It heals remarkably quickly and when we return for the shoes a couple of weeks later Jai asks him what it was. Toothpaste! Worth remembering.

Food experiences with Jai are a joy. We go to her 'local' café for lunch and sit outside ignoring the passing traffic and dust. She orders fish stir-fry, vegetable curry and plain rice. It is hot and we want to share the milk of a coconut—having the top sliced off a not-quite-ripe coconut and drinking the wonderful thirst-quenching milk through a straw is one of life's joys. Even with Jai's Khmer, gestures towards a coconut seller across the street and two elderly men from an adjacent table joining in, we cannot make the waiter understand and finish up with a bottle of water. But after more pantomime our coconut arrives, amid cheers from our two aides.

About 7.00 every morning the 'pan-pan' man cycles by Jai's house, calling 'Pain! Pain!'—think French, not agony. Which of course tells everyone that he has bread for sale; from an enormous pannier covered with a red-and-white kramer on the back of his pushbike. It is cheap, and deliciously fresh.

Jai and I discover a local produce market and riding through its narrow pathways on her motorbike is an

183

insight into the Cambodian psyche. No road rage, horns toot only to warn, and everyone waits patiently until there is space to move forward another few centimetres. Later with time to spare I wander entranced for over an hour, and use a whole film to capture images: stallholders crouched on the ground alongside their wares; beautifully stacked piles of eggs from white to duck-egg blue; tumbling green vegetables, some I recognise and many that I don't; fruit stalls with rainbow-coloured piles of orange mandarins and yellow bananas, of green mangoes and pink dragon fruit; seafood stalls with whole fish dead and alive, bits of fish, shellfish and eels; meat sellers with cuts of meat completely foreign to me.

The stallholders use weighing technology ranging from spring balances to kitchen scales—modern and old—and often they are hand-held. And if I want to buy, out comes a calculator and I'm shown the ridiculously cheap cost in *riel* (r).

I meet many young westerners, volunteers with NGOs aiding Cambodia's recovery. A Swiss woman helping train Cambodia's first wheelchair athletes in sprint and long distance for the 2008 Paralympics in Beijing; a man working with an environmental group encouraging villagers to save endangered birds as a tourist attraction rather than eat them; and Tom works in an area where another endangered bird will only survive if the villagers revert to traditional rice-farming techniques. And Katie and Hannah who manage Epic Arts in Cambodia, an organisation that trains people with disabilities in creative movement, music, art and craft.

184

My last evening in Phnom Penh on this visit is spent with Jai at Pontoon a floating nightclub on the Tonlé Sap River. It is years since I have been to a nightclub and the noise is incredible, but I am made so welcome by her friends that I don't care. I get another view of her life in Cambodia—and some flashy drinks. I feel overdressed, over-age and, by 1.30 am, decidedly overtired, but it is a great end to the intensity of the three weeks. At first I feel uncomfortable with the ostentatious spending of money just metres from Phnom Penh's poverty but then I look at all these young people—many of whom exist on a basic living allowance—and realise they need somewhere to relax with people from a similar background. It's incredibly hard working in a culture so different from your own, and trying to communicate with the nuances of its language. They earn their extravagant evenings.

A few days off, Cambodian style

Jai and I spend a few days in Kep, on the south coast of Cambodia. Originally known as Kep-sur-Mer, the remnants of the buildings show that Kep was once an affluent French colonial retreat, and it was also one of King Sihanouk's favourite spots. Due to the long years of civil war little is left except ruins of the once grandiose mansions. Some provide homes for squatters, others are completely abandoned, and now Cambodians holiday in Kep.

185

CLA holds a two-day conference here; Jai goes as part of their organisation, I go along for the ride. Even sharing the most basic room at Veranda Guesthouse with Jai (cold shower and all) is one of my most luxurious accommodation experiences in recent years. Individual huts on stilts with bamboo and reed walls and thatched roofs, large urns on the roof catch water for the bathroom, and a design feature is gaps in the walls and floor—luckily good mosquito nets are provided. All the huts, and the dining room and bar have west-facing verandas from which it is mandatory to watch the sunset over the sea every day. The bar does a wonderful line in daquiris (Jai's favourite tipple), reasonable red wine (mine) and thirst-quenching fruit shakes (both of us). Jai and I rack up over US$120 in bar bills in six days—and we aren't even trying.

Kep has the warmest sea I have ever swum in. It looks murky but I'm assured it is pollution-free, and my badly grazed knee (from an ungainly trip up a kerb) definitely benefits from a daily immersion in its warm, salty water. There is a fishing fleet at Kep—brightly coloured long boats with curved prows and single paddles—and the fresh fish at roadside stalls and in beachside cafés is wonderful. Crabs au naturel, or cut up shells and all, and baked in a piquant sauce; whole fish steamed with herbs or barbecued on a stick; fish soup with a meal of shellfish in each bowl; and always fish amok—a mild but tasty fish curry. A few of us eat at a café by the water—fresh seafood cooked true Khmer style is an extravagance at US$4 a head including drinks.

While here, I get confirmation of a theory I have long held regarding children's imagination. One of the delegates expresses concern that kids in a (seemingly) poor village have no toys. I believe children are born with imagination

186

and make up games with whatever is at hand. I describe Mancala, a game I play with my grandchildren that originated in Africa or South America, I think, that requires nothing more than stones and holes in the ground. Invented I'm sure by imaginative children. Just think about hopscotch, skipping, chasing games—all played with basic or no equipment. In Kep I'm walking by the shore next to a tree-scattered stretch of dirt on which a few boys are kicking something. The rules of their game are simple: the 'court' is a length of dirt between two trees; each player uses a thong (flip-flop); they get it as far as they can with a single kick from one end of the court and if they strike another thong they get a second turn. The one who gets his thong closest to the tree at the far end is the winner. Later in Siem Reap I see girls playing the same game on the footpath. Simple, but clever.

A rewarding experience in Kampot

Jai and I return to Phnom Penh via Kampot a small fishing town on the Prek Kampong Bay River. Downstream from Kampot we have to cross a wide fast-flowing river. The bridge is down: rumour has it that a 65-tonne truck went through a 10-tonne load limit bridge and was jammed in the river for two weeks, though it is no longer there. We are ferried across on a flat boat—Jai and I, our moto-dobs and drivers, a gaggle of schoolgirls with their bikes, and a farmer with his goat. The ferry master and his mate carefully load and tie down bikes and motos, there is a motor (of the chug-chug variety), and a large paddle on one side of the stern for steering. The gentlemanly ferry master and mate carefully hand us on and off.

In Kampot we visit the Epic Arts café and studio that Hannah and Katie are just opening, where they plan to employ disabled people and run classes and workshops.

Hannah wants to redecorate the café before it opens and asks if we know anything about paint. We do. Five minutes later I'm sitting bemusedly on Sophara's pillion as we go to buy paint: he is a young deaf-mute and I have neither Khmer nor signing—our communication is gesticulations and smiles—and he is driving in Cambodia's mad traffic. Juliette, a friend of Hannah's from the United States, has her camera over her shoulder; Katie's cousin Rose visiting from the United Kingdom comes along for the ride; Jai is interpreter and assistant paint consultant; Sophara is the colour consultant and I'm here because I know about paint—and never miss the chance to do something different.

The 'hardware store' is actually a marine goods store with paints for boats: enamel, long-lasting and waterproof, but expensive and difficult to use. This exercise needs to be cheap and simple for the novice painters. The shop owner, ably supported by two daughters, is wonderfully helpful. With his Khmer and their few English words, Jai's Khmerglish, my scouring of the shelves, and Sophara's expertise with the colour chart, we finish up with an enormous tub of white acrylic, tints in primary colours, a roller and brushes. I do a quick trip to the market across the road for plastic bowls, as roller trays and for mixing paints.

Returning to the Epic café on Sophara's moto I reflect on this afternoon's experience. An impossible one without my adventurous daughter.

Wonderful Wats— more than just Angkor

There are *wats* (temples) everywhere. Wholly restored and wonderfully painted with golden spires, red and blue decorations, intricate gold-painted panels, and red, pink or gold doors. Or under reconstruction, with finely detailed new cement structures mirroring the old, and large concrete Nagas; all awaiting their coats of splendour. Young monks wander about in their saffron robes, while the older ones seem to be on more serious business, and the wats are always awash with youngsters in navy and white from an attached school.

Ten months later in Phnom Penh I visit Wat Phnom with Naomi. An icon of this city built on Phnom Penh's only hill; supposedly the original temple was built on this site in the fourteenth-century and much rebuilding has been done since. There is an impressive staircase up to the wat with balustrades made of the largest Nagas I see in Cambodia. The rooms of the wat are brilliantly decorated with paintings on ceilings and walls depicting the Ramayana and Khmer history, and with carved shutters and wall decorations. Outside are beaten metal walls and immaculate statues, not to mention cheeky monkeys.

While in Siem Reap, Jai and I have a flying visit to Angkor. Knowing that we cannot do Angkor Wat justice in

189

the half-day we have to spare and that I will be back, we spend the afternoon at Banteay Srei, one of the smallest temples in Angkor and an excellent example of Angkorian art. Srei means woman and it is said that women must have built this temple because no man could have created such intricate and delicate carvings. And the beauty of the remaining carvings more than compensates for its size.

On the way back to Siem Reap we visit Angkor Wat briefly and walk the whole 800 metres of the bas-reliefs on the lowest level; I am astounded at the detail, complexity, and condition of the panels depicting battles of long ago. They whet my appetite for more of this imposing temple.

In Kep, Jai and I visit Wat Kirisan at Kompong Trach: a temple built in a complex of caves where a community of monks live. Having refreshed ourselves with coconut milk, we visit the monks' dining room, where the lurid paintings around the top of the walls depict Buddha's life from birth to enlightenment on one side, and on the other interpretations of hell—enough to set you back on the straight and narrow! A group of elderly women are cooking a delicious-smelling lunch for the monks and we are invited to join them for meal after the monks finish. Unfortunately Jai has another commitment for the afternoon so we must decline.

We choose four of the twelve or so children armed with torches wanting to be our guides, and agree on a price—selecting one entrepreneurial youngster with a twelve-volt battery over his shoulder and a serious torch. The boy who always shines his torch in front of me as I rock hop down into the caves gets my riels. Many of the large caves contain shrines and Buddhas, including a reclining Buddha at least four metres long and two metres high—getting him down into his cave must have been quite a challenge.

A nasty experience—
or grist for the writer's mill

As Jai and I chat in a tuk-tuk returning to her house in Phnom Penh from Kep, I forget anti-theft warnings; my daypack is looped over one shoulder instead of both and a couple of observant men on a moto snatch it and speed off. Our driver valiantly gives chase but to no avail. The majority of Cambodians hate thieves and apparently any they catch can be beaten to death so I'm glad we don't catch mine— angry and shocked as I am, death is a little extreme!

We spend a few tense hours getting plastic cards and mobile phone cancelled. Help lines are useless when your mobile phone has been stolen, your impoverished daughter has only a few cents left on her pre-paid phone, landlines are almost non-existent, and 'reverse charges' and 'telephone operator' are unknown concepts. Losing phone, camera and US$100 are an inconvenience, losing two-and-a-half weeks of journal is distressing, but nothing is life threatening.

The adventure of acquiring a police report makes it worthwhile. I'm going to claim my camera, mobile phone, the pack and assorted odd bits and pieces on my travel insurance—it's why I have it for goodness sake—but the insurance company requires a police report, and within twenty-four hours. I think the person who decided on that

191

'reverse charges' facility for help also put together the police report idea. Find a police station, find someone who speaks English and get a report in Cambodia, all within twenty-four hours. What a joke. It reminds me of Jai being robbed in Thailand years before—getting the police report wasn't *too* difficult, but when she returned to Australia she had to pay someone to translate it from Thai!

We do our best. Spending hours as Jai rings all her contacts looking for tourist police or a police station. Nobody can help until she calls Rit, a Cambodian who taught her Khmer when she first arrived. It's about 4.30 pm on the day after the robbery and he can help us immediately. We go to his house on one of Phnom Penh's main boulevards and I meet his wife and baby daughter. We sit on plastic chairs in his driveway, he fetches us water and makes a phone call. We drink our water and ten minutes later a policeman arrives. He too gets a chair and a glass of water, and interviews us with Rit interpreting.

'Please describe what happened.' So we do.

'Where did this happen?' he asks.

'In Monivong Boulevard, just past the intersection with Mao Tse Tung, close to the Vietnamese Embassy.'

In response to the 'Is there a witness?' question Jai replies, 'Yes, the tuk-tuk driver'.

'Where is he, what is his name, what was the number of his tuk-tuk?'

We don't have any of this information of course.

I ask Rit to tell the policeman that I spent hours cancelling my cards and phone, I wouldn't do that just to scam the insurance company and he can check with the bank if he doesn't believe me. Finally the policeman says OK, we must go with him to the police station for the report. I go on the back of his moto and Rit on the back of Jai's. We arrive there at 5.30 pm, too late for anyone to produce a report, but Rit kindly agrees to meet us there at 7.30 am the following day, well beyond twenty-four hours but nothing else to be done.

Next morning Jai is unwell but I tell myself I can do it, and Rit will be there. Grasping what little courage and Khmer I have, I walk to the police station which is actually quite close to Jai's house. It's a different policeman so, when Rit arrives, I tell the story yet again. This time saying that Jai is the witness and showing the graze on my hand from the strap as the pack was dragged off. At last we get the report underway with me filling it out—in English I'm glad to say— and as requested by Rit I 'write clearly'. It is a standard report, questions in Khmer but with English translations, thank goodness. I've stupidly forgotten my passport but luckily in this situation it's not a criminal offence. Rit waits patiently while I take a moto to fetch it, then leaves for work with the throwaway line 'Just wait for official stamp.'

I wait, and wait. The police person, an admin man not an action man, has some English and pores over the report finally asking me to add a list of stolen items. Then a real policeman arrives, gold spaghetti on the shoulders of his navy-blue uniform. I go through it all again in simple English, including where I think it took place. Then I must go on the back of his motorbike to show him where it happened. Down

Monivong across Mao Tse Tung, and when we get to where I think it was I say, 'Please slow down. Here, I think.'

'No!' is his response and he continues until we are in front of the Vietnamese Embassy. 'Here!' he states, categorically, no argument brooked. I'm a little nervous by now, so say, 'It was dark, maybe here,' and wait for him to return us to the police station. But no, he takes off into some back streets, which luckily I recognise as an area I have previously walked through. But what on earth are we doing?

'Where are we going?' I ask.

'Police station,' he replies. I have no choice but to stay with him, but it explains why he brought my report.

At another station he hands us (me and report) to someone else—also in a navy-blue uniform, with gold spaghetti but no apparent English. We go into his office, and sit for what seems a long time. He appears to read the report—very slowly, two or three times. He leaves the office. He returns. Half an hour passes. A few people have said it will cost US$5 to get the report and I'm seriously wondering whether I'm supposed to offer someone money. But what if it's the wrong man, or the wrong amount? I'm getting increasingly anxious, and vow *never* to break the law in a country where I don't speak the language.

He leaves and returns again. I ask 'Why do we wait?' He mimes stamping the report. At 10.30 am—and remember all this started at 7.30—I have had enough. I look at the clock. I look at my watch. I reach for the report, I look flustered (I am), but say bravely, 'I must go. I will take the report with no stamp.'

'No!' he replies—he has one word of English at least. He gets on his walkie-talkie and speaks to someone. 'Wait.' A second word I recognise. In less than five minutes another blue-uniformed man arrives with two stamps and stamp pad in hand. He hands them ceremoniously to officer one, who with just as much ceremony stamps both copies of the report—adds something by hand, and gives me my copy. I have US$5 in my pocket but nobody asks for it, and he waves me out. At 10.45 am I leave the police station, orient myself on a map I have in my bag, buy a bottle of water to celebrate my release and find my way back to Jai's house. Relieved, free, and remarkably calm.

NOVEMBER 2006

Back in Cambodia

Ten months later and I'm back in Phnom Penh with Naomi, and this time I have my own motorbike helmet. An investment for future plans.

As before Jai meets us at the airport. She now lives in a French colonial remnant—a first-floor apartment with large rooms, wonderful tiled floors, fans in every room, a housecleaner-maid called Puti, and Josephine and Annabel the cats who run the joint. She shares with three other young women one of whom is away temporarily, so Naomi and I have free accommodation as long as we don't mind sharing a queen-sized bed. Of course we don't.

Now it's three on the motorbike and Naomi surprises me with her lack of concern as we go off to the local market.

I have forgotten that decades ago one of her daughters was a bikie. We lunch at the market on pretty ordinary fish soup (Jai had expected better where the locals eat), herb omelette, which is delicious, rice, iced tea and a pork dish for Jai. We sit at a low plastic table on low plastic stools—normal at street and market stalls. It is an eye-opener for Naomi on her first visit to southeast Asia, but even with ice in the tea and the dirty conditions of the market we suffer no ill effects.

The balcony overlooking the street at Jai's house is a joy in the cool of the morning and evening, and on the first night we watch fireworks from here—cloudbursts and cascades of silver, red, green and gold. Are these just to welcome us? We like to think so.

Each day this balcony is our observation point for life on the street: laden motorbikes, tuk-tuks, cyclos and scooters coming around the corner; food stalls opening and the locals breakfasting; kids going to school, couples going to work; people pulling trailers loaded with hardware, cardboard, sugarcane, plastic chairs; anything you can imagine. The noise is endless—horns, engines, motos and the chatter of passers-by.

In the afternoons, food stalls across the road set up for the evening trade: a father and daughter pull a trailer with food, water and utensils; two women arrive with bright plastic tables and chairs in another trailer. There is constant chiacking and collaboration between children and parents.

Some stalls have old machines—with spoked driving wheels that were once turned by hand but are now powered by very dodgy electrics—that crush sugarcane to produce

196

pure sugar juice (drunk through a straw from a plastic bag and surprisingly refreshing). Others offer bright orange marinated and fried chicken wings on skewers, and bowls of boiled shellfish; both to be dipped into small bowls of sauce. The shellfish, like an Australian pipi or British cockle, is opened, the top discarded, the bottom dipped into the sauce and the fish sucked off. I wouldn't mind trying it but don't quite pluck up the courage—and Jai who might join me on this venture has deserted us.

Bananas from the local market are irresistible after ten months deprivation from Cyclone Larry's destruction of Australia's banana crop. We walk there often, on the way exploring the local streets with their art shops, woodcarving studios and stonemasons. We get sidetracked by Friends restaurant (part of an organisation that trains street kids in hospitality and manufacturing) that serves an excellent mix of Cambodian and western food. The service cannot be faulted and the youngsters are very proud of their restaurant, as they should be.

Only five minutes from Jai's house Friends becomes our 'local', the fruit shakes are fantastic, the Khmer dishes delicious and every bite is for a good cause. Trainees also make goods with donated materials that are sold at the Friends shop next door: bags in interesting shapes, clothes, greeting cards, and a range of jewellery made from beads that look like shells but are actually tightly rolled paper. About 1800 street kids have already been trained by the Friends organisation and most are employed. A successful locally run program.

197

Sunset on Sunday is *dalang* (promenade) time on Sisowath Quay alongside the river. We stroll past Cambodian picnickers on the grass, and stalls selling food, balloons on sticks, jewellery and jasmine decorations. There is no pressure to buy but we succumb to pineapple on bamboo skewers—peeled, cut and ready to eat. Adjacent to the broad esplanade and its smiling 'dalangers' is the never-ending cacophony and movement of motos, tuk-tuks, cyclos and the occasional four-wheel drive.

The Royal Palace is our final treat in Phnom Penh, and Jai joins us on this excursion. It is an enormous complex in manicured grounds with statues and shrines, and many buildings containing treasures of the royal family. We visit a throne room with immaculately painted ceilings and walls depicting the Ramayana and other traditional stories. The 'silver pagoda' contains an emerald Buddha and showcases of gifts to the royal family over the last few hundred years; and I lift the edge of carpet on which visitors must walk to admire the sheen of the silver underneath rather than the exposed tarnished stuff behind barriers. The outside walls of one pavilion have original paintings from the Ramayana, though they are faded and partly water-damaged. And a little piece of trivia amuses me: there's a display of clothes worn by maids with a different colour for each day of the week; royalty needs no diary, 'Pria is in green, it must be Friday'.

Where Elephants Weep

We are lucky enough to attend a rehearsal of an American–Cambodian opera, *Where Elephants Weep*. It is the

198

story of a young Cambodian–American, raised in the United States after escaping the Khmer Rouge, who returns to Cambodia to rescue its ancient music. He falls in love with a karaoke singer, an east versus west Romeo and Juliet tale. The music is contemporary but played mainly on traditional Khmer instruments, two of which have been adapted to handle the tonal needs of western-style music. The sounds range from the haunting notes of a buffalo horn to the sensitive playing of an electric keyboard by the youngest member of the group.

The musical is being produced by a team of Cambodians, Americans and a Filipino, and the lyrics are mixed Khmer and English. The orchestra and singers are polished and professional although they have worked together and with the production team for less than a week. It is a remarkable marriage of ancient and modern, of voice and instrument.

Siem Reap—
Angkor and the rest

In Siem Reap we attend a rehearsal of a different kind: a piece developed by Jai and Epic Arts using dance and puppetry with kids with disabilities. They have made life-sized puppets from bamboo and flat baskets of assorted sizes, and with which they dance. Their enthusiasm and ability is heart-warming, particularly as Hannah's iPod has exploded; we clap the rhythm and Jai, Hannah and Katie chant for the final dance.

Krom Ty Chean is a small family business outside Siem Reap, and Puon the puppet-maker is the grandson of

199

Ty Chean, the master who resurrected it after the Khmer Rouge left. Jai visits to buy a shadow puppet and I go with her. Puon is making a small leather puppet (*sbaek doit*), and I watch him draw the outline and patterns on previously tanned leather, cut out the body and arms and use fine, very sharp chisels to punch the design. Mind you, Puon holds an animated conversation with Jai as he does this. His wife highlights the designs with paint and attaches the sticks. The family has been making shadow puppets for generations, as well as performing with large shadow puppets (*sbaek thom*). It will be a while before Say-Haa, their six-year-old son, is ready to take over and I hope they survive. I am fascinated by Puon's skill with his chisels and Jai's skill with the language as she chats and plays with Say-Haa.

Vannak, a Cambodian friend of Jai's, takes us to a traditional Khmer restaurant and inculcates us into the joys of 'proper' Khmer food; and though he is disappointed that we aren't up for wild deer or boar he graciously accepts the peculiarities of Jai's mother and aunt. We sample instead delicious whole-baked fish with ginger and spices, prawns and baby squid in a tasty sauce, delicately seasoned morning glory and garlic (different to Australian morning glory), noodles and vegetables that melt in the mouth, and a tasty example of the fish soup we'd tried in the Phnom Penh market. And as a bonus Vannak tells us what we should visit in our limited time at Angkor.

Our three-day pass sounds enough, but it isn't. The days must be consecutive, the weather is very hot and humid, and we two older travellers find four hours traipsing is about all we can take. But Hinda, an understanding tuk-tuk driver, is at our hotel at 7.00 each morning and we manage to explore six of Angkor's treasures.

We devote one morning to Angkor Wat, which is as beautiful as its pictures, although those iconic towers are but the start. We do not make it to the top of the central complex—the stairs to the upper level are horribly steep with crumbling narrow tread and I freeze as I remember that people have died falling from here. I don't need the challenge and am happy to admit I'm too scared to proceed. The intricately carved bas-relief on the first level makes up for missing the view; scenes from the Mahabharata and the ancient history of Cambodia encompass images of Vishnu, Krishna, Hanuman the monkey king, Shiva, and Lakshmi the goddess of beauty. We spend two delightful hours trying to work out who is who—no black and white hats to differentiate the baddies from the goodies—and what exactly are these monsters and whose side are they on; and enjoying the strange sacred garuda, ganesh and goose. Even the awful depictions of torture, and the dead and dying can be admired for their enduring detail.

I revisit tiny Banteay Srei; and Bayon with its gigantic faces, where the bas-reliefs depict daily life—markets, dogs, children, boats and fish, men working and women cooking. I marvel at Ta Prohm where the wat is being consumed, and at the same time held together, by roots of towering banyan trees. And Angkor Thom, originally a fortified city, hides a variety of ruins—temples, massive gates with protective statues of gods and demons; and

201

terraces including one where an inner wall was hidden for centuries and hundreds of carved figures look as though they were carved yesterday.

Phare—an artistic school

From Siem Reap we go to Battambang by the 'fast' boat. Sounds very romantic, and it is for the first and last of the six hours! The young sit on the roof slathered in sunscreen and protected by kramers or sarongs, but Naomi and I opt for shade in the hot, crowded and uncomfortable interior. The passengers are mainly barangs, though a few locals are dropped off or collected from the floating villages on the way. A father and his little girl in a gorgeous aqua dress have been to 'the mainland' for shopping and are returning to an isolated house in the wetlands. From another we collect a young woman dressed in her city finery, including hat and gloves, for a visit to Battambang.

The images from this journey make the hot hours bearable. Most of the journey is on a lake so enormous we could be at sea, that turns into wetlands where 'islands' are already emerging and supporting crops and water buffalo only two months after the end of the wet season. There are floating villages, one with a wedding marquee, another with a café where the skipper stops for lunch and Jai and I refresh ourselves with coconut milk. Two villages have shops, and I wonder if another provides a school. Some isolated habitations have a floating barn or shed, and everywhere are slim, wooden boats transporting villagers or serving fisher people. The crews range from

202

children, perhaps as young as eight effectively plying their poles, to wrinkled grandparents. Nets of all shapes and sizes are suspended in the water with PET bottle floats, or are being thrown out or pulled in, or hung out to dry on massive frames.

Sometimes we meet and pass other boats—three in convoy have a cargo of saffron monks. Occasionally the channels are so narrow that luxuriant foliage scrapes the sides of the boat and passengers with window seats. As we approach Battambang the wetlands become the Stung Sangker River, crowded with fisher people. It's easy to understand why, in water-rich Cambodia there is always fish in markets and on menus.

We are in Battambang to visit Phare Penleu Selpak (cultural and artistic centre). A French woman began Phare to give children in refugee camps something to do. Now, with Khmer principals and worldwide sponsors, Phare provides formal and artistic education to disadvantaged children from Battambang and surrounding villages. Classes include circus, painting, drawing, carving, music, dance and singing. The arrangements for us to see a rehearsal of a circus piece are very Cambodian; it is over when we arrive, but we return later, meet Darren the English volunteer running the circus school and watch it on video. Performances in southeast Asia invariably educate and the circus piece we see addresses the problems of lack of self-esteem and peer ridicule. Darren says that the students have all been disadvantaged or abused in some way, and their work reflects their experiences.

203

A couple of
Cambodian weddings

The real highlight in Cambodia this time is attending two Khmer weddings. While with CLA Jai worked with Seng who is marrying Gina, and Ratanak who is marrying Sarin a technician in the CLA studio. Sarin lives in Cambodia but Charley (a co-president of CLA and one of its American philanthropists) describes him to me as his son by 'moral adoption'. Charley is accepted in this role by Sarin's mother and stepfather (his late father's brother). Hope you've got all that because it isn't easy. But it explains why Sarin and Ratanak's wedding is probably the 'wedding of the year' in Phnom Penh!

When a couple decide to get married, they visit a fortune teller who works out the most auspicious date for the wedding—and November is apparently a very favourable month, hence our invitation to two.

The weddings start at 6.30 am with a procession from the bridegroom's to the bride's house—it may be symbolic if the bride and groom's families live too far apart as they do in both these weddings. Any number of friends can take part and at the start are presented with a platter of food—fresh fruit, joints of meat, banana-leaf-wrapped sweetmeats, or packets and tins of food. The groom (in a golden suit) and his attendants greet everyone in the procession, the guests walk through a decorated archway into either the bride's house or, if it is too small, a hired facility. The bride, also in a golden outfit, is inside with *her* attendants.

204

As the ceremony is in Khmer I'm not sure exactly what is happening but the bride and groom disappear, there are a variety of formalities between the Buddhist equivalent of a civil marriage celebrant, parents, relatives and beautifully attired small girl and boy. These rituals include inspection and approval of the food brought, presumably so the bride's parents can assess how well the bridegroom will provide for their daughter, and readings of Buddhist texts and possibly other missives. Guests wander in and out, take photos, sit outside on gold-decorated chairs, talk with friends, and eat and drink until finally the bride and groom emerge and the ceremony continues. After about three hours the bride and groom, now in their third or fourth outfit, are actually married.

There is non-stop traditional wedding music and at Ratanak and Sarin's wedding it is live entertainment. First an instrumental group as the ceremony takes place, and later a CLA teacher and a young woman perform a routine of slick repartee that apparently is traditional and makes fun of members of the audience, the groom and his best man. Even non-Khmer speakers like us enjoy the banter, though it would have been wonderful to understand the words.

I'm not sure what the couple do for the next few hours but most guests depart to regain their strength for the evening. This begins at about 5 pm when invited guests arrive at another venue for the celebratory party, dance and real nosh. This is also when wedding gifts are given: cash only, in the envelope in which the invitation was delivered. A couple of family members sit at a table by the entrance receiving the envelopes and recording gifts in a ledger. Jai dances to the end at Seng's wedding and can't believe that at midnight the couple is counting their stash. 'It's their wedding night. After that day they should just have been drunk' is her comment.

The food provided at the morning ceremony is mainly a traditional meat-based porridge that Naomi and I ignore; a platter of fruit from the procession prevents starvation. The food at the evening parties is fantastic. Tables are traditionally set for ten and as you arrive you are allocated the next available seat regardless of where friends might be sitting, and no refreshments other than water are provided until the table is full.

Before Seng and Gina's party a group of us meet at the Raffles Hotel (Naomi and I each spend the equivalent of a night's accommodation on a tomato juice) and don't get to the party until 7.45 pm. Luckily this is not considered rude, but we are definitely the last to arrive. Being less than ten people we have to kidnap other guests to fill our table and get food. By the time it arrives the dancing has begun and I can never resist the dance floor, though it is incredibly hot. After a few dances and a nibble at a vegetarian spring roll Naomi and I go home—I hear about the feast later from Jai.

Ratanak and Sarin's wedding party is as sumptuous as all-get-out, providing more food than we can eat and even a table for vegetarians. And we are again entertained with live performance of traditional wedding dances and songs before taking to the dance floor ourselves.

By the end of the day the bride and groom have worn maybe ten matching outfits and the attendants perhaps five. Starting in gold and ending in white, through purple, green, shocking pink, red-trimmed white, and more. I'm told that the 'success' of a wedding is measured by the number of outfits, and that all of these are normally hired. Furthermore any guest turning up in the same gear to both parts of the ceremony, or to any one of the four ceremonies in the case of two weddings with some of the same guests, is beyond the pale.

The evening affairs require formal gowns but Naomi always looks elegant and I manage to mix and match a little, combining an uncrushable flowing white skirt from my local op-shop with two different tops, and an artistically draped scarf. After leaving Seng's morning ceremony Dewey, a young Cambodian–American, finds an apricot satin concoction for the evening party into which I'm sure she is sewn; while Jai is in a Cambodian-made maroon number that Naomi and I lace tightly with ties up the back. A stunning pair, they epitomise the glamour of Cambodian weddings.

SO WHAT ELSE IS CAMBODIA TO ME?

Widely smiling children and teenagers at the roadside, particularly in rural areas, waving and exercising their tourist-oriented English with 'Hello, what your name?' and thrilled when I respond with '*suasudi*' (informal hello) and '*lia hiy*' (informal goodbye). There are school children everywhere: alone on bikes or dinking their friends, little ones in cyclos with their older siblings, in carts, on motos and occasionally in cars; they are always smart in sparkling white and navy blue, despite unmade streets in cities and dusty roads in the countryside. Peals of joy ring out everywhere as mothers wash their children with scoops of water from plastic barrels, and the kids always have the widest smiles though they may have little else.

Most children want to be educated and schools usually run two shifts. I'm told that teachers are so badly paid they hold private classes, and children cannot get their school certificate without doing these extra lessons. So money must be found for uniforms, books and private lessons—not easy for many families. According to a CLA student it costs US$4 a month: not a lot to us but there are many orphans who must earn it themselves or depend on relatives.

The peacefulness of saffron and brown-clad Buddhist monks is tangible, and not only at the wats but also walking singly, in pairs or in small groups on the streets, particularly in the mornings when they collect food. Sometimes they are on motos, sometimes there seem to be monks' outings by bus or truck. And technology has not left them behind either; I see them in phone booths and internet facilities.

The lavatory systems remind me of other places I've visited. Flushing loos are rare and toilet paper must be used sparingly or not at all; when there is plumbing a hand-held water spray is the alternative, otherwise it is water containers and small pots for washing oneself. These are all fine with me on my fourth or fifth journey where alternative body-waste disposal systems are the norm.

Nowhere do I see garbage collectors or rubbish bins for public use; those insidious plastic bags, polystyrene

208

containers, non-refundable bottles and cardboard, paper, rags and food waste proliferate in backstreets. Every now and then someone sets fire to a pile, and clouds of toxic smoke join the rest of the pollution.

There are fewer beggars than I expect, but difficult to ignore for all that. Women with babies, children leading a blind parent who plays a drum or blows a whistle to gain attention, and old women and men just sitting on the footpaths. Most of those I see cluster around the tourist hotels, restaurants and nightclubs. There are some obvious land-mine victims, the most memorable is a boy in Phnom Penh who is maybe ten years old with the most appealing eyes and whose only complete limb is one leg with which he scoots himself on a trolley. I see him first on the footpath above the bank of the Tonlé Sap River and vow to return to give him something before I leave. I next see him one evening when I am on a moto, then on my last day I walk the length of the river bank where the beggars collect, but he isn't there. I should have given him something the first time I saw him but feared being mobbed—it's only later I realise how gentle and unthreatening the Khmer people are.

Memories that will always be with me are the friendliness of the people, and the experiences that I could not have had without Jai introducing me to her Cambodia.

209

'Tell me and I'll listen. Show me and I'll understand. Involve me and I'll learn.'

—A Lakota Indian saying

TEN

CAMBODIA, KIDS AND CULTURAL REGENERATION

In January 2006 I am on a bus travelling north from Phnom Penh to Siem Reap, learning how to sing in Khmer. The passengers include a few westerners, about fourteen Khmer teenagers, and maybe five Khmer adults. I have already met some of the students and their teacher Ieng Sithul, and we are travelling together because they are going to perform for us at one of the wats (temples) outside Siem Reap. There is another teacher with them also, a slim, gentle and elegant woman whose name I never hear. She sits with the kids and encourages us in our attempts to exchange culture and language.

One of the other westerners on the bus is Barbara Walker, an American and mother of Trent who is living in a remote village with the family of Master Prum Uth with whom he is studying *smot*. Smot is an ancient form of Khmer chanting (described also as a melodic poetic recitation) that is often religious in nature, and frequently performed for the dying and at funerals.

Barbara starts the inter-racial communication by asking the students to teach her to count in Khmer; I join in and it takes off from there. They teach us the numbers from one to ten; they sing the Khmer version of 'She'll be coming round the mountain when she comes' and teach us the chorus; we sing the English version while they join in, in Khmer. Then, under the musical direction of Chris a young musician from London, we teach them 'Row, row, row your boat' with translation by a Khmer–English speaker, and we sing the round in a mixture of both languages.

INTRODUCING
CAMBODIAN LIVING ARTS

My enjoyment of the three weeks I spend in Cambodia starts as I zip around Phnom Penh on the back of my daughter Jai's motorbike and finishes as we pay a final visit to the Russian Market in Phnom Penh for presents. But one of the highlights is taking part in a program run by Cambodian Living Arts: a not-for-profit Project of World Education and hereinafter referred to as CLA. Jai is working on a cultural project with CLA and without her introduction to them I would have seen a very different picture of Cambodia.

CLA is provided with office space and administrative assistance by World Education, a Boston-based NGO; but is also made viable by donations, and the efforts of two American philanthropists. In Cambodia CLA is run by a Cambodian–American field officer and local staff, and helped by local associates and volunteers, such as Trent and Jai. CLA funding helps performers, teachers and students to revive traditional dance, drama, puppetry and music and to develop contemporary artistic expression. When I join them in January 2006, they support some twenty Masters and between 250 and 300 students who range in age from six to twenty-four.

Much of a country's history is reflected in its traditional arts. Under Pol Pot and the Khmer Rouge teachers and performers were slaughtered and this aspect of Cambodian history was almost eradicated. Pol Pot's intention was to cut all ties with the cultural past, while the Khmer Rouge wanted to transform Cambodia into a peasant-dominated

213

agricultural society. Under these regimes there was no place for traditional cultural art, or its proponents who kept artistic expression and the 'old' Cambodia alive. But a few artists survived.

A child, Arn Chorn, also survived although most of his family didn't. He was taught to play *khimm* (dulcimer) by an old teacher in one of the labour camps, and flute by another music teacher, Yoeun Mek. The Khmer Rouge left Arn alive to play their military songs, and he risked his life stealing food to keep Mek alive. When the Vietnamese arrived they expected Arn to kill but he wouldn't, instead escaping to a refugee camp in Thailand. There he was adopted by Peter Pond an American and continued his life and education in the United States.

Sixteen years later Arn (now Arn Chorn-Pond) returned to Cambodia and found Yoeun Mek. They located two other Master artists who had survived and children with the ability and desire to play traditional music, and this became part of the arts revival. Arn's initiative, originally called the Cambodian Master Performers Program, developed into Silapak Khmer Amatak or Cambodian Living Arts (somewhat easier for western tongues). Arn still trains students in traditional and contemporary music, and with other teachers has rescued many youngsters from prostitution, begging and child labour along the way. Ten years on his enthusiasm for saving the culture of his country has not waned.

I meet many of the CLA-supported Masters and we exchange traditional greetings and *sampehs* (bows of respect); theirs are usually accompanied by a grin because I am Jai's mother. She is a puppet-maker spending a year working on projects to restore shadow puppetry to its rightful place as an historic and well-loved medium for entertainment and education; in fact *sbaek thom* (large leather) shadow puppets have been declared 'a masterpiece of cultural heritage'. When I'm here Jai has already been around for a few months and is known and respected by the teachers, and loved by the students, and I suspect the grins are because she wears a lip ring—probably the only one they've seen in their lives in Cambodia.

CLA runs 'delegations' to raise awareness of their work with Cambodia's cultural arts. The participants are 'delegates', so if I use this term please picture a disparate group of people from all walks of life, many backgrounds and countries, and assorted ages. We are not a high-flying group of business people or representatives of anything except the human race. What we all have in common is a wish to learn more of Cambodia's culture and to find how we can assist CLA in what they do. It would be impossible not to be inspired to help after sharing performances, bus journeys, meals, laughter and tears with the students and their teachers.

The students all attend classes with faces glowing with enthusiasm, spotless school uniforms (where possible they also go to a local government school), and love of what they are doing. And sometimes they introduce themselves to us, giving their age and name, some in English, some in Khmer.

When we meet them in a different environment they are like children everywhere, jostling to have their photos taken, messing around with each other and any westerner who will join in, or practising their English. But dress them in the traditional costumes of *yike* (Khmer musical theatre) or dance, or put an instrument, unchanged for a thousand years, into their hands and they take on the mien of the people who have presented these arts for centuries, and perform with pride, joy and professionalism.

Once the students are trained, if possible they will return to their classes as teachers, to become both role models and the new Masters. Many of the Masters I meet are in their seventies and eighties and protégées are needed to continue their work if traditional skills are not to be lost, and the cultural history of Cambodia as told through the arts is to survive.

Although most of our experiences involve the teachers and students of traditional arts, CLA also commissions new works to ensure that the arts move forward, and we see examples of contemporary dance, music and opera as well.

BEGINNING
THE CLA EXPERIENCE

I am already in Phnom Penh and have explored it on foot and from the back of various motorbikes. But now the delegates are trickling in and I must become a little more respectable—I'm a delegate after all, and as Jai's mother don't want to put her to shame. I am staying with her instead of at hotels with the others so turn up at events on the back of a moto; stashing my motorbike helmet somewhere while we go off on a day's expedition, or I play the lady for an evening.

216

Our first 'official' experience is a tour of the old quarters of Phnom Penh by bicycle rickshaw (cyclo). This mode of transport doesn't seem right, one human having to work so hard and for so little money to transport another. We are assured that these are genuinely poor cyclo drivers who would otherwise find it hard to survive. Jai also tells me that cyclos are dying out because people want to travel faster, so we are helping those in need rather than those who can afford to own a tuk-tuk. Even so I feel uncomfortable. Our tour is a quick look at a variety of architecture: the American Embassy, an enormous edifice, heavily guarded and certainly not old Phnom Penh; Wat Phnom atop the only hill in the city; the grandeur and ochre-coloured art deco of Central Market; and the Tonlé Bassac area with its rundown flats and shanty dwellings. We end at the Tonlé Sap River for a sunset cruise and enjoy the food, drink and company far too much to notice the sunset—philistines!

We are joined on board by two of the Master performers in CLA's program who play the *chapei dong veng* (a long-necked guitar): Kong Nai who is blind and known as the Ray Charles of Cambodia, and Suon Peng who still suffers from his ill treatment by the Khmer Rouge. Chapei was a traditional court musical form for hundreds of years: a satirical improvisation in which the singer pokes fun at officials as part of a lively social commentary. Chapei musicians were unable to perform under Pol Pot and the Khmer Rouge, and even while the Khmer Rouge vied for power under the United Nations the chapei performers who had survived sang a sanitised version. Kong Nai and Suon

217

Peng sing about Charley and John, Americans who are with us and who give much of their time to CLA. It is translated for the non-Khmer speakers but it is obvious from the laughter of the Cambodians that we're not getting the nuances; however it's impossible not to laugh—satire's intonations and facial expressions are international. Kong Nai seems quite serious in his presentation, but I enjoy Suon Peng's wicked smile and seeming irreverence.

ARCHITECTURAL HISTORY AND CONTEMPORARY CREATIVITY

On our second day we see some of the work of Vann Molyvann who was responsible for many of Phnom Penh's Art Nouveau buildings under the sponsorship of King Sihanouk and the arts renaissance of the 1950s and 1960s. We start in the Tonlé Bassac area where two of his apartment blocks still stand; though after the years of civil war one of these once desirable buildings is a shell inhabited by squatters—including some CLA teachers and students.

There was a vibrant artistic community in Cambodia in the 1960s and the cream of Vann Molyvann's work was the Preah Suramarit National Theatre. It survived the bombing, Pol Pot and the Khmer Rouge only to catch fire in 1994. Apparently Vann Molyvann was on his way back to Phnom Penh and could see his theatre burning as the plane flew over the flames. He raced there but could do nothing except stand atop a fire truck, tears rolling down his face.

The shell is still there and architectural remnants can still be admired—the skeleton of a windowed pyramid that

218

crowned the stage, beams at interesting angles, black-and-white floor tiles, and walls constructed of hexagonal concrete frames around art-deco glass. But the theatre is again being used by the arts community—classes and rehearsals being held in areas protected from the weather— and in one corner is a tiny Buddhist shrine complete with candles, incense and flowers.

A little history will help here. During the 1980s the Ministry of Culture tried to find surviving musicians and entice them back to Phnom Penh. The returnees set up makeshift homes on Dey Krahom (Red Soil), the central strip of land between Vann Molyvann's two apartment blocks in the Tonlé Bassac area, because of its proximity to the National Theatre. Apparently people who worked for the Ministry were given, or could buy, small plots of land here and had permission to build small houses; and artists without official 'permission' also settled on Dey Krahom. A large cultural community was formed in the shantytown and ruined apartment block. But when I am there developers plan to raze both and build new high-rise flats.

According to authorities quoted in an article I read in *Phnom Penh Post*, people who thought they owned their land and home at Dey Krahom discovered that they did not. None of the residents have titles—some squatters assumed that five years' occupation gave them ownership but the land law of 2001 excludes land owned by the government or municipality; other people paid corrupt middlemen so the land never belonged to them, and yet others believed they owned the land they had been given permission to build on.

219

In Phnom Penh I meet two young English women: Katie, a dancer was one of the founders of Epic Arts in the United Kingdom and started Epic Arts/Cambodia in Phnom Penh in 2003; Hannah joined a couple of years later and now manages the performance program. They run art and dance classes and workshops for people with disabilities, and organise dance performances all on the smell of an oily rag. Our architectural tour is followed by a performance by Epic.

The performers include two dancers in wheelchairs: a young man and a woman possibly in her forties who was one of Cambodia's top classical dancers until a car accident left her a quadriplegic. Another performer is a deaf and mute young man who is a wonderful mime artist, and there's Katie. The dance is based on an old folk tale called 'Wolf Mountain' that is full of humour and adventure, with musicians under the direction of Chris from the bus journey. The performance is a superb mix of contemporary music played on traditional instruments; a traditional story with choreography inspired by sign language, traditional Cambodian and modern dance; and contemporary costumes and stage set. The disabled Khmer dancers are far more able dancers than I could ever be.

Over lunch at Friends restaurant I talk to Andrew whose skill has raised enough money to rent and renovate a house for the Masters who live in the Tonlé Bassac (hereinafter called CLA house), and Dickon another financial wizard who decided that he should stop making a fortune for himself and put his skills to better use. Dickon wrote an internet web page about the imminent Tonlé Bassac destruction that

220

inspired Andrew to become involved. The two are now friends and associates in helping save Cambodia's arts and its artists. Talking to them starts me wondering how I can help—without their money-making skills.

The afternoon is unforgettable. We meet four teachers in the Tonlé Bassac and about fifty of the hundred students who live there. Kong Nai teaches chapei, Ieng Sithul and an assistant teach classical and folk dance, Khi Mom teaches yike, and Tep Marie runs a singing and *pin peat* class (pin peat ensembles accompany court dances, plays and religious ceremonies). Two classes are held in the shell of Molyvann's abandoned apartments, the other two in huts at Dey Krahom; and these kids, living in the poorest conditions, sing, perform opera, play their instruments and dance for us—all with the widest smiles. There is no air of depression or sadness here; making our way between huts and up dingy stairways, we are surrounded by smiling faces and children's laughter.

The Masters will move to CLA house, but where the students, their families and the other people from this shantytown will go to live is still undecided. The developers and local government are trying to relocate them 20 kilometres out of Phnom Penh, but they were part of the artistic community that settled here decades ago and their lives are in the hustle, bustle, noise and dirt of this old area of Phnom Penh. Why should they be forced to move out of the city?

To digress: when I return with Naomi in November 2006 I revisit the Tonlé Bassac where students and their families still live and classes are still held. Some shanties have been demolished and the holes filled with barbed wire and concrete to deter squatters. The welcome given to us by these families, many connected with the arts and often five or six people to a spotless single-roomed dwelling, makes the label 'slum' meaningless but the inhumanity of their impending eviction is unforgivable.

The contrast between the Tonlé Bassac and the venue for that evening's entertainment is incongruous, almost immoral. We have a buffet style Khmer meal with lovely wines at the old Phnom Penh home of Nina a Cambodian–American. 'Cambodian-style dressy' is the request so we are attired appropriately. Knowing my style of travel Jai has warned me I might need something dressy for a couple of evening affairs, but my uncrushable black dress stays in my pack—far too hot. Instead I wear a gold-patterned, purple wraparound skirt—a 'welcome to Cambodia' present from Jai—with a blouse from the Russian market and one of her necklaces.

THE MEKONG AND THE HORRORS OF TUOL SLENG

The delegation travels by bus to Arn's house on the Mekong River, and it's a chance to get to know each other a little better. I enjoy the company of Marj an American on her first visit to a third-world country whose husband Ralph is a volunteer consultant to CLA. He has been to Cambodia before but it's an eye-opener and a big adventure for Marj.

222

Arn tells us that when he was growing up in the United States he never imagined owning his own house, particularly in Cambodia, but he loves it. In the garden is a small hut that has a large platform in front, where we sit to hear a little more about CLA, enjoy light musical entertainment, and to eat a delicious Khmer lunch. Arn also built a small theatre as part of his house and here we are treated to a performance of wedding music by Master musicians and their *mahoari* class—in mahoari the singer tells a story, weaving the musicians in without warning and they must immediately play a solo.

Arn is currently training a group of young musicians in modern techniques and they play us pieces combining the old and new of Cambodian music. Our final treat is Seima (pronounced Sreima), a beautiful young woman with a wonderful voice, whom Arn had heard of as a young female singer on the streets of Phnom Penh and who he is now training. Her voice soars towards the roof as she sings a haunting love song of the sixties.

In the afternoon some of us visit the Tuol Sleng genocide museum; originally a high school, it was taken over by Pol Pot's security forces and became the largest detention and torture centre in the county. Rooms full of photographs taken of people as they arrived, of the bodies found at liberation and of the mass graves at the killing fields, and an obscene glass-fronted cabinet filled with skulls, all contribute to the horror of these 'ordinary' buildings. It is easy to understand why Cambodians continue to fear the Khmer Rouge some of whom, we are told, are still hiding in rural areas.

The contrast to the positive feel of the last two days is palpable and I am deeply saddened. Master Prum Uth joins us at Tuol Sleng and chants smot to help the souls leave this place of torture and death. A smot is performed every year on the anniversary of the prison's liberation—only seven people were found alive—to help the tortured souls that are still here to depart. It is an emotional experience: Prum Uth chants something I cannot understand but I sense the peace in what he is doing. Months later as I write this the memory of Tuol Sleng still sickens me. The men, women and children in those photographs were tortured and sent to the 'killing fields' though innocent of any crime. And the record keeping was so meticulous that there is evidence of every one.

The evening is a good antidote. We meet at the Romdeng, a restaurant run by the same people as Friends, and are entertained by a group of musicians and singers who perform pieces from CLA's first commercial CD of traditional Khmer music—and again we hear Kong Nai, definitely the most feted chapei musician.

THE CONTRASTING MUSIC FORMS OF SMOT AND YIKE

The area around Phnom Penh is quite flat but as we drive to Kompong Speu province we see an occasional hill in the distance. Our destination is a pavilion adjacent to a simple wat on the highest point in the area. From here we look down over fields—dry and dusty but seemingly supporting the local farmers—and onto another much more highly decorated wat in an oasis of greenery. Trent tells us about

224

smot and why, at eighteen, he is spending three months studying this rare and ancient form of chanting. The book of Buddhist prayer, which he reads with no problem, is a marvellous fan-fold of exotic and colourful characters, and Trent's demonstration of smot, a sung chant unlike anything I have heard before, is just as enthralling. Strange to hear and see a young American so intensely interested in this ancient art form.

After lunch we drive to Prum Uth's village to attend Trent's smot class where the students, in spotless school uniforms, show pride in what they do and great respect to their teachers. Prum Uth's assistant teacher Keot Ran is a blind woman perhaps in her fifties, and the warmth of the children towards her is obvious. We sit in a room with large openings that let in the breeze (and noises from outside and the students, like kids anywhere, are distracted by chickens, cows and motorbikes). Smot, sung by these students, who range in age from twelve to eighteen, is very moving. Prum Uth compliments Trent highly for his behaviour, respect, ability as a student of smot and as a house guest, and makes a comment that is translated as: 'If he was a girl he would be most beautiful'—a first-class Khmer compliment I suspect!

CLA house is now ready for the Masters from the Tonlé Bassac and we are here for the grand opening. Jai and I arrive early because she is to help students from Khi Mom's yike class get ready for a performance. The students greet Jai and Dickon, who is also there early, with obvious affection, understanding that both these people are working for their futures even if unsure about how. A small girl presents each of them with cotton friendship bracelets that she has made and which they put on immediately.

This is the first performance I have seen with students in full costume and make-up. It is impressive, both the quality of their performance and their understanding of the words and music. It is a story about a prince, a princess and a wicked witch who wants to marry the prince (of course) and bewitches him, but the real princess saves him in the end. Behind a curtain the rest of the class play instruments and sing. It is the first time the students have been to CLA house and the excitement over their new school with its performance room is terrific to see.

TO SIEM REAP
AND A PICNIC AT ANGKOR

The rest of the CLA activities take place around Siem Reap and we get there on the six-hour bus ride described at the start of this chapter. We stop for a picnic lunch alongside a river at Kompong Thom where Sinat, one of CLA's advanced students, plays a piece for us on the *khse diev* (pronounced *sidieu*). This is one of the oldest known Khmer instruments where the player plucks a single string while holding the sounding box, a half gourd on the neck of the instrument, against his chest.

226

As usual I am doing this journey on the cheap and Jai is working, so we stay at the guesthouse 'around the corner' from the delegates' hotel—but comfortable beds and a bathroom with shower are all we need. CLA staff members, and Ieng Sithul and his assistants and students also stay here, and we are close enough for Jai and I to walk to the hotel where most of the delegates are ensconced to join them for breakfast.

We have a few hours to spare the first afternoon and make it to the last day of a silk fair. Most stalls are selling high-quality silk products: garments, scarves, fabrics, cushion covers and other decorative pieces, and many are from villages where the industry supports those in need— land-mine victims, widows and the poor. I happily buy scarves for me and the women in my family, well within my budget and luggage limitations.

On the first evening we go to Angkor for an exploratory drive, all being shoestring travellers for a moment: by arriving after 5 pm we can get into the complex free! We get just a brief taste of its history.

We meet up with students and teachers from both Ieng Sithul's class and the local wedding music class. All the children have been across the causeway into Angor Wat and those from Phnom Penh are on a high; for many it is their first visit to this historic place of worship. Cambodians pay no entrance fee so visit frequently, and locals often come at weekends to picnic at sunset—which we are also here to do.

As the sun goes down the towers of Angkor are reflected in the moat, and it is beautiful. For those willing (and with settled stomachs) there is a Khmer picnic at the water's edge. Trent, Jai, Dickon, Elliot (a young musicologist intern with CLA) and I sit on the ground sharing food from roadside stalls with adults and students and I wouldn't miss it for anything. The exuberant chatter is mostly in Khmer and I understand little, but I enjoy the interaction between people: Cambodians, Cambodian–Americans and westerners.

As we are packing up we are surrounded by children, some as young as five I would guess, begging for leftovers and unfinished scraps. Of course we hand them over—who could throw anything away in the face of hungry children? But deciding how to share out the food is hard; luckily Jai takes over, and in her Khmerglish, makes it quite clear that nobody gets more than one serve, that the older children are not to take from the young, that it is to be as fair as possible in an impossible situation. But they respect her authority, and behave fairly and peacefully; well, most of them.

We return to Siem Reap where I catch up with journal writing while Jai goes out for the evening. Ieng's class is rehearsing down the hall from our room and I glance in but decide not to stay—it may not be appropriate and I don't want to spoil my enjoyment of the performance. But the beat of the drum accompanies my dreams.

PERFORMANCES, PERFORMANCES, PERFORMANCES

It's an early start the next day to catch the sunrise at a wat; unfortunately the arrangements are very Cambodian and the sun is well risen before the bus leaves! But it's a lovely ride alongside a river and through country roads to a remote area that doesn't see many visitors. We are entertained in a pagoda adjacent to the wat by *troeming* students and teachers (troeming is ancient instrumental funeral music). Master Ling Srei is also pretty ancient. I cannot take my eyes

228

off him; his face is classic Asian, his head a skull covered with leather-textured wrinkles, but his hands on the hammers when he plays the *korng vung* (circular frame gong) are as steady and sure as they must have been when he was young. His assistant is not a lot younger and plays traditional multi-reeded flutes.

There are four instruments: drums, a gong, flutes and the korng vung—the number of gongs vary based on the type of music being played, for troeming it is nine. We are told that when CLA found Ling Srei, by word of mouth as often happened, all the troeming instruments had been destroyed. But he drew what he wanted then worked with Sok Duch, a maker of traditional instruments who survived Pol Pot, to construct them correctly. He even remembered the exact pitch of each small gong in the korng vung. Amazing!

In the afternoon we go to Wat Bo, one of Siem Reap's oldest temples and the home of one of the two professional shadow puppet companies in the area. Jai gives a presentation describing her background, the history of shadow puppets in Asia and the projects she is working on while in Cambodia, and demonstrates different types of shadow puppets.

Sbaek thom are made from the hide of a single cow that is cleaned and tanned by the puppet-maker before the character/s or event to be depicted are punched out and it is mounted on two poles. Jai has done this, including scraping the flesh from the hide, and shows us photos to prove it. Heavy is an understatement, and each sbaek thom is operated by a single puppeteer whose body becomes part of

229

his puppet as he dances with it. Traditionally the puppeteers are male maybe with a female as narrator, however women now dance with sbaek thom in contemporary works.

The *sbaek doit* (small leather) are single characters or objects that may be articulated with up to three sticks, and they also have a design punched out. In all these puppets the leather can be subtly coloured.

We spend the early evening at Wat Dam Nak, which was a royal palace in the early twentieth century but is now a wat, and the centre for Khmer studies. I relax and watch the preparations taking place in the grounds while Jai works. The students from the bus are made-up and dressed, becoming professional performers as they don their costumes: silk blouses and silver- or gold-trimmed wraparound skirts (girls) or cotton shirts and the traditional *kben*, a length of material that is wrapped around, pleated, fed between the legs and tucked in to create gold-trimmed baggy pants (girls and boys). Gold jewellery, ornate belts, headdresses, and swords or other weapons complete the costumes.

Each performance piece is a combination of pantomime, drama and dance portraying a classical or traditional folk story; and staged with the pride and professionalism I now associate with these students.

We end the day with sbaek thom in the grounds of Wat Bo. The puppets tell traditional tales from the *Reamker* with monkey armies, kings, princes, and the odd god thrown in— all the usual suspects. I love the way the puppeteers become part of the puppet, beginning behind a large screen (at least four metres high by 15 metres long) when all that can be seen are enormous shadows, before moving to the front and continuing in full view. I am spellbound. We are invited to go behind the screen and it is fascinating. Not only the gymnastic puppeteers, but also people drumming, making sound effects, singing and narrating; and the light source— a massive bonfire of burning coconut husks on a large platform about a metre above the ground, the huge flames leaping another two to three metres. It is fantastic to be under the stars for this performance; a tradition of so many of our Asian neighbours.

ANGKOR EXPLORATION

One day we *do* manage to see the sunrise; at the Bayon temple that is unlike any other wat I visit. Although much of the original detail has eroded since it was built for Jayavarman VII in the twelfth century, many of its enormous heads still gaze down solemnly. The temple is a confusion of passageways and tiny shrines where even at 6.30 am there are wrinkled women with incense, candles and a blessing to exchange for US$1. The atmosphere is sober—maybe a combination of the ridiculous hour and the stone watchers—until I come upon Ieng Sithul and his students and the place fills with light and laughter. Everyone must have their photograph taken, and we westerners are treated like favourite relatives. At ground level are small bas-reliefs overshadowed by massive faces, and among them are ancient musical instruments: a khse diev, and a *memm* (a single-stringed instrument made from wood, vine and lizard skin where the sound travels up to a

231

lizard scale held between the player's teeth and his head is the resonating box). And Sinat joins us to play his khse diev beneath its thousand-year-old image.

Man Men, another CLA-supported Master, normally holds his classes at Wat Bo but a few students live in his village and are to perform for us there. It seems remarkably poor: dry and dusty, and not much sign of crops or livestock other than a few scrawny cows, and chickens pecking in the barren dirt. But this is a western perception of poverty; what I really see is the artistic wealth in Men's hut where the students play.

Wedding music combines instruments and male and female singers, and we hear two pieces before the students tell us about themselves and demonstrate their instruments. Some members of this group perform professionally at weddings and for western visitors in Siem Reap. Sinat, one of Men's students, hopes to be a teacher and performer when he finishes his studies, and he is also to learn how to make khse diev with Master Sok Duch.

After the class we are divided into small groups, and go with a student and a Khmer interpreter to meet and talk with a student's family. My group goes with Khossal a flute player who had told us that he was fourteen years old and an orphan. We sit on a platform near the house in which he lives and try to find out a little about him. Briefly, as told by Seng our Khmer interpreter, we learn Khossal's mother is alive but 'not suitable for him to live with' and that when his father died his grandmother looked after him until she too died. He now lives with an aunt and uncle. He says he cannot go to

232

school because it costs too much—Seng tells us that the cost of uniform, books and private lessons (necessary to complete one's education) are quite high in Cambodian terms.

Khossal has a small vegetable patch behind his grandmother's house and I ask whether he grows vegetables but Seng tells us he is growing gourds because he wants to make himself a khse diev to play in Men's class. To cut a long story short, I find out from CLA that Men can use another khse diev player and that they can arrange for Khossal to go to Sok Duch with Sinat in the summer. I tell the other delegates this story and say that between US$10 and US$15 donated by each delegate will allow this to happen. Not only do we raise enough money, but two friends from New York offer to pay the cost of at least two years' schooling for him. In our terms an inexpensive gift, in Khossal's terms hope for a future.

When I return ten months later Khossal has recently moved to Phnom Penh, is to board with Sok Duch in his village, and learn to play and to make the khse diev— a great outcome.

We have a free afternoon on this day. Yay! Not long enough to explore Angkor Wat—that will have to wait for my return—but Elliot joins us and at Jai's suggestion we go to Banteay Srei. It is over 30 kilometres from Siem Reap and an hour in a tuk-tuk, but we organise one at a reasonable price and it is more comfortable than motos on those unmade roads, even though tuk-tuks don't have much padding on their metal seats. We go through delightful rural areas: past shady gardens, green fields, smallholdings with

233

interesting crops, and stalls selling lotus pods, sugarcane, timber and carved souvenirs.

Banteay Srei is considered to be the jewel in the crown of Angkorian art. It is a Hindu temple built of bricks in a pinkish-orange hue, and many of its carvings are well preserved. Whether due to durable material, the depth of the bas-reliefs (said to be the deepest of any of the temples) or that it is better protected from the corrosive effects of wind I don't know, but it is beautiful. The carvings include male and female gods and finely detailed patterns and images from nature. The small site is crowded with a mixture of Cambodian and foreign visitors; I could have stayed for hours had there been less people.

We pay a flying visit to Angkor Wat on our way back to Siem Reap: I can't leave Cambodia without at least a taste, and it might be Elliot's only chance. Angkor Wat is the best known of the temples, the best preserved in the Angkor complex and believed to be the largest religious structure in the world. It must be seen and not in a rush, but today I have no choice.

Our tuk-tuk driver drops us at the back of the temple and says he will wait for us in front. We wander through the gardens admiring the iconic towers with their cupola-like pinnacles, and take time to walk all four sides of the central temple where almost perfect bas-reliefs still tell the stories of epic events in Hindu religion and Cambodia's history.

We cross the causeway over the moat to the front where we expect to find our tuk-tuk: we all noted the colour of the awning and the garb of the driver so it should be easy. We

234

wander in different directions, meeting again at the steps. No sign of it or him. And time is running out—we have a date at a flashy roof-top restaurant for dinner and entertainment and it will not do to be late, unshowered or unkempt. It's a mystery. We haven't paid for the afternoon why would he take off? When we can wait no longer we find three motos (the quickest way to get back) agree on a price and set off.

Suddenly we see our tuk-tuk speeding towards us. Instant recognition—we owe him a lot of money so he *would* be looking for us! We quickly halt our motos, luckily I have learnt '*Chop! Chop!*' (stop)—strange that, in pidgin it means go faster. We get no explanation from the driver but I suspect he over-estimated how long we would be, returned someone to Siem Reap, and didn't get back in time. But we feel a duty to him because he *has* spent the whole afternoon with us. We abandon three disgruntled moto-dob drivers (Jai at her most charming explaining what has happened) and race into town.

A quick shower and change into a kaftan I brought with me for just such an occasion, swish earrings and necklace, and I'm ready to face the world. The Amansara Hotel and restaurant are *very* luxurious and the manager, an enthusiastic supporter of CLA, is hosting this dinner, or I wouldn't be there. The restaurant is on the roof top with comfortable mattresses for lounging at low tables rather than formal tables and chairs, and the food is excellent. Yoeun Mek and Man Men entertain us with songs and instruments, then we are asked to reciprocate. I have drunk

235

enough wine to do a rendition of 'Waltzing Matilda' with a two-way translation: me (Aussie slang into English), and Arn and Seng trying to translate it into Khmer—just imagine! It causes much amusement, and Jai says she's not embarrassed, she just didn't fancy joining me in a duet—with my singing skills I don't blame her. A couple of Americans, not to be outdone, give us renditions of classic American tear jerkers: details of which are lost in the wine haze and my stolen journal.

ARTISANS D'ANGKOR

I have a lazy start to the last day of the delegation, breakfasting with those still able to eat. I'm very grateful to my iron constitution—I've been adventurous with food with no ill-effects, while others have been careful and unfairly suffer from gastric nasties; but all the preventative and curative medication I carry is put to good use.

Artisans d'Angkor was created in 1999 to provide an artistic workshop centre in the Siem Reap province where young artisans could learn to make quality Khmer handicrafts, before returning to their villages to start up workshops. Artisans is now completely self-sufficient, making pieces for tourists, specially commissioned items and works purchased by hotels. A visit here is our last organised activity, and we see young men and women making wood and stone carvings, sculptures, lacquer work and painting. A group of silk painters composed entirely of young deaf-mute women take a break to joke in sign language—at our expense I suspect—before posing for photographs.

236

Jai and I take an afternoon off and lunch at The Blue Pumpkin—an amazing out-of-place European-style internet café where the coffee is perfect, according to my barista daughter. Wide settees run the length of two walls upstairs, and you can order luxurious coffee or fruit juices, and just lounge. The Blue Pumpkin is a wonderful haven away from the heat and dust of Siem Reap, and is the hangout of young western volunteers like a couple of similar oases I visit with Jai in Phnom Penh. It is a place where they can sympathise with each other over the inequities and difficult situations that they are trying to address, and a supportive environment in which to regain perspective on what they are doing and recharge their emotional batteries.

In the evening we dress up again, for our last formal CLA function: a buffet dinner at the house of Phlouen Prim, a Cambodian–American living in Siem Reap and a deputy director of Artisans d'Angkor. The house is modern, large and sumptuous and although I find it hard I accept the contrast with what is outside: this man is doing much for Cambodia and Cambodians.

These eight days change my life. I return home determined to go back to Cambodia; to tell the story of its artistic revitalisation through the people involved.

237

'Avoiding danger is no safer in the long run than outright exposure. Life is either a daring adventure or nothing.'

—Helen Keller

ELEVEN

VIETNAM: SAME, SAME, BUT DIFFERENT

An elderly woman grinning widely, gaps in her betel-stained teeth, her face a wrinkled map cannot stop touching us. She and Naomi are both aged 67, sisters under the skin though no words in common—but smiles and gestures say it all. Mui translates: 'I wish I could speak English and talk to these two all day'. She and Naomi are a perfect illustration of the Vietnamese adage: 'Same, same, but different'.

We discover neither her name nor that of her neighbour, a younger woman in whose house we are sitting and whose Vietnamese green tea we are sharing. The householder and her husband were heroes of the Vietnam War; we are shown her husband's uniform, still immaculate, medals still pinned on the jacket. I capture images of her in the uniform on my camera, then Mui takes a photo of us with both these women. I'll have that betel-stained smile forever.

We are here because the householders supplement their income from a small coffee plantation with another crop. There is a large shed on the property filled with hanging plastic bags of fermenting bamboo shreds, rubber tree sawdust, limestone, old mulch and spores. Wonderful fungi sprout through holes in the plastic, bright orange for medicinal purposes and fans of pale grey and cream straw mushrooms for eating. We buy some of these for that evening's dinner.

I suspect that we are also here because Mui is obsessed with the war.

240

EASY RIDING THROUGH
THE CENTRAL HIGHLANDS

The bus to Dalat takes us through hectares of fertile fields with fruit and vegetables growing almost wild, and roadsides lined with drying coffee beans. The market in Dalat is a palate of this fresh produce and it's great fun to buy, when all we have in common are fingers for bargaining: two tomatoes, one carrot, six bananas, two mandarins, three rolls, and thousands of dong.

The 'Easy Riders' take people to villages in the Central Highlands to which tours don't go, to visit locals and learn about their lives. It seems impossible to go off the tourist track without our own transport so they are a justifiable extravagance.

We think two days in the highlands then back to Dalat for the bus to Nha Trang makes sense but Mui and Trung, whom we meet outside the Peace café, have other ideas. Their 'good guy, bad guy' team persuade us to take three days to go to Nha Trang with them. They know roughly where we'll go but make no promises about what we'll see— that depends on everything from the weather to who is at home when we arrive. Their price of US$100 a day for the two of us is non-negotiable; though there are 'faux Easy Riders' who offer cheaper deals, Mui says, 'We give value for money, take it or leave it.' We take it.

We have two days to explore Dalat before beginning this adventure. We try to visit the Lam Dong Museum—on a Monday when it's closed; wander the market; walk around and picnic by the lake; tramp kilometres up and down hills

241

to find an eccentric poet/calligrapher and an even more eccentric artistic monk; and discover areas of faded French colonial beauty, unfortunately some now up for redevelopment not restoration.

Then begin three days with our bikies. 'Can you manage large luggage?' we ask (our eight weeks' gear includes wedding outfits for Cambodia and warm clothes for North Vietnam). They can. Our bags and theirs, wrapped tightly in plastic, are secured to the motorbikes with assorted straps.

Trung and Mui order lunches and dinners and eat with us, so we get authentic Vietnamese food at Vietnamese prices. They find fish and vegetable dishes, which we all share, and occasionally a meat one, which we don't. Lunches are at roadside cafés where the food is cheap and tasty; and there are squat toilets with baskets for the paper and containers of water for washing hands—part of the challenge of travel like this.

The evening meals are fantastic. At Lak Lake guesthouse and restaurant the baked fish, rice-paper rolls and fish soup are delicious and almost too much. Mui entertains us with the story of wooing his wife; he couldn't afford an expensive birthday gift so bought ten pairs of underpants in different colours and says he won her heart because it was imaginative and they fitted her. I'm not sure that I believe him.

Our second evening is at the Trinh Nu waterfall guesthouse, on the edge of the wide Krong No Stream. Dinner here is also delicious and includes the mushrooms we bought from the mushroom farm. Unfortunately Mui's

242

idea of haute cuisine sees them crumbed and deep-fried, their delicate flavour lost. Ah well! He didn't profess to be a gastronome.

Much of the Central Highlands is volcanic and fertile: hundreds of hectares of coffee plantations fill the landscape, their trees covered in clusters of beans or wonderful jasmine-like flowers. We are told Vietnam is the second largest exporter of coffee in the world—utterly believable. The roads are edged with coffee beans: pink, green and fawn during the first drying cycle and dark brown in the second. People, cows, dogs and chickens constantly walk on the beans; and family members turn them regularly—children kick them up, adults use rakes and paddles. Once fully dried two outer layers are removed and the dimpled, green coffee bean is roasted. Trung tells us that this is when secret ingredients (like fish sauce) are added.

Because coffee is an annual crop families must participate in alternative endeavours also. We visit a coffee farmer who cultivates a few mulberry trees, and the government gives him silkworm eggs that he tends, plants on frames when they hatch, and feeds on the leaves until they spin silk cocoons. The only unsmiling child I see in Vietnam is here; she looks eight years old but is probably older and her job is to drag these cocoons off the frames.

At a silk-production facility—the closest we get to mechanisation—we see the cocoons spun into silk thread. The cocoons must be wet for the ends to be found and the silk to separate; young women stand for up to eight hours,

243

their swollen hands immersed in water, attaching the silk of five cocoons to a steam-driven spindle.

My favourite visit is to a family, originally from Hoi An, who makes rice paper: ladling rice 'batter' onto a hot plate, spreading it with the ladle, then a moment later lifting it off to dry on a rack. This rice paper is made with black sesame seeds to make *banh dap*, a Hoi An speciality. One rice-paper circle is grilled and spread with oil and chives, a soft one is placed on top, then they are folded in half and broken into pieces to be dipped into soy sauce with chives and chillies before eating. It is delicious.

Another family produces rice wine for their whole village using a simple method and the most basic equipment. A large quantity of rice is boiled, or soaked for days, placed in big earthenware pots with yeast (or a local leaf that also starts fermentation) and left to brew until it is ready—trade secret I assume as nobody tells us how they know—then cooked in a still where the steam condenses and runs into a large vat. The first output is 76 percent-proof, and 20 kilograms of rice produces over 20 litres of wine. Nothing is wasted—the dross is fed to pigs, providers of fertiliser for the rice crop and eventually pork.

Another family makes the large decorative garden pots we have admired in shops and markets. The 'potter' pours fine concrete over sand moulds on the ground, rotates a shape-former in a frame to create an up-ended pot that is left to dry for a couple of days before being painted.

Mahogany cannot be felled legally but the dense stumps and roots can be dug up—Trung says they 'turn to stone' if

244

left too long. These are intricate shapes with beautiful grain and colours, and we visit a family who transform them into ornate pieces of furniture and statuary often decorated with carved animals and birds. The carpenter—artist and sculptor—uses a small chainsaw, patient chiselling, fine sandpaper, and finally pine sap to enhance colour and produce a wax-like sheen.

Numerous minority groups live in the highlands. Many speak their own dialect, and in the villages where they speak no Vietnamese Trung uses their language. To get to a Mnong village we cross a narrow bridge constructed of tapering bamboo tied with vines, and a bamboo handrail that almost peters out. Stumbling and clutching the rail I think of the villagers, young and old, who cross it daily without hesitation. The village comprises long houses on tall stilts with floors made of bamboo bark tied to bearers and walls woven in intricate patterns, and we enter by steps cut into a tree trunk. Inside there are cooking fires; and traditional tools, baskets, pots and utensils are used for household chores, farming and fishing.

In another village we visit a kindergarten where the children cannot speak Vietnamese and are taught in their own language. Their teacher encourages them to interact with us but they are too shy. The village looks to be at subsistence level but I'm impressed with their ingenuity: Trung demonstrates blacksmith's bellows comprising two large bamboo tubes, through which air is pumped into a narrow tube at the bottom by pushing a stick with a plug on the end up and down. The plug is made of some hard

245

VIETNAM: SAME, SAME, BUT DIFFERENT

substance with an outer coating of chicken feathers. Fascinating and very effective.

I've always loved motorbike riding and these three days are no exception. We pass mountains and valleys, jungle and rainforest, bamboo stands, rice paddies and lushness, occasionally scarred by a bare hillside. Mui says some is caused by erosion but the rest from defoliants dropped during the war and only now, thirty years on, is revegetation occurring.

Naomi's bikie is Mui; he is brash, opinionated, doesn't really listen to anyone else and could do with a charm course. More than once he says, 'No questions yet, I haven't finished,' as he describes something to us. The Vietnam War is still important to him: three of his five uncles were with North Vietnam troops and two with the South; he's knowledgeable but becomes quite aggressive when he talks of battles and atrocities.

Trung is quieter and we discuss many things as we ride: life philosophies and how things work in Vietnam—school hours, government policies, people's attitudes to education. He's a gentle man with an obvious love of his country, and his knowledge of the environment and farming adds to the experience for us both.

Many of the people we meet are as interested in us as we are in them. They are used to Mui and Trung having pillion passengers—but not women of our vintage. It's a great experience filled with people we could not possibly have found on our own.

THE MEKONG DELTA

Getting there

Our boat journey from Cambodia to Vietnam is delightful—
not too hot, not too long, plenty of fresh air, fishing boats and
river banks dotted with villages—but crossing the border is a
novel experience. We disembark first on the Cambodian side
of this imaginary line, an exit date is stamped in our passports
and we return to the boat to cruise 100 metres down river. We
disembark again, this time clambering up the dusty river bank,
to Vietnamese passport control where entry forms are taken,
visas checked and an official heads off with our passports
leaving us at a picnic table under an umbrella of palm fronds.
As we wait people badger us to change money and buy goods;
and after the gentleness of Cambodians the Vietnamese
assertiveness takes me by surprise.

Our passports returned we re-embark at a different spot.
This section of the Bassac River—though I'm never sure
when it's Mekong and when Bassac—reminds me of the trip
from Siem Reap to Battambang in Cambodia: fishing boats,
houseboats, groups of floating houses, nets being thrown in
and hauled out, young and old working the water. Many
boats have beautifully painted eyes on the prow, perhaps to
help them find fish or their way home.

If the rat's not on the table …

We reach Chau Doc an hour later and climb rickety steps to
exit through a restaurant with tables outside, delicious
smells and Vietnamese diners; Naomi and I agree we'll

return for a meal. Emerging into the street we are grabbed by a couple of cyclo drivers who say, '$1 each' and, having no idea where the Trung Nguyen Hotel is or how Vietnam works, we don't barter. We should have—it is less than two kilometres and definitely not a dollar job—I bet they love ambushing new arrivals!

The hotel room is clean, big enough for two, the bathroom looks adequate and we only plan to stay a couple of nights. But the best laid plans …

The balcony of our room is a window into the vibrancy of southeast Asia. There is constant activity at the market diagonally across the intersection—all modes of transport, kids going to school, people going to work and stallholders setting up. Opposite our first-floor window an existing building is being extended upwards, and the construction work is fascinating. The scaffolding is cobbled-together bamboo and planks, safety helmets are optional, young men lean out to yell to mates below, concrete for the pillars is mixed at ground level and pulled up in buckets, and timber forms for pillars are constructed at assorted angles from vertical without plumb line.

The market, where we are often the only westerners, has a great variety of produce and goods, including aisle after aisle of fabrics wonderfully displayed—luxuriantly embroidered, bolts in the brightest of colours, sombre men's suiting, and at one stall a woman holds the fabric between her toes as she cuts lengths.

After the humidity of Cambodia, we enjoy the weather of Chau Doc. Walking ourselves weary, gaining familiarity with this small fishing and port town, learning how to say 'No' to cyclo and moto drivers and market stallholders, and how to keep smiling as the twentieth child says, 'Hello. What's your name? How old are you?' Twice we revisit the area where we docked to find the restaurant, but it is not there. Does it only open when a boat is coming in or was it a figment of our imagination?

A few kilometres from Chau Doc is Sam Mountain and we spoil ourselves with motos to the top—a hairy five-kilometre ride of steep bends on potholed asphalt. We look across the Mekong Delta to Cambodia over rice paddies, stretches of water, occasional buildings and small settlements; a patchwork of yellows, greens, greys and browns.

The walk down winds through tiny villages, each with 'hello-ing' children, old women and roosters, and small hammock-filled cafés whose owners try to entice us with tea or soft drink. Many villages have temples; one is protected by an enormous golden dragon, at another an old man—his face a sculpture of wrinkles, straggly beard and benevolent smile—invites us in and gives us glasses of green tea as we struggle with Vietnamese.

We know there are buses back to Chau Doc from the village at the foot of the mountain but can find nobody who speaks English or understands our faltering, mispronounced Vietnamese. Two moto drivers hassle us non-stop but cannot point out a bus stop or tell us when the buses come—strange that! It's hot, we don't want to wait for a bus that may not arrive, and we finally give in to the moto pests. Riding back we see buses and bus stops—of course it would have been possible.

On the day we plan to leave for Saigon we come down with what I call Asian belly. The young people at hotel reception are sympathetic and helpful—we can stay indefinitely; they re-schedule our journey, and even buy ginger at the market to put in green tea to settle our stomachs.

Two nights earlier I had eaten at a vegetarian café where Naomi accompanied me though ate nothing. It was pretty disgusting; not only a menu of faux meat made from soy when Vietnamese non-meat dishes are absolutely delicious, but it was dirty and had at least one resident rat. I ordered before noticing how grotty it was, and the rat didn't appear until I'd almost finished eating. This is where infection should have come from, not a clean café with good food and no litter or livestock where we both ate next day. When later describing this to my daughter-in-law Kate she asks how I dealt with the rat, I reply, 'If it's not on the table, don't worry about it.' Cheap travel certainly changes standards.

Two International Sculpture Symposia have been held in An Giang Province that incorporates Chau Doc and Sam Mountain. International sculptors stayed in An Giang, toured the area and met its people, then designed and created outdoor sculptures that reflected their feelings. They are exhibited near Sam Mountain: huge representations of people, creatures and the environment in marble and granite with touches of bronze or steel.

250

In the Delta

Finally, though still a little queasy, we leave for Saigon via two days in the Delta. We'd booked onto a tour by boat and bus with a home-stay in a village; but with dubious guts we play it safe, taking an overnight stop in Cantho instead. Tan collects us from the Trung Nguyen and she's a delight—so much depends on the guide that we think this tour might be OK—but she hands us over to Nhi who is officious, abrupt, rude, unfriendly and definitely in the wrong job. She is disinterested in us and the places we go to, dispenses minimum information, and talks endlessly to the bus driver and on her mobile phone. I note in my journal: 'As a guide she'd make a good plumber'.

We visit a Cham minority village where weaving is a speciality, and although traditional fabric is being woven on a loom it is just a sales exercise—the room is full of scarves, sarongs and skirts. Nhi is honest enough to say that they are not all made in this village; one skirt is very like one I have from Thailand and I even wonder if they are Vietnamese. I'm interested in the social aspect of places: how people live, education, agriculture and their manufacturing processes, and have an aversion to buying from these outlets. But I'm an idealist, they need to make money and tourists are a cash supply.

At another village we see incense sticks being manufactured and the roadside is lined with brilliantly coloured bundles fanned out to dry—yellow and red sticks, and incense in different shades of brown. Walk into any temple or shrine in Vietnam and the smell of incense

251

surrounds you; whatever your beliefs it is lovely to pay a few dong for a couple of incense sticks to light and wedge in an urn of sand.

In many of these rural areas wide drains run alongside the road, spanned by an assortment of bridges from utilitarian concrete and beautiful arches, to rickety sticks I'd think twice about crossing. In these ditches are flocks of ducks, kids fishing and manoeuvring boats, and men up to their armpits in water sorting out fishing nets. Assorted habitations crowd the other side and small boats are moored where there is no bridge.

I'm puzzled by white 'houses' on mounds in the rice paddies and ask a trainee guide who is travelling with us. He explains that they are tombs for members of the family that owns the paddy field. They are quite small so I hope they are for ashes—the alternative doesn't bear thinking about.

Cantho is a thriving town and gateway to the waterways of the Mekong. We explore the market, and narrow streets and alleyways, eventually ending up in a 'boys play area': stall after stall of new and used spare parts for bikes, motos, cars and other machinery—pulleys, ball-bearings in their casings, nuts, bolts, tools, tyres, plus unidentifiable bits. We enjoy the evening streets as we search for a cheap meal; ending up at a café next to our hotel that's busy, good value and with no visible livestock.

The two floating markets we visit are bottlenecks of wooden boats owned by local farmers who sell their produce on the water. Some are also homes with flapping washing and children playing. Wares are advertised

252

by samples hung on a bamboo pole at the prow: capsicum, pumpkins, bananas, pineapples, potatoes, onions, sweet potatoes.

Dong, our guide this day, explains that farmers started selling produce from boats when the government stopped taxing businesses on the water. He also says they make about US$100 a month, but don't see education as important and often won't keep their kids at secondary school. When a son gets married, the family buys another boat and he stays in the business, so maybe education doesn't seem relevant.

I have heard about monkey bridges that connect villages and a couple of times ask our guide, 'Is that one?' to be told with amusement, 'No, that's a tiger bridge!', or 'No, that's an elephant bridge!' I eventually realise that slender pieces of wood or bamboo strung between rickety uprights are what I'm looking for and understand the mirth—'bridge' is a generous description. I'm sure the locals cross with loaded baskets, at a run, probably in the dark and with their eyes closed.

A rice-noodle factory is an interesting stop; the process is like the one on our Easy Rider trip but on a larger scale, the rice batter contains sago and the paper circles are lifted off the hotplate and laid on the drying rack with a beautiful woven bamboo cylinder. Once dried in the sun they are cut into fine vermicelli with a hand-turned pasta cutter.

253

I have lovely memories of the Mekong: endless water, colourful and vibrant floating markets, fisher-people and narrow canals with impossible bridges traversing them.

PEACEFUL SOJOURNS
IN NORTH VIETNAM

We arrive in Hanoi nine days before we fly back to Australia and want to explore some of the area's attractions. Luckily we find Viet, at Vega travel, who understands what we want and works out an economical way to get to Halong Bay, Sapa and Tam Coc—though we have to abandon Cat Ba Island in Halong Bay. But if we miss something so be it—we'll just have to come back.

Halong Bay—
water and peace

We share two days and one night on Halong Bay with seven other tourists and Hiep our knowledgeable guide. Halong's wharf is crazy with thousands of people and hundreds of tour boats; Hiep says 400 boats leave Halong daily. Constructed of brown-stained timber, yellow bamboo trim above, green-painted trim below, some boats are fancier than others but all fly Vietnam's red flag with its gold star. Our economy option model lost her mast in a storm but the sails are for show so it's no big deal—and the service, food and our small group couldn't be bettered.

The scenery is stunning; there are not enough superlatives to say more. Publicity photos show the islands against brilliant sun-drenched sea and sky; we see them in misty clouds against a grey sea. As we cruise, their sombre shapes materialise evoking thoughts of mountain gods or island spirits. Atop one is a tiny pagoda, and eroded tunnels cut under others; Hiep tells us there are over a thousand islands. The area was designated a World Heritage site in 1994 so hopefully will remain unspoilt—though isn't '400 tourist boats a day' and 'unspoilt' oxymoronic? While Vietnam's popularity as a holiday destination continues to increase, so too will Halong Bay's. I appreciate my hypocrisy, I'm one of those tourists.

Hang Sung Sot is my first dry limestone cave, where stalactites and stalagmites no longer grow. I've always been a 'cave nut' and Sung Sot is one of the best, with rock formations and the scalloped surface of the arching roof in pink, white and cream. It was formed beneath the sea, lifted by earthquake, discovered by man over a hundred years ago, and is part of the Halong Bay World Heritage site. Hiep says Sung Sot is 10,000 square metres—it's enormous so I'm not about to argue.

The grey morning of the second day brings another journey highlight, Naomi's first kayak experience. We paddle into a lagoon through the arch of an island and the surrounding grey-green walls are so close that we can see eroded caves, rock textures and tiny trees clinging to seemingly vertical cliffs. For a while we are alone, the only sound an occasional splash as we push ourselves into another glide. We return to our boat cold and wet but don't give a damn.

Tam Coc— 255
Halong Bay of the rice paddies
The bus ride to Ninh Binh, to visit Tam Coc, takes three-and-a-half hours instead of two, making us realise we are either fortunate with Viet's other arrangements or unlucky

with this. Luckily a helpful young man with a mobile phone rings the hotel for us and arranges for the motorbike to collect us at 10.30 pm instead of 9 pm. And Tam Coc is worth the worry.

As we are rowed through the paddy fields, sharp-edged grey peaks cut the sky, reminiscent of the islands in Halong Bay. Tam Coc means 'three caves' though they are really tunnels through the mountains; their roofs gently eroded scallops dappled by the water, with an occasional stalactite for unwary heads. The sun is a pale circle through the hazy morning clouds and it's incredibly peaceful, the only sound the swish of paddles and occasional Vietnamese between our skipper and her off-sider. As we glide we see a pagoda, graves, cattle, people fishing and working in the paddies, and occasionally rowers lying back and using their feet to 'pedal' the oars. Unfortunately the peace is disturbed a couple of times: first when vendors approach and make us feel guilty because we don't buy drinks for our rowers, then our skipper tries to sell us embroidery. She also puts the hard word on us for a tip but I only tip as thanks for an unexpected service; she hasn't been unpleasant but has ignored us until she wants to sell us embroidery.

On the recommendation of two different people we stay at the Xuan Hoa Hotel in Ninh Binh—supposedly excellent with the 'best' Vietnamese food. But it's a little costly at US$16 when we're only paying US$15 in Hanoi; and after Tam Coc we have lunch at the hotel—it either has a new cook or the two enthusiasts haven't eaten decent Vietnamese cuisine. We cancel our second night and return to crazy Hanoi.

The trip back on a local bus is almost as interesting as Tam Coc. It leaves promptly, has room for our luggage (horror stories of local buses include luggage piled on knees) and is half empty. Mind you en route they cram in as many passengers as possible, pulling in to bus stops long after I would have admitted defeat. The conductor moves everyone closer together and finally hands out small plastic stools on which passengers sit in the aisles. At 3000d each it's a steal—we paid 64,000d for the tour bus *to* Ninh Binh. All this and more; we are entertained for the whole journey with schmaltzy English Christmas songs—no matter that it's 31 December.

Finding the right bus at Hanoi South bus station to take us back to our hotel is tricky, but another young man rescues us and tells us the bus we need and where to catch it. We are back at Prince II in time to celebrate New Year's Eve with savouries and cake—and ABBA's 'Happy New Year' echoing up the staircase all night.

We should have gone to Ninh Binh the same way; but how do you find out except by 'doing' or asking a lot of questions—assuming you know who to ask. Travel books are useful, but without real tourist information it seems impossible—and we try all modes of transport except camel and bullock cart (I'm joking about the camel).

An expedition
to Sapa in the Highlands

Our last excursion out of Hanoi is northwest to Sapa. At an elevation of 1650 metres it nestles in the towering Hoang

Lien mountain range that includes Fansipan, Vietnam's tallest mountain.

The overnight train to Lao Cai is a dream—but I'll be honest, we have 'soft sleepers'. We are met by the Mountain View Hotel's minibus and driven the 35 kilometres up to Sapa—a journey that can take two hours. The evening we return to Hanoi it has rained all day, is still drizzling and I describe the journey down to Lao Cai as 'hairy'.

At the weekend hill tribe people come in to Sapa to run market stalls so it's the popular tourist time. We go mid-week when it is quieter and, I think, more interesting: the locals come to shop and the atmosphere is wonderful. We see old women haggling; young mothers chattering vivaciously with babies slung on their backs; older women selecting produce; schoolgirls giggling and bargaining for mandarins; and men poring over strange electrical bits.

We book ourselves onto a 15-kilometre trek to three hill tribe villages for the next day and maybe that's what brings in the clouds and drizzle. When we wake, the mountain view is just a memory but six of us trek regardless: two young Australians who had thought this was a five-kilometre ramble but manage remarkably well and cheerfully, a couple from Paris who are mountain goats in disguise, and us. Two return to Sapa dirt-spattered after many mud slides, but I'm not saying which two.

Chu, a young Black Hmong woman, is our guide; knowledgeable, patient and caring she helps those who need it down the slippery slopes and as a bonus she's quite a chef. Not only does she tell me how to cook three of my favourite

Vietnamese dishes, but at our lunch stop she cooks us a delicious meal. It would have been lovely to see the views hiding behind the clouds, but even the sliding and falling on steep clay tracks with just a bamboo stick for support doesn't spoil our enjoyment. And for the first time on this journey we *do* tip.

IDIOSYNCRASIES OF CHEAP HOTELS

Every hotel we stay at has a list of regulations, in both Vietnamese and English, even in Bau Loc where western guests are the exception. Here are a few for your enjoyment:

- During your stay if you need any allowed requirement please do not hesitate to contact reception to have instructions in details
- You should return to Hotel before 23.00. If you are in special case please inform guard in advance
- Any activities such as cooking, ironing, washing, moody shoes or boots (*this in Sapa and it takes me a while to translate moody to muddy*), using hair-dryer for other purposes are not allowed in the room
- Do not drink too much, make noise, influence on the others
- Guests will respect public hygiene and order at the Hotel. No animals, strong smelling goods or cooking are accepted in the hotel room.

259

Most hotels prohibit washing in your room—they offer cheap laundry service though it is often returned un-pressed and still damp. Naomi and I, covert washers of undies and shirts in showers, resort to assorted subterfuges to keep them hidden as they dry.

And you must *never* bring prostitutes into your room, use electrical equipment or move the furniture.

But what can you do except rearrange the furniture when the room is an odd shape, the queen-sized bed is jammed against the wall on one side and the other side is so close to a large wooden chair that you cannot get out without stubbing your toe, smashing your knee, tripping over it or all the above. I'm not joking, this describes our room at Prince II in Hanoi where we quietly move chairs and tables each night and just as quietly reconstruct the room before breakfast.

Don't get me wrong, the Prince group are great places to stay but another idiosyncrasy is that booking a room is meaningless. We end up staying at all three hotels because when we arrive back at the one we booked for our return to Hanoi, we are told, 'Sorry, no room, there is one for you at Prince III (or II or I) we will take you there.' They don't mind opening the safe for our secure envelope or finding motorbikes to transport us and our expanding luggage.

Despite strange-shaped rooms, bulky wooden furniture with hard wooden seats, having to hurdle fridges to get out of bed, showers that drown you, freeze you, or just trickle down your back while soaking the floor, I wouldn't stay anywhere except these cheap hotels. The staff are welcoming, friendly, and helpful beyond what is required. Breakfast is included in most of those we honour with our custom, or costs an extra dollar. So what if it is Vietnamese soup with noodles, or their idea of a western breakfast of

fruit, eggs, and rolls that are chewy outside but like the diet
rolls my mother used to eat inside, and served with syrupy
strawberry jam or processed cheese.

EATING IN VIETNAM
IS A JOY

I quickly find my favourite foods: water spinach, morning
glory or bok choy stir-fried with garlic; vegetarian Cao Lau
in Hoi An; fish in clay pot in assorted places; fresh vegetable
spring rolls; calamari with vegetables; tofu with tomato
sauce (not the one in a bottle!). And sesame snacks we
discover in Hué—chewy or brittle and both delicious.

But some things I find difficult. 'Baby eggs'—duck and
chicken eggs served hard-boiled complete with embryo that
a child tells me are 'delicious but head is crunchy'; whole
dead pigs and even a bullock tied across the back of
motorbikes; dog parts on market stalls; livestock in eating
establishments—dogs, on the menu or roving around and
sitting on chairs, a chicken in one café struggling on the
floor with its legs tied together (I assume until someone
wants to eat it) and the odd rat.

Cafés and restaurants

There are many highlights in our cheap eateries. The top
one, for uniqueness of food and its intransigent approach,
is Cha Ca La Vong in Hanoi that has been in business
since 1871. On arrival you are handed a card that says, 'We
only serve Cha Ca, it costs 70,000d a person', so take it or
leave it. Cha Ca is a traditional Hanoi dish of small pieces of

261

fish and chopped greens you fry over a charcoal burner at your table, serve with steamed rice and sprinkle with chopped coriander and crushed roast peanuts. Delicious, and our most expensive meal in Vietnam.

Making our way back to Hanoi's Prince III we pass the Ladybird restaurant; an unlikely name but we go twice for the best cheap food we find in Hanoi and tables on the balcony from which to watch the street—a fascinating pastime.

Our favourite café in Hoi An is Son Vy where we become regulars. The food is delicious and they serve vegetarian Cao Lau, a Hoi An dish of doughy noodles in soup (traditionally made with pork) with bean sprouts and greens and sprinkled with crispy rice-paper pieces. A Hoi An speciality because seemingly it must be cooked in water from the local Ba Le well. Son Vy is cheap—a meal for two of Cao Lau, the best fresh spring rolls, and Vietnamese tea is a steal at 28,000d; the owners are friendly and their ten-year-old son Vy goes to the market on his bike to get fresh ingredients for our order.

On our first visit I am curious about something being cooked and sold outside and the owner buys us a piece to try. It is son dap, steamed rice pancake with a topping that tastes like chopped peanuts, sugar and soy sauce—interesting but once is enough. Though we *do* buy a sinful sweetmeat of chewy peanuts and caramel; our dessert for a few sticky-fingered evenings.

The Xuan Trang cafetaria in Hué is another favourite. They also do a great line in fresh vegetarian spring rolls, their tofu in tomato dish is one of the best we try anywhere,

262

as is their stir-fried water spinach and garlic. These three dishes, along with fish in clay pot and squid with vegetables, constitute our Christmas dinner.

We had thought that food could be a problem because we don't eat meat, but not so. We don't try *pho* (noodle soup) at the street stalls—they always have large pots of beef for *pho bò* and chicken for *pho ga* bubbling away—but find it vegetarian style in a few cafés.

In Dalat, the Peace café where the Easy Riders hang out is close to our hotel and becomes our local; its two women chefs cook delicious food using whatever is good at the market that day. And it is in Dalat that we invent an Australian twist to Asian food. After a morning's exploration, in need of lunch and away from our familiar eateries, we see a cabinet with some food and a small area behind with tables and chairs. At our request the owner makes us rolls with La Vache Qui Rit and slices of something pale green that we assume is a vegetable; but he is puzzled— obviously it is not normally served this way. After we finish eating, with my dictionary and struggling Vietnamese, I ascertain that the delicious 'vegetable' is unripe mango, traditionally eaten dipped in chilli and sugar.

Markets

We only shop for ready-to-eat food in the markets but that doesn't stop us enjoying and wandering through stalls of produce so fresh it is almost growing: mounds of every colour; tofu fresh and cooked with plastic bags of sauces for dipping; dried herbs of assorted colours and aromas; fish—

dead, alive or somewhere in between swimming or gasping in stainless steel or plastic bowls, and more dried fish than I could imagine a whole population eating; raw and cooked meat from tiny birds to recognisable dog. The produce might be on tables or on the ground, or swinging from a shoulder yoke, in plastic bags or baskets, in a 'proper' shop or under a striped tarpaulin. One thing is certain, however it is displayed it is fresh.

We occasionally buy something cooked in the market or on the street and it's always interesting even if not my taste. In Sapa it's a couple of sweet delicacies—bananas fried in batter, and bean paste somehow coated in flour and fried. In Hanoi we hunch on tiny stools to agree on a price and eat a surprisingly good slab of deep-fried sticky rice and bean paste served with pickled vegetables. In Chau Doc it is tiny steamed potato-like vegetables eaten with toothpicks, and strange-tasting sweet cakes. And though Naomi isn't interested, I often enjoy sweet potato roasted over roadside fires.

Market stalls spill from covered areas to streets and squares, and their wares bombard all the senses. I'm sure you can imagine the colours of shrimps, grains, garlic, chillies, rice and other produce; smells from spices to fish and meat; and sounds from baskets of squealing pigs or squawking chickens, birds in cages, and vendors calling their wares trying to attract our attention with 'Madame you want …'

Unfortunately my pleasure in this country, the wonderful things we see and do, its food, and its cultural, religious and civil history is marred at times by the

264

aggressive demands of people wanting us to buy. Even small children asking 'Why you no buy?', and shopkeepers insisting 'You buy from me', 'I have more inside', 'I can make in one hour, no problem'. I understand why, but it doesn't mean I like it. Don't get me wrong though, wearisome as it might be constantly saying 'No' to heckling hawkers and trying to organise things where 'organise' is 'same, same but different', I wouldn't have missed a moment of Vietnam.

265

'Certainly, travel is more than the seeing of sights; it is a change that goes on, deep and permanent, in the ideas of living.'

—Miriam Beard

TWELVE

VIETNAM'S CITIES
OF CONTRASTS

On a trip through the Central Highlands, Naomi and I enjoy a wonderful delicacy called *banh dap* made from special thick Hoi An rice paper with sesame seeds that is dipped in soy sauce seasoned with chives and chilli. When we get to Hoi An we go looking for it, the delicacy is disappointing, but the experiences aren't.

We go over the river to a local café, where no English is spoken and the menus are boards showing dishes served— and follow a sign down a side street; perhaps the first westerners to visit the tiny garden café. The banh dap is disappointing: no black sesame seeds, no seasoned oil spread on the rice paper, and served with fish sauce instead of soy with chilli and chives.

But at this café our waitress fetches a neighbour, a young high school teacher who also runs private English classes. We spend almost two hours with her students, a wonderful bit of cross-cultural conversation. Using their whiteboard we draw pictures and small family trees, and write words and sentences. At first the students' English is limited to questions from their textbook but they become a little more linguistically adventurous. They are all around 15 years old and it's their first chance to really converse with native English speakers.

Another day we find a larger café that serves banh dap but are again disappointed; perhaps those we ate in the Central Highlands had been improved by the cook. But we enjoy struggling with Vietnamese–English conversations: first with a young man who is in Hoi An on business and cheesed off that he has only US$2 for his day's expenses;

then with two young women who are eating something interesting. Using gesticulations and phrase book we discover that it contains no meat, they write the name on a piece of paper and we order it. Thirty minutes later we realise the waitress must have just thought we were showing her our piece of paper! I love the experience of sitting in these cafés on small plastic chairs at child-size tables, ordering in Vietnamese, and trying tastes and conversation.

SAIGON: WIDE STREETS AND WONDERFUL BUILDINGS

Naomi and I like getting into the countryside, but we perhaps spend as much time in Vietnam's cities as outside them. I'm using the term 'city' loosely here but I'll start in a proper city, Saigon.

Saigon to the Vietnamese (Ho Chi Minh City to the politically correct) is bustling and noisy. We've booked a hotel in Pham Ngu Lao, a budget traveller's haven, and arrive at Madame Cuc's Hotel 64 to discover we have no room. We did postpone our arrival but it happens to others who haven't changed bookings and I conclude that's how it's done in cheap hotels—first in gets the room; last in gets sent elsewhere. We are taken to number 74 Bui Vien with the assurance, 'There'll be a room for you tomorrow. No problem.' Number 74 is OK but the atmosphere not as congenial and Madame manageress is out of a French colonial time warp—all gentile behaviour, black dress and graciousness but hard as nails underneath; unlike Madame Cuc who's a bit of a softie as reflected in her 'girls' who run

269

the place. Next day we are back early at Hotel 64 to guarantee that room.

By the end of our first day we feel like successful DIY travellers. We want to break the eight-hour bus journey to Dalat but have heard horror stories of journeys on local buses so want a tour bus. A Dalat specialist has been recommended but he's not what we need; we visit a tour office where we can plan our own journey but not on our budget; finally on our way to a Sinh café we see the Linh café (the 'L' on the sign cleverly painted to look like an 'S'). The team of Linh and Vi find a tour bus company who'll drop us off at the Tran Anh café in Bau Loc, collect us there the next day and, we are told, we can drink free tea and coffee while we wait. Collect us maybe, free tea and coffee we doubt.

As always we walk our legs off, exploring and getting to know the kilometres around the hotel. Despite having to cross horribly busy roads, we return again and again to the huge Ben Thanh market with its incredible food section—where we wander, smell and salivate—and stalls of everyday things for the Vietnamese and traps for the tourist. I buy a few gifts, loving the bustle, the bartering and the bargains.

Of course we do the tourist things in Saigon: the Reunification Palace, Notre Dame Cathedral, the historic post office and a trip to the Cu Chi tunnels. The tunnels were used during the Vietnam War and I should have known—those who want to visit war zones and hear stories of atrocities are welcome; I just hate anything perpetuates the horrors of war, and don't believe these 'tourist attractions' prevent them. It's worth it however for

270

the workshop we visit briefly on the way where people, disabled as a result of agent orange, create timber carvings, paintings, lacquer work, and eggshell mosaic which is exquisite. Most pieces feature the Vietnamese icons of girls in ao dai, people on bikes, water scenes and fishermen.

En route we also visit the Caodai temple at Tay Ninh: a stunning piece of architecture, large and ornate with carvings and statuary that include brightly painted dragons and serpents curling round pillars. The vivid embellishment is complemented by monks in red, gold and blue, and nuns and novitiates in immaculate white. Caodaism combines aspects of most of Vietnam's religions but its proponents were politically and militarily involved during the twentieth century; however what remains with me from their midday service is the peace within the temple and the beauty of the ceremony.

The Reunification Palace was completed for the French governor-general in 1868, and became South Vietnam's presidential residence until Diem's own people bombed it when he was there—how's that for unpopularity? After rebuilding, it remained the presidential residence until the end of the war in 1975. It is a striking example of 1960s architecture, but the gold, red and black drapes and nacre-inlaid furniture have an air of faded grandeur. The basement contains the war rooms and communication centre frozen as if the president has just ducked out for a cup of tea, and a room of photographs illustrating the history of the palace and its occupants.

Notre Dame Cathedral is an elegant 1870s' brick building with high square towers supporting iron spires and crosses.

271

I like the simplicity inside: white walls, painted stone arches, a mixture of stained and plain glass in the windows. The neighbouring 1880s post office bustles with people performing their postal business under the benevolent eye of Ho Chi Minh, while tourists gawp at its towering white, gold and green arches, old timber telephone booths, striking floor tiles and wrought-iron decorations.

The Fine Arts Museum is housed in a slightly rundown French colonial building that works well as a gallery. My favourite exhibits are wooden figures from early twentieth-century highlands mausoleums, Cham sculptures and contemporary paintings of minority group women.

We add a Saigon experience of our own. After walking numerous kilometres we decide to treat ourselves to *kem* (ice-cream) and happen upon Kem Bach Dang where we have delectable ice-cream and fresh fruit served in a coconut shell. Naomi has coconut and taro, I have coconut and coffee—luckily my caffeine intolerance doesn't extend to ice-cream. The most expensive and unhealthy lunch of our whole journey.

HANOI IS CRAZINESS AND BEAUTIFUL SURROUNDINGS

Saigon was interesting but I fall in love with Hanoi. Our Halong Bay guide tells us that Saigon is 300 years old; Hanoi is 1000. Maybe that's what it is: the ghosts of Hanoi past beckon me in the historic city where we stay, in every old shop, around its winding alleyways, across The Hoc Bridge. The city almost beggars description. Wonderful, crazy, noisy, polluted, traffic as chaotic as in all Vietnamese cities but exponentially worse in the old town's narrow streets—anyone who hasn't experienced Hanoi traffic couldn't imagine it.

With genius Viet at Vega travel we do what we want outside Hanoi, and have three and a half days to enjoy the city. We wander the old town for hours, finding most of the thirty-six streets whose names indicate the merchandise that was originally made and traded in the street and is often still sold there. The name usually starts with Hang meaning 'shop' and we get to know those close to our hotels: Hang Bac is silversmiths and silver jewellery; Hang Bo has basket ware; Hang Dao with silk bolts, scarves by the thousand, dresses, shirts; Hang Gai with hemp and cotton products; Hang Thiec where tinsmiths make everything from woks, to letterboxes to tin boxes; and gloriously decorated coffins are manufactured on Lo Su.

This area is a collection of wonderful buildings, original or faithfully restored—a potpourri of ochre or dark-stained wooden walls, wonky balconies and roofs, and uneven cobbled streets.

The streets are always crowded with pedestrians; small stalls selling raw or cooked food; and women gliding with baskets suspended from shoulder yokes filled with fruit or vegetables. Motos and scooters weave, and an occasional car adds to the chaos. In the market Naomi and I exchange a few halting words of English or Vietnamese with older stallholders, who like to touch us. Most people purchase indescribable bits of meat for their bread rolls; I buy triangles of La Vache Qui Rit cheese when I need a cheap savoury fix. A stallholder and I manage a transaction with fingers in the air for three rolls, one cheese triangle and the cost of 9000d—the laughter, gesticulations and confusion are free.

The water puppets of Hanoi began in paddy fields in a rural area of North Vietnam over a thousand years ago, relating traditional tales and satirical stories of local personalities. At some point they disappeared until Hanoi's Municipal Water Puppet theatre opened in the 1960s. The puppets are carved from water-resistant wood of the fig tree and painted (and some of the characters are remarkably lifelike) but last for less than fifteen performances. And although it all happens on or in the water the tales make sense—if you find a program in a language you understand!

Dong Xuan is another market to delight, with hectares of fabrics from spider-webs embroidered on brightly coloured bolts to men's suiting and flimsy wedding stuff. Stall after stall of shoes: children's in pink, yellow, silver and red, adults more sober brown and black; clothes from ordinary to garish; and of course, assorted foods and unrecognisable condiments in packets, bottles, bowls and bags. We find chopstick rests here—Naomi's are small blue and white porcelain fish, mine are tiny wooden curves inlaid with a dot of nacre.

274

We are assured by a couple at the hotel that the driver of the number 14 bus will understand us when we ask for the ethnology museum. Well I don't know about that! Nobody seems to speak English and 'ethnology museum' is not in my phrase book. But a young woman with whom the conductor is flirting willingly takes the Lonely Planet guide and its map, and turns it in all directions. She seems not to understand it, but won't admit it in front of him. Eventually we work out where we are and as I prepare to press the bell to stop the bus the conductor taps me on the shoulder, points ahead and nods. He has understood all along. Very funny!

The building design is fascinating; the exhibitions and dioramas of minority groups' histories, costumes and lives are interesting and informative; and there are stunning photographs. Traditional tribal houses in the grounds are open to visitors, and there's a slightly dilapidated water puppet theatre.

The Temple of Literature was Vietnam's first university founded in the eleventh century. It remained a university until 1802 when the new capital Hué opened its National University. It is a collection of temples and pavilions in extensive gardens; a peaceful haven in Hanoi's bustle. My favourite is the red and gold Khue Van pavilion filled with shrines, altars, urns, dragons and elephants. On this day we lunch at Koto—like Friends in Phnom Penh it's not just a restaurant but trains street kids in hospitality; a good cause making the cost of eating worthwhile.

Although we cannot see inside Hanoi's Opera House, we admire its early twentieth-century architecture, and thanks to this foreshortened visit arrive at the History Museum during its lunchtime closure. We have over an hour to browse the antiquities in the garden: stupas, fragments of very early temples and pagodas, and statues of sacred elephants, dragons and lions. The museum building combines French and Vietnamese architecture, a magnificent venue for an interesting collection spanning pre-history through Champa to the mid-twentieth-century emergence of the communist party.

I love Hanoi's craziness, crowded old city and brouhaha.

AN UNSCHEDULED STOP
WITH AN UNEXPECTED DELIGHT

In spite of our concerns about breaking our journey at Bau Loc we are not stranded there forever. We are perhaps the only westerners in town, certainly at the Bau Loc Hotel, and after registering we visit the Tran Anh café where we *do* get free tea and coffee, and plates of delicious sesame sweetmeats—to encourage customers to purchase tea leaves or coffee beans.

We have time to wander and find a market (of course), an unusual blue-and-white-painted catholic church, and a 'two-dollar shop'—as they are called in Australia—where, with much pantomime, we find two *cai muong* (spoons) for our growing collection of picnic accoutrements, and a bad-taste card for my son Dave's birthday.

A group of people, including children in dance costumes, are dining at the hotel. We discover from Vien who speaks a little English, that they are from Binh Phuoc province northwest of Bau Loc and here as part of a tour to 'engender understanding between children of different provinces'. We ask if we can attend their performance and he says we are very welcome. A taxi is arranged, we have a speedy shower, tart up a little (mustn't let Australian women down) and arrive with time to spare. We are treated like visiting dignitaries: seated at a table and fed roast melon seeds, oranges, biscuits and Vietnamese tea.

The children dance and sing, and participate in games and competitions led by gung-ho young leaders. The evening ends with a stick dance; pairs of people crouch on the ground striking long bamboo poles together in time to music, while dancers jump in and out trying to avoid smashed ankles. We are encouraged to join them by children and adults taking our hands, and once I work out the rhythm it is great fun—and not a bruise to show for it. We return to the hotel with the children who kiss us goodbye (girls) and shake our hands (boys). It is an unexpected and joyous evening's entertainment.

Saturday is wedding day and the hotel entrance is framed with pink and white balloons. Six hundred guests are expected and a reception room is a wonder of flowers, crates of beer, more balloons, lights and a fountain in a pond. We ring Vi in Saigon who says the bus will stop for lunch at the Tran Anh and we must be there by midday. Strange, because *we* lunched at a tiny place an hour before Bau Loc, but that's what Vi says so we obey. When we leave the hotel the wedding is underway; every guest being photographed with the bride and groom, but an hour-and-a-half later it's all over, people leaving even before our bus arrives.

At the Tran Anh we enjoy more free tea and sesame biscuits before moving to a front veranda at 12.30 pm worried we'll miss the bus. While we wait guests to three more weddings pass by and we talk to women in beautiful *ao dais* and modern Vietnamese-style formal wear; and are amused by elegantly dressed and shod women arriving and leaving on scooters and motos.

At 1.30 I request the assistance of a Vietnamese woman from Perth, Western Australia to whom we had talked earlier. I have the bus driver's mobile phone number but he doesn't speak English, so she calls him on my behalf. He's on the way 'no problem', eventually arriving at 2 pm. They had already stopped for lunch—why does this not surprise me?

WE DIDN'T ACTUALLY WANT TO STOP IN NHA TRANG

Nothing we hear or read about Nha Trang (pronounced Nya Trang) tempts us to visit, but it's the easy way to get from Dalat to Hoi An, and there has to be *something* of interest. Mui recommends the Sao Mai hotel and he and Trung drop us there. It is cheap, comfortable and clean, and Mai at reception is friendly and helpful, but Mui's assurance that they will speak English is a slight exaggeration.

We try to arrange a stopover in Qui Nhon—hoping for another Bau Loc experience. Thinh, a helpful tour agent around the corner, explains there are no daytime tour buses from Nha Trang to Hoi An and that a stopover in Qui Nhon is impossible. Oh for another Linh.

Instead he books us 'soft seats' on the daytime train to Danang. We also decide to make life easy for ourselves and use Hanoi as our base to explore the north, and Thinh arranges a cheap flight from Hué to Hanoi. All this planning and organisation probably takes a day—but that's independent travel for you.

The hotel is two minutes from a beach where we walk in the winds of a typhoon crossing Vietnam, and one afternoon spoil ourselves with expensive tea and cakes at the elegant and decadent Louisiane.

The Po Nagar Cham towers were built between the seventh and twelfth centuries on an ancient sacred site and they are still used for worship. Enough remains of the brick and sandstone towers for me to appreciate their interesting shapes and delicate decoration.

On our way to the Cham towers we cross the Cai River, where scores of fishermen shanties on stilts crowd the shoreline, large fishing boats and their coracles shelter from the typhoon and a lone fisherman in a narrow boat pulls in his net as he drifts under the bridge.

And though we didn't expect to enjoy Nha Trang, of course we do.

HOI AN,
AN UNEXPECTED DELIGHT

The Reunification Express leaves Nha Trang at 5.40 am so Mai arranges for us to be collected at 5 am, and wakes at 4.30 in case our alarm fails. When we get on at that awful hour people are sleeping on their and other people's seats, on the floor between the seats and under tables, intertwined, stretched out with legs up windows.

Thinh said there will be lunch and I naively picture a buffet car or food trolley; instead it's free breakfast, lunch and bottles of water. Breakfast is a container of instant noodles, and a machine dispenses boiling water so you can reconstitute them. Going by the cow on the front of the box and the word *bò* (beef), the seasoning is meat-based; Naomi reconstitutes the noodles and eats some plain, I stick with my bananas. Lunch is a poor man's aeroplane meal—a tray with containers of rice and three different accompaniments. Mine are definitely all meaty but I extract a few cabbage leaves to eat with some rice; one of Naomi's is tofu so she's a little better off. But I'm not complaining—it's a great service, I'm the fussy one.

The passengers are a mix of young and old, many doing thirty-three hours Saigon to Hanoi. The most memorable is a spry older man who watches everything around him, uses the boiling water machine for a constant supply of green tea, eats breakfast and lunch with relish, gives himself a serious face massage (so good I'm tempted to ask if he'll give me one) and occasionally dozes.

There's more impressive service when TV is due to begin—an official 'luggage organiser' moves overhanging bags to ensure that everyone can see the screens unimpeded. The first show, a Vietnamese-style *Mr Bean*, takes place on a park bench and is funny even though I can't understand the dialogue. But I spend most of my time watching the now familiar sights: rice paddies with flocks of ducks, people in straw hats, oxen and water buffaloes pulling ploughs, and white egrets.

We booked a car for the 20 kilometres from Danang to Hoi An, an extravagance I appreciate because by the time we

280

arrive I have a rotten headache. Not the fault of the train per se, more a combination of the ungodly hour of waking, a long nine hours, the young man in front of me who keeps his seat angled back as far as possible so he can sleep undisturbed, and being imprisoned by the tray on the back of his seat falling down whenever he moves. The joys of cheap travel!

Apparently there are 600 tailors in Hoi An; every second shop with bolts of cloth, dressmakers' dummies clad in today's 'fashion' and people slaving away at sewing machines. Shopkeepers tell us we can have anything we want in an hour—but those in the know say to leave a few days up your sleeve for final fittings. There are almost as many shoe shops, with a thousand styles and hues of leather. But we aren't buying and the touts outside the shops cheerfully take our 'No thanks, just looking' and leave us alone. Luggage shops flourish—all those new clothes must be taken home. We meet a young Australian couple who have purchased their complete wedding outfits from expensive tailors and shoemakers, as well as cheaper clothes—and an enormous suitcase.

Our real joy is the old town. We explore thoroughly, fascinated by streets filled with small wooden houses, shops with stone floors, and the river with its adjacent market and wharf. Although Hoi An has been a trading port since the Cham period many of the ochre-painted and timber buildings date back only to the late eighteenth or early nineteenth centuries. But they are delightful, and traditional methods and materials are used when

281

maintenance or rebuilding is needed. My favourite is the Museum of Trading Ceramics, a two-storey timber building where one exhibition details the history of movement of ceramics in Vietnam and its trading partners, the other shows when different parts of Hoi An were inhabited and by whom—information for both obtained from archaeological finds. Japanese, Vietnamese and Chinese people lived in some areas of Hoi An 300 years ago.

Tran Duong, a retired mathematics teacher, lives in a 200-year-old French-built house that has been in his family for four generations. He loves showing it to foreign visitors, and relating its history and that of the furniture and his family. He has a visitor's book and requests vehemently that we add something *and* contribute a donation. I note in my journal: 'He's a wonderful old man (same age as me actually) with badly dyed grey hair, blackly combed over his head'.

Our favourite shop is a jeweller's that we just happen upon in a street near the market. It's run by a young couple— he designs and makes silver jewellery and she is the sales person. There's no hurry, nor pressure to buy; she is helpful, and if we can't find what we want her husband can make something for us. We talk about our families and hear about her husband, their twenty-two-month-old son, her seven-month-old niece, and her sister and brother-in-law who are tailors working out of the same shop. We trust her because when we ask a price the piece is weighed, the cost calculation is shown to us and it is non-negotiable. We finally purchase four pieces. On our second visit we meet the son, a brown-eyed scamp who is into everything including taking a water

282

bottle from my pack and carrying it around like a toy. His mother and I try to persuade him to hand it back but he's not interested in the pen I offer in exchange, so I draw a picture of him in my notebook—wide smile, spiky hair and all. He recognises himself and is prepared to swap, but insists on the pen too. Definitely a future asset to the business.

We meet two Italian Hilarys, the two Ilarias as we call them, and share a taxi to My Son. Construction and occupation of this ancient Champa site began in the fourth century and development and occupation continued for 900 years. From then it was continually pillaged by Chinese, Khmer and Vietnamese people until, used as a Viet Cong base during the war, it was almost destroyed. The remaining fragments illustrate how beautiful it must have been and the orange brickwork and delicate carvings remind me of Banteay Srei in Cambodia. I find My Son a place of sadness.

Hoi An is a delight from the old buildings to the market, shopkeepers, cafés and restaurants. I can't decide whether to settle in Hoi An or Hanoi.

HUÉ: CITY OF HUSTLERS

Disembarking from the bus when we arrive in Hué is a nightmare that should have prepared us for the sharks ready to circle whenever we hit the streets. A 'feeding frenzy' is how Naomi describes it as we are surrounded by a mob of touts: shouting, screaming, forcing cards into our faces. When we say we have accommodation they demand to know where we are going, insisting their hotel is better. Eventually one young man stops yelling, offers to get us a taxi, spirits one up and tells the driver who doesn't speak English where we want to go. It's not far and after he takes our luggage up a lane to the guesthouse we offer him the 15,000d on the meter, prompting a heated discussion between driver, guesthouse manager and an unknown woman in black. They side with us, 15,000d is reasonable; he grudgingly accepts the cash and leaves.

The Mimosa Guesthouse sounds fine in the Lonely Planet guide and Long, the manager, is charming. But it is shabby, the room dark and dismal, and when we sit on the loo a pipe in the ceiling drips cold water on our heads. Age must be catching up with us because we no longer want to 'do' shabby just to save a couple of dollars. Also I enjoy somewhere to sit, eat and hear stories from other travellers, and Mimosa's tiny reception area has just two chairs and a television. So it's down the lane to the Phuong Hoang Hotel which, by contrast, is sparkling, has internet (though it doesn't work while we're there!) and a dining area. US$3 more gets us a double room with window and breakfast, available the next day. We pay a deposit on the spot.

In the morning Mimosa seems a little better, with the best shower we find in Vietnam and a sunny balcony for eating breakfast. But the room is still depressing and we are in Hué for five days so want our 'home' to be pleasant. We tell Long that at our age we need a little more comfort, he apologises and explains he is poor and trying to make his hotel better. We feel bad but have to think of ourselves.

In the daylight we discover the window at the Phuong Hoang is cheek by jowl with the bright pink building next

284

door and any natural light seeping in is cerise. My Vietnamese is challenged as I try to explain to Moon at reception that daylight is necessary for my wellbeing; finally she understands and another dollar a day gets us a room with a window overlooking roof tops—a favourite city view.

Most of the places we want to explore around Hué we can reach on foot, but as soon as we walk out of the laneway it's on. Non-stop harassment by moto and cyclo drivers: 'Where you going?', 'You want to go to market?', 'One dollar one hour tour on cyclo, cheap.', 'You want to go to Imperial City? I take you, wait for you.'. Everywhere else—and I mean everywhere—a 'No thank you, we want to walk' causes amusement, amazement, even occasionally a 'Why?' but is respected and the hassles stop. We are here for Christmas and it's during our search for a church at which to attend a service that I've had enough. I explain to a pushy cyclo driver that I'm now angry, 'No!' means 'no', and if we want a cyclo we'll be unlikely to use him. Maybe in Hué it's the only way to get that tourist dollar but we become weary trying to be polite and finally resort to curtness—not like us at all.

But having got all that off my chest, some of the people we deal with are lovely. We visit a patisserie on our first day and mistakenly leave without paying for cups of tea, the waitress also works in a shop near our hotel and that evening recognises us, explains and we give her the money; we often see her after this and she greets us with smiles and hugs. A young man and woman at the CL Travel kiosk on the river bank where we organise a boat trip to a pagoda and get help with translation of Notre Dame's Christmas services

285

timetable, smile and wave at us as we pass each day. And Moon at the Phuong Hoang, who makes us feel guilty when we arrange our own moto drivers for Christmas morning, surprises us with a gift of bananas on Christmas afternoon.

In the Citadel we hope to get similar feelings to those engendered by Hoi An's old city—but don't. There are streets filled with small houses, kids, a few shops, but the atmosphere is not the same. However, one of the bloodiest battles of the Tet Offensive in 1968, and North Vietnam's later invasion of Hué resulted in the almost total destruction of the Citadel. So it's not surprising that the atmosphere is heavy. It must be strange for locals who survived to observe the tourists, people who cannot possibly imagine their suffering.

But within the Citadel is Hué's Fine Arts Museum, housed in a beautifully restored wooden building originally constructed in 1845. Its roof is striking: old traditional tiles with ornate dragons decorating the peaks and corners. Many of its antiquities disappeared during the war but those remaining are worth visiting. Outside is ancient statuary and bronze verdigris-covered bells in carved frames, while inside is an eclectic collection mainly from the Nguyen period of 1820 to 1945. My favourite is a filigree gold-painted wooden sphere about half a metre in diameter, representing dragons hiding in clouds (very symbolic in Vietnam) sitting on the tails of four up-ended dragons.

What remained of the Imperial City in 1975 and its subsequently restored buildings are impressive: gates decorated with ceramics and three-dimensional mosaics

286

made of bottles, plates, pieces of glass; Thai Hoa palace built in 1805 in the original architectural style; fragments of early splendour include the red and gold Mieu Temple dedicated to the Nguyen emperors; nine dynastic urns with Chinese decorative designs dating back 4000 years; and the entrance gate with dark ochre-tiled roof and decorated with stone dragons. A restored theatre has an exhibition of theatrical memorabilia and a troupe sometimes perform traditional music and dance, but regrettably not for an audience of two.

We take a painted boat on the Perfume River to the Thien Mu Pagoda. The female skipper has no idea of customer relations—unusual in our experience of Vietnamese women so far. When we arrive at the steps leading up to the pagoda, she curtly tells us to be back in twenty minutes, and brooks no argument. The pagoda is a striking hexagonal brick structure of seven levels, small pavilions on either side contain a massive bronze bell and a stele dating back to 1715, gardens with a lotus pond, statuary, bronze ware, a small monastery and a building housing assorted Buddhas. You can see why twenty minutes is not enough.

But the boat journey is enjoyable. We see fishermen of course, but more unusual are narrow dredge boats where a square bucket is dropped overboard, filled by hand if necessary and wound up manually, until the full boat chugs down the river to unload onto sand piles on the river bank.

The morning we leave Hué the oxymoron of 'Vietnamese organisation' is epitomised for me. At the hotel is a sign 'Bus to airport, any time $2.50'—much easier than getting our luggage to a bus stop and cheaper than a taxi. We arrange it through Moon, checking three times, agreeing 12.30 pm for a 1.30 check-in makes sense—we've no idea how far it is to the airport but an hour seems reasonable. At 12.45 Moon says 'Don't worry', but by 12.50 she is on the phone asking where the bus is. Finally one arrives at 1 pm. The angst is unnecessary, the minibus full of people and luggage reaches the airport at 1.35 and five minutes later we're checked in.

HUÉ AT CHRISTMAS

Christmas in Hué is a fusion of kitsch and curiosities. The swish Imperial Hotel has a Christmas tree built entirely of Heineken beer bottles, possibly 15 metres tall, adorned with the usual decorations and a 'Merry Christmas from Heineken' banner. Alongside is a large sleigh carrying Santa and presents pulled by three bucking reindeer, which by Christmas Day look decidedly jaded. There are traffic jams every night as teenagers, young couples and parents with tots in tiny Santa outfits fight to have their photos taken with a Vietnamese Santa.

Shops, travel agents, hotels and eateries all have fantastic Christmas trees and decorations, but no special Christmas items to sell. And the lights in trees, shrines, windows and doorways are impressive, each set going through up to ten changing sequences. The Trang Tien Bridge is given the same treatment, with constantly changing sequences of coloured spotlights on each span. We watch in awe for ten minutes— and don't see a pattern repeated.

288

On Christmas Eve we attend a children's service at the simple but beautiful Notre Dame Cathedral. Young women in long white dresses begin the service with a dance which Naomi thinks is liturgical, there are fairy-like angels and three children do readings that end with a few lines of singing that everyone (except us) joins in. And it is irrelevant that we don't understand a word sung by the children's choir. The priest is young, theatrical, colourfully garbed and intense as he tells what I assume is the nativity story. The first carol we recognise is playing as communion begins and we lapsed Jewish sisters leave.

We decide that on Christmas Day we will visit two of the Royal Tombs and explore some of the local countryside on motorbikes. Moon at the hotel can arrange bikes and drivers but our experience with Easy Riders has spoilt us— we want English-speaking bikie guides. At the Xuan Trang café a sign advertises guides on bikes and serendipitously Tu our waiter is one of them; we book him and an off-sider for Christmas Day.

Our first destination with Tu and Phuc—don't try to pronounce that—is Tu Duc's tomb. Mostly ruins, but there are fragments of its original beauty: an elephant statue, details on roofs, a little bridge and a wooden pavilion where Tu Duc relaxed and fished. And Minh Mang's tomb has been much restored—a temple and a pavilion are in good condition and there are beautiful fragments of carvings and fretwork.

The highlight of the morning for me is a monastery that Tu says is also a university of Buddhist studies. Here we sit with Buddhist monks in a ceremony of chanting, drums and bells. There are only five participating—four fully initiated monks and a novitiate identifiable by a partly shaven head and his grey robe—and I irreligiously wonder if the others have gone home for Christmas. The gardens are extensive and include a lake with bridge and wooden pavilions where people go to meditate—a tranquil place to visit on Christmas morning.

Finally we pay a brief visit to a village where they make incense using sawdust from local cinnamon and sandalwood trees, before lunching at a café in another small village. Tu orders two different types of rice cake with dried shrimp that are specialities of the area, one in a light sauce, the other steamed in banana leaves. Both unusual, delicious and, because we are with locals, the grand total is 28,000d. We feel a little conned because not only do they expect us to pay for their lunch—though it would be churlish to ask them for their share of such a small amount—but we paid for seven hours and get five. And they aren't a patch on the Easy Riders. But who could be?

Back in Hué we feel like a cup of tea with Christmas cake or mince pies. The best we can think of (other than blowing a month's budget at the Imperial) is to go to the patisserie. The pastries are pretty average and they've run out of black tea, but the day improves as we chat to Ann and Lyn, other sisters from Australia, and agree to meet for dinner. The Imperial offers Christmas dinner at a mere US$45 a head but we decide against that; instead dining deliciously at the Xuan Trang for a cost of about US$8 for four.

Of course we enjoy aspects of Hué that balance the feelings of constant harassment: the walk alongside the Perfume River and through the park with sculptures from Hué's International Sculpture Symposia; the Trang Tien Bridge that we probably cross twenty times; the market for bananas; the stalls for cheese triangles and bread; the Citadel and Imperial City that dominate the north side of the river; the excellent Xuan Trang café; the not-so-excellent Lac Thanh restaurant where Mr Lac, who is deaf and mute, greets us like friends, imperiously waves us in and serves fairly ordinary food; the patisserie on Hung Vuong where on our first visit I have a delicious olive bread roll, Naomi has a raisin scroll and we share a chocolate croissant (very Vietnamese!) and we return for tea and pastries on Christmas Day. And those Christmas wonders in this confusing city.

'There is a peculiar pleasure in riding out into the unknown. A pleasure which no second journey on the same trail ever affords.'

—Edith Durham

THIRTEEN

GOING SOLO:
ANXIETY AND ADVENTURE

By the time I get to Barrow Creek Roadhouse in mid-August 2003 I've been on the road long enough to be a little adventurous. I'm looking for unusual places to stay and Barrow Creek, 200 kilometres north of Alice Springs, certainly satisfies that requirement. It comprises a roadhouse, an adjacent property with a house close to the road, and an Aboriginal reserve. I arrive in the late afternoon wanting to go no further. The walls of the bar are covered in postcards, assorted banknotes, odd bits of clothing and photos of transient visitors—the normal décor of outback pubs.

A woman, who I later learn is half of the management team, comes out from the kitchen. I ask, 'Have you got a campervan site for tonight, please?'

She responds with a question, 'Are you sure you want to stay here?'

Of course I do. 'Yes, thanks. How much?'

'Five dollars for power or three-fifty without.' So I take a powered site—even for me, the last of the big spenders, it would be silly not to.

'You'd best go and have a look. The electric pole's in the middle of the paddock—park anywhere. Then come and grab a beer and watch the sunset.'

I drive into the piece of dirt that's the 'paddock' and I'm the total camping population. I get as close to the one scrawny tree as possible, set up and go to freshen up. The water-saving shower makes sense in this arid land, though when I turn it on the trickle is way less than any water-saving device could devise. But it is cool and clean, and I even wash my undies and T-shirt as is my wont.

294

My washing line goes between two uprights on a couple of motel units under construction. By the time the washing's hung other campers have arrived: five Japanese youngsters with a station wagon and a large tent, and a German couple to whom I later chat.

When I mention the shower trickle Ian, the other half of the management team, says, 'It depends on the bore—whatever it brings up.' For five dollars I'm not about to complain.

Carmel and Ian—from Sydney and in the middle of a 'round Australia working trip'—had lucked onto this job only a couple of weeks before. With no experience of running a pub (including keeping the alcohol register of Aboriginal people who come for grog), they are on a fast learning curve but thoroughly enjoying it. 'Better than working at The Alice', they reckon.

The three of us sit together on the west-facing veranda and yarn over our beers as we watch the vivid red clouds on the horizon disappear into the purples of the night sky. These sunsets and people are part of what my travel in the outback is about.

I am subsequently reminded that Barrow Creek is where an English backpacker was assumed to have been murdered and his girlfriend was kidnapped—I wonder whether this was behind Carmel's first question.

It's strange the coincidences that occur on the road. Three years later I'm at Downfall Creek on Lake Tinaroo in the Atherton Tablelands. There are many spots for Ski2 and I choose one that is level, close to amenities and has a view of the water. When I share a bottle of wine with my camping neighbours it is Carmel and Ian, on the road again.

ALONE INTO THE OUTBACK—
MISERIES AND MINING

I take off with Ski2 to Darwin on our first extended trip together—the longest previously being four days when I took her to Hattah Kulkyne National Park to prove to myself that I could do it alone. I reckoned if I was OK for four days I'd be OK for four weeks—or months. I haven't checked but know that Darwin is a large number of kilometres away, though it can't be as far as Perth—and that seems unreachable.

Then shortly before leaving Melbourne I go to an exhibition of Sydney Nolan's *Drought* series paintings, and among them is a map of Australia showing the places he and his wife visited while he painted, and the distances between cities. And guess what, Melbourne to Darwin is further than Melbourne to Perth. Suddenly it feels like I'm taking on too much, but I've promised myself I'll go—and go I will. I'm incredibly anxious for the last couple of weeks before I leave, but won't change my mind. I'd have to be half dead to let myself down that way, thank goodness.

The first few days are difficult, I can't pretend otherwise: I feel lonely, I worry each day that Ski2 won't start or will let me down and I'm concerned about the distances I intend to cover.

My confidence improves with my first taste of a dirt road in Ski2. Though it is only 88 kilometres, it also

296

provides a salutary lesson about dirt-road driving. I'm en route to Lake Mungo National Park, and the road is rough, dusty and corrugated in parts so I take it gently. A car follows me for a while until the driver gets tired of my snail-like behaviour and speeds past. About half an hour later a police car and an ambulance overtake me; a few kilometres further the car that followed me is front end into a tree. Luckily the driver looks to be only slightly injured, but I stay tentative.

It's worth the tense drive: Mungo's history interests me, the camping area is wonderful and I watch the sun rise over the dry lake as the moon sets behind me. I also ride my bike towards the ancient Walls of China but the gears are most unhappy so I stop. Luckily I meet up with a serious cyclist who knows what he's doing. He cleans off the grit, re-greases my bike, tries to fix the gears and tells me how to take care of it better. Having the bike on the back of the van over that dirt road was the problem—the dust flying up behind onto the oily gears and chain. Why didn't *I* think of taping plastic bags over the gears and derailleur?

Broken Hill in New South Wales is a town that's very much part of Australia's mining history and its name has always attracted me. But surrounded by slag heaps and dross it doesn't look like a good place to get over miseries. However the bike must be repaired so I stay for a couple of days. I'm sure my doldrums are exacerbated by my incompetence with the bike and uncertainty about what I'm doing. I send an email to my family to let them know that I'm still alive—my kids *might* be worrying—though have no

297

happy tales to recount to friends. My journal says it all: 'Overdosed on chocolate biscuits—why do I do that when I'm miserable, it doesn't help. I'm so cross with myself about the bike'. I do give myself a hard time.

Exploring Broken Hill's art galleries and interesting architecture on foot improves how I feel—walking is always good for my mental state and small galleries are my cup of tea. Artist Pro Hart grew up in Broken Hill and started painting here. So once the bike is fixed (*and* I've bought very expensive cleaner and re-greaser) I ride to see his house, and visit a nearby studio showing his brilliantly coloured contemporary art.

I try hard to visit an Aboriginal art centre: on my first visit it is closed, due to open at 10.00 next morning, so I take my time arriving about 10.15. At 10.30 a cheerful Aboriginal woman arrives; this looks hopeful but she also hangs around by the door. I ask if she is an artist, she is. I ask what time the centre is likely to open, to which her response is, 'Who knows? Bloody blackfella time, I'm going home.' I'm not being racist here; she says it and my disappointment is tempered with amusement.

Coober Pedy, another evocative but depressing mining town, is my next destination. Dry and dusty, surrounded by the ghosts of the past in the shape of abandoned diggings. I'm told by a miner who moonlights as a guide that nowadays it costs $500 a day for equipment and diesel just to look for opal. I do a guided tour to see what makes Coober Pedy tick and learn a little of its history, and most interesting to me is a subdivision where enormous chunks

298

of rock are carved into stone houses that are all in one piece: solid, cool in the summer and warm at night.

Other establishments are below the ground—and underground hotels are a major tourist attraction. I visit an underground catacomb church, seemingly based on one in Rome where bodies of martyrs were buried for a few of centuries.

From Coober Pedy I start on the hundreds of kilometres north to Uluru–Kata Tjuta (Ayers Rock–the Olgas) and Alice Springs before the long haul to Darwin.

THE SPIRITUALITY OF ULURU AND KATA TJUTA

I had thought that Uluru was just left of Alice Springs and I suppose it is if you look at a map of Australia. But luckily I check before it's too late and realise I must turn west quite a long way south of Alice. And it's exciting: the Rock is such an icon that however much I try to avoid tourist attractions there's no way I'm giving this one a miss.

The Lasseter Highway runs almost straight towards Uluru so as I drive I'm looking for the Rock—it is so large it must jump out. Suddenly there it is and I'm ridiculously thrilled but puzzled; it's in a national park yet there is none of the surroundings I expect. It's tantalisingly close by the time I reach the Curtin Springs Roadhouse and I look at my map. Of course it's Mount Connor, a large mass of the same geological make-up as Uluru but it's not just one rock. A stunning mountain, even if it is 130 kilometres too far east, and I feel absolutely stupid—though I'm not alone in making this mistake.

More exciting to me is that Curtin Springs advertises camel rides and has a camping area behind the roadhouse. I'll definitely be stopping here on my way back but for now I continue the search for the genuine article.

When I get closer to Uluru it is obvious—signs, warnings about not being able to camp at the Rock, distances to Yulara (the only accommodation here) and to Uluru itself. The Rock may be evocative and iconic but to me, who just wants to put my van under a tree, Yulara is awful. It's the only place I've found so far where I cannot park in the 'camping' area but must go with caravans into a miniature city of numbered rows, and no choice of where I might like to be.

With hundreds of tourists a day Yulara offers everything from tent sites to top resort accommodation, so must be easy to manage. You can't have people like me wandering around willy-nilly. I accept that I won't want to sit outside enjoying the surroundings, and go off on my bike to explore.

And my bicycle comes into its own. It's 20 kilometres from Yulara to Uluru and I do it twice. On the first evening I visit the cultural centre and cycle back to watch Uluru change hues as the sun sets. It is stunning as it turns countless shades of orange, mauve and grey then disappears into the darkening sky. I use a whole film but just a few photographs are enough to remind me of the magic of those changing moods.

300

Next day I chain my bike up at the cultural centre and spend hours getting an insight into how the local Aboriginal people live with their land and view the landscape as part of their history. Then I walk the 10-kilometre track around the massive edifice—quite moving with all I've read. Much of the site is significant in local Aboriginal ceremonies and visitors are requested not to photograph or walk in certain areas, nor climb Uluru. And I respect their wishes: I have a self-guided walk booklet that describes places of cultural significance that I can go into, and there is no way I'll climb the Rock.

I'm not only moved by the historical significance of the Rock, I'm blown away by its enormity and variations in geological structure. As I walk I find changes in colours, shapes and textures: oranges, greys and browns; overlapping folds, large cracks, rounded silhouettes and sharp-edged cavities; rough conglomerate and smooth granite—all enhanced by a brilliant blue sky.

I had met Nigel and Gina, and their children Ruby and Hugo, days earlier at the camping ground at Orooroo where nine-year-old Ruby and I had talked about bird-watching. They are at Yulara and offer to take me to Kata Tjuta; I accept gratefully—back then packing up Ski2 seems a major task. We stop at a viewing platform and the whole of Kata Tjuta can be seen, a grey-mauve curve of rocks in the distance. We do two walks each different but each provides stunning colours and shapes, again enriched by bright blue through gaps and gullies. To me Kata Tjuta is more beautiful and spiritual than Uluru.

Returning along the Lasseter Highway I reach Curtin Springs just in time for the sunset camel ride to Mount Connor, that faux Uluru. I have never been on a camel before but love the motion. I get the baby of the camel string and

301

she's cute and gentle—with me anyway—though she does keep turning round and nipping the leg of the young woman riding behind me. Our guide/camel boss tells us a little history of Curtin Springs Station, including that this area was too dry for ancient Aboriginal people hence it doesn't have the cultural significance of Uluru. We watch the sun set over the mountain and take some striking photos of shadows thrown by the camel string onto the orange ground.

A TOWN
CALLED ALICE

The name Alice Springs has enchanted me since I read Neville Shute's *A Town Like Alice* eons ago—a name that evokes images of pioneers, flying doctors, Australia's red centre, and a tiny town surrounded by kilometres of scrub. But of course it cannot live up to these expectations; it's now a vibrant city with a population of almost 30,000 and suburbs sprawl into the outback.

I find a street of caravan parks and choose G'day Mate— I like the name but it's definitely not the best on offer with tiny sites and no cheap options ($21 a night for me and my little van seems quite unreasonable!). But it's only five kilometres on a bike track next to the (dry) Todd River to the city, and by the time I've been there a few hours, visited the supermarket and explored the city centre I feel at home.

Over three days my bike takes me everywhere. I do most of the touristy things and, feeling more enthusiastic about this journey, send my first email to friends. Among happier news I look for sympathy with 'The nights are

302

freezing, it was –1°C at Uluru'. But the days are gorgeous, I'm into shorts and T-shirt and the nights will get better as I move north.

Desert Park is my favourite place in Alice. There are three central desert ecosystems with imported indigenous flora, birds and reptiles. Interpretive rangers, many of whom are Aboriginal people of the central desert, run tours and give presentations about the Arrernte culture, food and medicine, and the plants and creatures that live in the environments. I start with a twenty-minute film that illustrates the desert's development over millions of years since its origins as an inland sea. The presentations and activities are continuous and I stay for six hours.

At the art gallery in the Araluen Centre I catch the last day of the Alice Springs Beanie Festival—a collection of hand-made beanies in a variety of designs and materials. And an 'Australian Royalty' exhibition by Gaye somebody who has used flotsam and jetsam to manufacture costumes, furniture and crowns in bizarre materials: a dried, bleached cane toad waistcoat; bathers made from dried and tanned chicken foot skins; and other pieces created from seaweed, shells, emu feathers and driftwood.

There is also a museum that specialises in the geological and biological history of the area—all right up my alley. The top floor of this building has an exhibition about Ted Strehlow, an anthropologist who wrote a book based on artefacts, sacred objects and songs he collected from the Arrernte people in the mid-twentieth century. The Aboriginal people felt Strehlow had betrayed their trust by

303

reproducing these extracts; and controversy continued after his death when his widow obtained some of the artefacts and sacred objects.

Next to the Araluen Centre precinct is a shrine to Eddie Connellan who started Connellan Air in 1939 and operated the Royal Flying Doctor Service: old aircraft hangars contain two of the early flying doctor planes and an assortment of aeronautical bits and pieces of that era. As someone who loves small aircraft and hands-on history, I wander happily for ages.

The best thing about Alice Springs for me is that it's the gateway to the MacDonnell Ranges, both to the west and the east.

INTO THE MACDONNELLS

The West MacDonnell Ranges are more popular than the east, and I can understand why: imagine a mountain range thrusting out of the surrounding flatness in which gorges and river systems are found—that's the West MacDonnells, the most memorable Northern Territory geology I've yet discovered. Namatjira Drive runs west to Glen Helen at the end of the mountain range, and short side trips take me into the gorges; each is different but all stunning—some even have pools of still water within their walls. A rough road traverses Aboriginal land from Glen Helen to Kings Canyon and those with four-wheel drive vehicles can get a different aspect of this glory, but sadly not me.

The West MacDonnells offer a great variety of walks— some easy, others a challenge but all with stunning

304

views and vistas. I visit ochre pits—still used by local Aboriginal people—composed of soft rocks of white, yellow, red-brown and almost black. Ormiston Gorge is the most popular camping spot in the West MacDonnells with solar-heated showers and flushing loos, but I discover Ellery Creek Bighole by accident and stay two nights happily using pit toilets and washing in Ski2's sink for solitude not found at Ormiston.

The East MacDonnells, though not officially a national park, is almost as stunning as the west. The road east passes Emily and Jessie Gaps and Corroborree Rock—all of which tell me a little of local Aboriginal history. I fall in love with Trephina Gorge Nature Park and stay for three days, camping under trees and alongside the gorge in which the river flows metres below the ground. I do most of Trephina's walks, but must return one day to finish the 20-kilometre Ridge Top walk.

At Trephina I meet up again with Alex and Chrissy and their four kids Chloe, Amy, Stuart and Tim. We'd met at earlier camping spots and quickly become friends—Stuart sees me as a surrogate grandmother, I think. One night we have dinner together at their van and I teach them a dice game called Krunch, and another day they take me to the John Hayes Rockhole where access is by four-wheel drive only. We climb and scramble all afternoon among the water holes and beautifully shaped and coloured rocks.

My friendship with this family from Nyora in Victoria has continued; whenever I visit them the first question from Stuart is always, 'Can we play Krunch?'

I also catch up with the Chaux family—Yves, Jocelynne and their two daughters—from Brittany in France. We'd originally met over a picnic table at Kings Canyon Station, and there they are at Trephina—one of the lovely reconnections made on the road. Yves has just rented a four-wheel drive and they offer to take me to the N'dhala Gorge Nature Park. I leap at the offer because I've read that it includes unusual Aboriginal art: finely etched carvings on rocks scattered in the gorge, and quite different to anything I've seen previously. We have a wonderful afternoon of wandering and getting excited as we find another elusive carving.

There are not enough superlatives to describe the MacDonnells. The colours, the thrusting peaks, the rounded and fan-shaped extrusions from the surrounding landscape, the strata in layers from vertical to horizontal and with all possible curves, waves and angles. Gorges, gaps, water holes and the ten-metre wide sandy river beds with the water so far beneath the surface that only the red river gums that thrive in this environment seem to know it's there. I'd love to be here on the few days in the year when it rains enough for water to flow for a few hours before leaching away.

Staying in the MacDonnells gives me a taste for camping grounds rather than caravan parks and I decide that wherever they exist I will use them regardless of how basic their facilities are—the trees, peace and other campers make having to wash in my van sink unimportant.

IT'S STILL A LONG WAY, BUT I GET TO DARWIN

I leave the peace of the MacDonnells, call into Alice to fill the fridge and food boxes then hit the Stuart Highway again for the long straight run to Darwin. At least that's what I think, but of course there are diversions along the way.

The Devils Marbles Conservation Park is just up the road from Barrow Creek and I camp beneath towering orange spheres and ovoids, many of which look as though they might roll away in a stiff wind. The formations are amazing: perhaps hundreds of rocks, some split to show brilliant blue sky through their orange edges, others are complete, a couple seem to be resting on impossibly tiny points. There are no 'keep off' signs or apparent concern about people damaging the rocks and I clamber madly.

Most exciting, the watercolour paints I bought myself in Alice get their first use. I've never painted before and I have to say that my attempts would not win any competitions, but it's fun to carry a chair away from the camping area and experiment peacefully with colours and brushes; with dusty greens, bright rocks and shadows; to spend hours puddling in paints.

Hundreds of kilometres of Stuart Highway pass under my wheels. But I always stop at easily accessible historical monuments and sites. I knew that Darwin had been bombed in the Second World War and that there was real fear of a Japanese invasion, but I learn that Katherine was also bombed with loss of one life and many injured. I also discover that US airmen were stationed at airfields as far south as Daly Waters (and hated it); and that stopping places were built to accommodate and feed the personnel on convoys from Alice Springs to Darwin.

I call into the Didj café in Katherine, an Aboriginal art gallery run by an Aboriginal barista offering internet on the side. I buy a delicious coffee, two dollars' worth of internet time to put my travel tales into the ether, and a small but delightful painting of two white cranes. Then as I continue north I have that moment we all dread—I can't visualise replacing my credit card in my wallet and sure enough it isn't there.

It takes me an hour to get back and I finally find it hidden under a pile of paintings. I don't really think that anybody has copied the details—until I reach Litchfield a few days later where a machine tells me 'card not valid'. I immediately assume that someone has taken my details and emptied my bank account. Irrational, illogical or what! It's just an electronic glitch of course but there's always something to produce another grey hair or wrinkle.

I find the Leprechaun Caravan Park in Darwin in the Yellow Pages. It's perfect; only $12 with power— incredibly cheap for the Northern Territory's capital—with a swimming pool, and only five kilometres from the city so my bike is well used again.

308   The park is a haven for international backpackers and within fifteen minutes of arriving I'm in the pool chatting to an Israeli I'd met in Coober Pedy and three Germans I'd shared a camping site with in Litchfield. Next day it's three young men from England who are working out how

to get decent jobs here and throw away their British passports. I chat with a Swiss woman who has been living in an on-site van with her partner since their daughter was born; now that she's two months old they're continuing their Australian explorations. And Marcel and Reineke from Holland who camp next to me are still firm friends.

Leprechaun is crowded, as I'm sure all caravan parks in Darwin are, but I find a spot in a corner with vegetation on two sides to provide shade and a degree of privacy. That's lucky because I develop a foot problem that curtails my walking for about four days; though I can still read, improve my ability to paint trees, chat to co-campers, and hobble to the amenities and swimming pool. Marcel and I commiserate over my collapsed arch and his leg damaged from an argument with a low fence post.

By the time my foot disaster starts I have already restocked the pantry, replaced walking sandals, bought a mobile phone car charger and got a decent pair of small binoculars. Expensive, so thank goodness for plastic—pay now regret later! Luckily it's a Friday: I have already contacted Liz, a friend of a friend, and she chauffeurs me around over the weekend, spoils me and becomes my guide to Darwin's markets, cafés and pubs.

Once mobile again I go to Bathurst Island, one of the homes of the Tiwi Islanders, but I'm not confident enough to go alone so extravagantly take an organised trip. It's a fascinating day: we fly over on a ten-seater plane which is fun and the pilot is *very* casual: 'I have to do this safety talk.

If we get into trouble here's the door and I go first'. The return plane is a 25-seater—quite large really—with two pilots and far more formality.

I see differences between the Tiwi Islanders and the mainland Aboriginal people with whom I've had contact on my travels. Their build and facial features are different, they seem much more relaxed around non-Indigenous people— maybe because the majority of the population on their islands is Tiwi, and their art is unlike anything I've seen on the mainland.

The Tiwis seem to combine their traditions and beliefs with other religions. When we arrive we are welcomed with a traditional 'smoking' ceremony, performed to smoke out the bad spirits and bring in the good. At the end the dancers chant something as they tap our heads and shoulders with leafy branches, then wish us well with: 'May God take care of you for the rest of your journey'. And we visit a beautiful catholic church: white-painted western architecture outside but Tiwi art décor and altar inside.

Darwin is a patchwork of memories. I ride my bike to Fannie Bay Jail and hobble around a sad collection of buildings with photographs of the jail when it was filled with Aboriginal and white inmates. I get to parliament house— a striking building with architecture I really like. The botanical gardens are lovely but divided by a main road. I have a sunset picnic at Mindl Beach with the daughter of a Zimbabwean guide on the Roper River. The bike path to the city snakes across the Stuart Highway and is edged with sprinklers that wet me as much as the grass.

I'm there for the tail end of the Darwin Festival and I see a fascinating piece. A slide show about a woman from Broome who discovers when she's ten years old that the man she thinks is her dad isn't; her biological father was a Japanese pearl fisherman. At forty, having never left Broome before, she decides to go to Japan and find him. A Sydney-based, Japanese documentary maker goes with her and records the journey as a series of photographic slides with narrative and dialogue—an effective medium, a successful search and a moving tale.

Darwin's art gallery is showing the Telstra Indigenous art award entrants with works ranging from traditional to contemporary, from ochres to acrylics, from dots to strong brush strokes. All so interesting I could spend a day with them.

Unexpectedly I love Darwin. I didn't think I wanted to be in a city again but I enjoy its noise, crowds, grime and the buzz.

HEADING EAST
INTO OUTBACK QUEENSLAND

South of Darwin I turn east off the Stuart Highway to Cape Crawford and Borroloola. These outback roads are accessible to me in a conventional vehicle though almost deserted. I don't feel afraid but decide I should try my UHF radio just in case I have an emergency; and it may be working but there's nobody within cooee. I don't worry: I've done the right thing with petrol for once, the road though narrow is surfaced, I have food and water, and if I break down someone will come along—today, tomorrow, the next day.

My first reason for going to Cape Crawford is to get off the main highways and drive as far as possible on secondary roads; the Carpentaria, Tablelands and Barkly Highways are the way to do it. Though wide red stripes on the map, one truck wide in reality. I see few other vehicles but go half onto the shoulder in the face of oncoming cars or vans hoping they will do the same. Mainly it is road trains rushing towards me—in either the rear view mirror or through the windscreen—up to 50 metres long and with no intention of slowing down. These I treat with absolute respect, taking to the shoulder completely. I cannot lose concentration for a moment. I must also watch for kangaroos and cattle (dead and alive), and wedge-tailed eagles feeding on the carrion and likely to add to it. But I love the remoteness of these roads.

Cape Crawford where the Tablelands Highway turns south off the Carpentaria is a natural stopping place on this route. The roadhouse here is known as Heartbreak Hotel; apparently when the owner built it everything that could go wrong did and it broke his heart. As I don't want power I can choose my camping spot anywhere on an enormous grassy area with plenty of trees. Once settled I gravitate to the pub's veranda, an ideal spot to drink a beer and chat. The truckies doing the run between the McArthur River mine and Mount Isa stop here for refreshments—and I join Joe, Barry and a couple of coldies during their stopover.

Heartbreak Hotel is also on the road to Borroloola where people come from all over Australia to catch the barramundi when they are running—as they are now. Fisher people fill up with petrol and grog before completing the journey: I meet one in the ladies loo at 6.30 am and our conversation goes something like this:

'D'ya know what time it opens?' (The 'it' being the office.)

'Sorry, I don't,' is my unhelpful reply.

'Our Mazda uses a lot of fuel towing the boat. Bin on the road from the Isa since eight last night. Had a cuppla hours' sleep. Hit a few roos, but!'

It's the 'hit a few roos' that haunts me.

The other reason I'm staying at Heartbreak Hotel is for the helicopter ride to the Lost City in the Abner Ranges. But the helicopter pilot will only go up with three people so I stay for a second night hoping to find someone to share the cost of the flight with me. The pilot finds a couple who do want to go up, and though it's dusk and later than he usually takes off, he agrees. It's wonderful to watch the sunset as we fly through the Lost City, skim over an escarpment and drop below its rim. This amazing geological formation of sandstone, eroded by the wind into sculpted pillars up to 40 metres high, is estimated to be 1.4 billion years old.

I travel the 400 kilometres south from Cape Crawford to the Barkley Homestead in five hours and see only six vehicles. But about 100 kilometres from the Barkley Highway I pass a ute with a boat on the back and two fellows with their heads in the cab—it looks serious. A couple of kilometres on it occurs to me that they could be in trouble, and if nothing else I can get help for them at the homestead. I do a U-turn and they are just leaving, but stop as I slow

313

down. I'm amused to discover they'd just been rearranging the Esky (car fridge). They are so grateful they insist on giving me a cold beer. It wouldn't occur to me to fear for my own safety and offering help is what you do 'on the road'.

I'm drawn to Queensland's gem-field areas and it's fun talking to all the mad enthusiasts. However, fossicking in piles of rock and dust and patiently sifting buckets of rubble isn't my cup of tea. But good luck to those who happily spend hours on their little stools searching for that magic gem.

NOT A FOUR-STAR CARAVAN PARK IN SIGHT

Of course Barrow Creek and Heartbreak Hotel aren't the only interesting roadhouses or camping spots I find. Once you leave 'proper' caravan parks the world is your oyster and not only is camping at roadside pubs free or cheap, the pubs are a story in themselves. Enjoy three with me.

Curtin Springs, Northern Territory

On my way back from Uluru–Kata Tjuta I stop at the Curtin Springs Roadhouse for that sunset camel ride. I pay an extravagant seven dollars for a powered site beneath a tree in the large camping area, only to discover later that it's free if I don't want power.

At night the manager of the roadhouse lights an enormous fire and campers gather round to exchange stories. On the first night someone sets up karaoke and after a couple of glasses of wine I join in, assuming I will never see any of them again. But of course I do, and they remember me and my singing! Over my frittata and wine at the camp fire I chat to Heather who gives me advice about places to stay and introduces me to the concept of free camping spots around Australia.

Curtin Springs' atmosphere is so relaxed and friendly that I stay for an extra day to wander around the area, read and write, and learn more about these families doing what I wish Ian and I had done.

Daly Waters, Northern Territory

I hear about Daly Waters from travellers I meet along the way. There's a conventional caravan park at a roadhouse where the Stuart Highway intersects the Carpentaria—but that's not it. The Daly Waters pub is a little further north, and west past the turn-off to an old Second World War airfield that's worth a quick visit. The pub has the usual outback décor, a dark and smoky atmosphere you can cut, a bistro in the bar and live entertainment each night.

The camping area is a large patch of dirt offering sites with or without power, plenty of self-contained portable shower/toilets and lots of campers. The ground is red and dusty and the floors of the showers have reddish-grey puddles collecting in the corners, but the water is hot and clean and there's plenty of pressure—the bore here definitely beats Barrow Creek.

I emerge clean and refreshed near where a couple of young English women, travelling in a beaten-up station wagon, have just pitched their tent.

'Fantastic shower,' I say, but their reply of 'You're joking,' doesn't surprise me.

I explain that the facilities may not look the best, but the water's hot, they're roomy and worth a go. As we chat I discover that they are running out of food and offer to share mine. They say they'll buy something in the pub later and invite me to join them. They brave the showers, and like me are glad they do.

We meet up in the bistro (a generous description) for a meal of reasonable quality and price before I make a beer last for two hours as the entertainer, a middle-aged singer guitarist, plays the crowd beautifully; bringing kids up onto the platform to perform with him and getting us to sing along.

Winton, Queensland

I spend two nights in Winton behind the North Gregory pub. The asphalt car park has been converted to a free camping area though only for vans I suspect—I can't imagine hammering in tent pegs! It's dry, dusty and wouldn't be my first choice—I like a tree or two—but by now I'm right into free spots. It turns out better than I expect: compatible co-campers to chat and dine with at the good-value smorgasbord, *free* hot shower and close to Bladensburg National Park.

316　　Winton's fame is based on a story that the song 'Waltzing Matilda' had its first public airing at this pub. How a town's whole tourist attraction can be based on a song is thought provoking. But the Landsborough Highway to Winton has even been renamed the Matilda Highway.

OF COURSE
THE JOURNEY IS THE THING

These 15,000 kilometres over two-and-a-half months are my first real on-the-road adventure, and full of marvellous experiences.

Darwin was always my goal and it feels good to have covered the kilometres that had seemed so daunting on Nolan's map. But of course things go wrong, the most memorable are running out of petrol on the Lasseter Highway—my fault and inexcusable—and getting bogged at Bladensburg where, thanks to Judy my friend and proofreader, the carpet I carry gets us out easily. Both situations initially bring some anxiety but I take them a step at a time, do what seems sensible (dirty word to this 'efficient' sister) and feel fantastic once they are sorted.

Two of my greatest delights are wandering in tiny townships and meeting others on the road. Travellers who include other grey nomads, adventurers from many parts of the world, and families doing what Ian and I never quite got round to—taking their kids off in vans, tents or campers and teaching them about more than just the '3Rs'. The number of families surprises me, and they travel for anything from four weeks to two years, with babies through to teenagers.

But when I make friends on the road, or just meet people I like, it's a two-edged sword. Leaving them can be hard even when I know we'll meet again. And just every now and then it hits me that I am on my own in this adventure. Though the evenings to myself in Ski2 are wonderful—no feelings of loneliness at all. I have two CDs that I occasionally play at night: an Andrew Lloyd Webber collection and *Songbird* by Eva Cassidy; both now bring back wonderful memories.

I had expected the long distances to be monotonous so have an eclectic collection for driving relief—The Beatles, The Seekers, and Simon and Garfunkel to sing along to; Mozart, Vivaldi, Beethoven and Brahms for peaceful listening. But I rarely play them. For the first time in my life I enjoy the voices in my head. If nothing else, on this first solo journey in Ski2 I learn that I am OK alone and that I like my own company. An important lesson.

The Northern Territory is new to me and I love its constantly changing landscape. Alongside the highway might be flat; horizon to horizon, mulga and scrub, then suddenly hills blanketed with trees or a mountain range appears in front or to the side. The journey is a canvas of stunning colours: the orange red of the earth dazzles between the greens, greys and browns, bright blue sky, oranges and browns of rocks, muted greens of the desert plants, then further north the lush greens of life-saving wet seasons proliferate; the black of moonless night skies lit by millions of stars, and the Milky Way is *so* milky.

My interest in Aboriginal culture and history grows apace. Their displacement by white settlers resulted in many generations of disaffected people but their cultural history is fascinating. It ranges from stories of the making of the land told through narration, song and dance to their traditional and contemporary visual arts of paintings, textiles and carvings. In the Stockman's Hall of Fame in

Longreach is a map of Australia's Aboriginal language groups—hundreds of small segments covering our massive land—and it enriches Bruce Chatwin's story *Songlines* that I have been reading.

This journey is a feast of national parks. I love the diverse Australian flora, the bird life, our elusive native animals but best of all is the peace; to describe them in detail would fill another book. There are two, however, I will never be able to go past: Carnarvon Gorge in Queensland and Edith Falls in the Northern Territory. Others that come close are the World Heritage listed Kakadu for its natural beauty and Aboriginal cultural history, though I prefer the less ostentatious Litchfield; and Kings Canyon where the landscape and geology are awe-inspiring.

Even with the freedom of the road there are rituals. One begins on arrival at a stopping place; I realise this one afternoon when I overhear my neighbours and know that I've heard it all before. No matter how large or small the mode of accommodation the first thing is to scrabble through the boxes on board with accompanying dialogue (even if travelling alone). 'Where did I put the cups?' 'Did we buy milk?' 'Where's the bloody bucket?' 'Why did we buy another bowl, we've got ten at home'...

Some people's departure is dead efficient: on the road by 7.30 am and off in a swirl of dust to travel for perhaps eight hours at 110 kph to reach their next destination in record time. The slightly more relaxed have a bite first, are on the road by 8.30 am and enjoy their drive. Then there are a few, like me, who walk a little, stretch a little, listen and look for a few birds, have brewed coffee, fruit salad and muesli, and hit the road at 10 am.

To be honest when I must cover the kilometres I leave before 7 am, though I have discovered that travelling at 85 kph instead of 100 cuts my fuel consumption by a significant 10 per cent.

I develop a morning ritual on this journey that I still use. It's a mantra I chant before leaving an overnight stop to remind me what I *must* do before moving off. SPEWWG-BBMFP, pronounced something like 'spewewg-beebee-emeffpee'—it's quite catchy and works well when I remember it:

S   Sliding window closed—if not it destroys
     the flyscreen

P   Pop-top down—no explanation needed

E   Electricity disconnected—driving off still attached
     would not be good

W   Water topped up—if available and good water

W   Washing taken in—you can work that out

G   Gas turned off—for safety in case of accident

B   Bucket emptied and on board—I've run over five!

B   Bike on board—sounds obvious but nothing is
     certain with my grey-nomad brain

M   Mat on board—I've replaced six 'outdoor' mats!

F   Fridge switched to 12 volt for driving and door
     properly latched

P   Pump (water) switched off—I'm not sure why but I
     do what I'm told.

Ski2 is more than a vehicle to me and we are a good team over all those kilometres. I always speak to her kindly and thank her for her dependability—I'm big on apologies and thanks—and I often pat her on her dashboard. We've been together for six years and 90,000 kilometres, and if we haven't been anywhere for a while she nags me gently as I pass her in the carport, 'When are we going away again? Come on, I've been sitting here for weeks, take me to a national park!'

'The only aspect of our travels that is
interesting to others is disaster.'

—Martha Gellman

FOURTEEN

MISADVENTURES WITH SKI2

Naomi and I are trying not to panic. It is raining and getting dark, and Ski2 is across a dirt road, on a downhill curve. The back wheels are in a ditch and the surface is wet clay.

En route to Canberra, our plan is to spend the night at Jindabyne in the foothills of the Snowy Mountains. We decide to take the road through Mount Kosciuszko National Park as an alternative to the highway, though we can tell from the map that part of the road is unsealed. I'm not worried, Ski2 and I have done dirt roads before, but as we leave Bruthen the rain starts—not heavy just persistent.

At the start of the dirt section the sign simply says 'gravel road for next 40 kilometres', with nothing to suggest a dry-weather road or that four-wheel drive is recommended. I have now learned that 'gravel road' is an all-encompassing term for an unsealed road, and where a gravel surface might be OK in the wet, this certainly isn't!

I am driving, and after a few kilometres I feel the back of the van trying to get away from me so I proceed with caution and stick to the middle of the road where the rougher surface offers better traction. Now, after years more experience, at the first feel of slip I would stop, retreat and take the non-scenic route. But I'm still learning a lot about the 'Ski2 and me' team. We even stop twice just to enjoy the scenery—the trees misty in the rain, the silence, the smell and colour that pervade the wet Australian bush.

For much of this drive we are winding around part of the mountain range, with the slope rising to our left across a ditch that carries a small rushing stream of water, and

324

dropping away to our right. The rain is light but steady—the rain that saturates. We would have made it, slowly and safely, but for an oncoming four-wheel drive. Like me the vehicle holds the centre of the road, but I see it's a four-wheel drive and think that he (generic 'he', might be a 'she') is better equipped to cope with it than Ski2 and can take to the edge, but he doesn't. He stays firmly in the middle. I have nowhere to go except towards the left, which I do gently.

After he passes I move gingerly back towards the centre of the road and as I do, the back of the van goes. We spin 450 degrees and finish up, hearts pounding, adrenaline rushing, with the back wheels in the ditch and the front facing the drop. It could have been worse—we could have gone over the edge.

But it's bad enough. The van is a rear-wheel drive and those wheels are in the ditch; the surface of the road is a slurry of water and clay. We picture something coming around the curve above us and not being able to stop. I have no emergency lamp or reflective triangles, and nothing to put on the road at that curve to warn people. Frightening. Even worse, dusk is falling and we don't want to be across the road all night. I have a mobile phone—very efficient—but in the middle of the mountains have no hope of getting a signal.

We collect all the branches we can find and pull small plants out of the ground, placing them under the rear wheels. To no avail, they just get muddier and wetter. I cannot possibly get a jack under Ski2—she's rear-end into the ditch and I'll get no purchase on that surface anyway. But I have recently read a book about a four-wheel-drive trip

325

where the author describes letting his tyres down to get out of sand—and I understand the theory: more surface area so more traction. We let out some air although I don't have a compressor to re-inflate and don't know how little pressure the tyres can be driven on without damaging them.

After two hours, though it seems like an eternity, Ski2 is out; the final solution is softer tyres, Naomi pushing at the side, and me gently accelerating and using the handbrake to stop her after every little gain. It takes me a while to realise that the centimetres gained from Naomi's push are lost in the moment of moving my right foot from accelerator to brake; and using my left foot on the brake doesn't compute as a possibility in my inflexible brain.

We are unbelievably lucky that nobody comes along from above us, and that we are both determined not to give in.

An amusing (in retrospect) postscript to the story is that by the time we've done all this, the petrol empty light has been on for a while and the nearest town is Jindabyne with no petrol between here and there. We sigh with relief as we pass each milestone on the way: leaving the slurry surface; leaving the dirt road (from here we can camp by the side of the road if necessary); reaching the lights of Jindabyne; and the last as we drive into the caravan park. It is still pouring as we eat peanut butter on toast for dinner, and the facilities are a trek away from our site. But we don't care.

326

Next morning there isn't even sufficient petrol to start Ski2. We borrow a jerry can from the manager of the petrol station at the park and buy enough to start her, and then pull in to fill the tank. After telling our tale to the manager his response is, 'If it's been raining nobody uses that road for forty-eight hours.' A sign on the road or a symbol on the map to indicate a dry-weather road would have been useful. A disaster averted by mere chance, I think.

On my return home I write to the Mount Kosciuszko National Park administrators and describe the circumstances and lucky outcome. I suggest that maybe a 'dry road only' sign would be useful—that was four years ago and I'm still awaiting a reply.

EXPERIENCE IS A TEACHER, BUT I'M A SLOW LEARNER

That Mount Kosciuszko incident is the worst I've had to cope with to date and I couldn't have got out had I been travelling alone. I now have better emergency equipment and more experience in dealing with unexpected events. At the suggestion of a friend who heard my sorry tale, I now carry pieces of carpet to use in similar situations. I also have reflective triangles to warn oncoming motorists of a problem ahead, already used twice: once by me and once to assist in another driver's drama. I now have better knowledge of tyre pressures and a compressor that runs off the cigarette lighter socket that has been used many times to inflate Ski2's tyres after I've been on dirt roads.

There have been other mishaps, too, some of which I should have avoided.

Early on I made a rule that, whatever the price of petrol, I will *always* fill the tank when the gauge falls below half. That was way back when, on one trip, the empty light had

327

been on for over 80 kilometres, and Ski2's 70-litre tank took 64 litres—a close call. It's not an easy rule for someone who watches their cents as carefully as I do, but it should be mandatory even for a compulsive petrol-price-watcher! On at least three other occasions Ski2 has been so close to empty that despite coasting down slopes and minimal acceleration she takes more than 60 litres to fill. Running out of petrol in that Mount Kosciuszko drama was inexcusable: about 15 kilometres before the skid when the gauge was well below half, we had passed the roadhouse at Seldom Seen but decided to continue. I'm definitely slow at learning how to avoid anxiety.

Then I actually run out of petrol. My mental conflict is always about price. I can ignore 1c or 2c a litre extra but in remote areas that impost might be as much as 20c. That's a lot of money in a 70-litre petrol tank—at least one cappuccino, food for dinner or two lunches, a small glass of plonk ...

Returning from Uluru I'm staying at Curtin Springs Roadhouse where the petrol is $1.26 a litre (long before it hits a dollar a litre in the cities) so I don't fill the tank—first mistake. I am going to Kings Canyon and reckon I have enough to get me there without falling far below half a tank, and there'll be petrol at the Kings Canyon Resort.

328   I stay a couple of nights, do the walks and set off back towards the Stuart Highway in the early morning. Way below half but the petrol is $1.35 a litre and I refuse to pay that—second mistake. There are two alternative routes to the Stuart Highway: a short one using Ernest Giles Road

that is unsealed, and a longer one on bitumen roads. There will be no petrol on the Ernest Giles and the surface looks dubious, and it's only 180 kilometres to Mount Ebenezer Roadhouse on the longer route. Perfectly manageable I think—third mistake. After 125 of those 180 kilometres the empty light is on. Nerve-racking, but if I go easy on the accelerator it will be fine.

I arrive at the Mount Ebenezer Roadhouse to be greeted by a sign on the pump. 'No Petrol'.

'Shit, shit, shit!'

A four-wheel drive diesel vehicle is just pulling out. I ask if by any chance they are carrying any unleaded petrol—for a mower, speedboat, anything. Of course not. So I adopt my best helpless female look and enter the roadhouse.

'Do you have *any* unleaded petrol? Please.' I'm pleading now.

'Nup. Might get some tomorrow,' says the young lady behind the counter.

'I'm already running on the empty light. Don't you have a can? I'll pay extra. Just enough to get me to the highway.' I know there's a petrol station at Erldunda on the Stuart Highway, another 55 kilometres.

'Nup. Sold out first thing this morning.'

'Thanks, anyway,' I say, though not sure for what.

'What'll youse do? Better stay 'til tomorrow.' The Mount Ebenezer Roadhouse is in the middle of nowhere, without even a camel ride to enjoy. No thanks!

'I'll get as far as I can then hitch a lift to the highway.'

And that's what I do.

I play the accelerator so delicately, let the automatic transmission ease me along, and coast where I can. Luckily it's not a hilly part of the world and I take the few uphill slopes very gently. I am four kilometres from the Stuart Highway when Ski2 gently dies and I glide her onto the shoulder.

I apologise to her and assure her that it's not her fault, that she has done very well and just needs to be patient. We'll get going again.

I check the mobile phone I carry for just such emergencies and unusually I have a signal, although only one bar of charge—my cigarette-lighter phone recharger hasn't been working. I have the highest level of cover with the RACV for just such emergencies and use a free call number to Victoria. They transfer me to Northern Territory, who take their time as I keep watching that one bar come and go.

Eventually I am told that they *can* deliver petrol, but it will cost me $45 for delivery, plus petrol of course. The petrol station at Erldunda isn't an authorised NTAA dealer so it has to come from Stuarts Well (and that's not even on my map).

Wondering why I paid extra dollars for all the RACV luxuries, I turn down their offer and go back to Plan A. I put the phone away (absolutely no battery now), slather myself in sun block, and with hat on head and credit card in wallet, I'm ready to thumb my first lift for decades. The traffic on this road is grey nomads, young families and tour buses so I feel quite safe—and if I don't like the look of a driver I don't have to get in. I stand by Ski2 with her emergency lights flashing and, within minutes, a Victorian couple stop and are happy to drop me at Erldunda.

A lovely fella at the petrol station (who calls me 'mate') lends me a jerry can with a flexible nozzle so I don't have to dismantle the bed to get to my jiggle siphon. I buy ten litres of petrol—another mistake. Two litres would have been enough and a lot lighter to carry. I approach drivers of the vehicles in the petrol station but no-one is going towards Uluru, and thinking about it now I should have gone into the café and yelled out.

So walking with thumb out I set off with my ten kilograms of petrol (yes, that's what it weighs!). About ten cars pass me, a couple of them slow down to take a look then pull away. I don't think I appear dangerous: I'm walking, on my own, there's no foliage to hide accomplices and I'm carrying a petrol can—what I'm doing must be pretty obvious. But is that the problem? Is it something to do with carrying petrol in the Northern Territory? I continue walking, knowing that I can make the distance if I must, but those kilograms get heavier with each step.

At last a four-wheel drive vehicle stops, another Victorian couple about my age; I suspect he was the instigator of the stopping because she is quite ungracious. I explain that my vehicle is only three kilometres along the road; grovel a little—I will be extremely grateful, forever in their debt. By now it is almost 10 am and the day is heating up.

The wife (I assume) says, 'I don't know if we can fit you in, we've got a lot of camping gear.'

'I can squeeze into a very small space, and the petrol can sit on my knee.' Wondering why they stopped at all, but not wanting to let them go.

331

'Of course we can fit her in.' Hubby joins in and now it's two against one so I think I'm OK.

And I am. She grudgingly puts a few packages into the rear of the Land Rover, making enough space for me on the back seat. I express my gratitude again and nurse my petrol. In ten minutes I'm back at Erldunda, returning the can and filling with 60 litres of petrol.

In my journal I castigate myself with: 'Well, I did it. I ran out of petrol! Stupid (and at Erldunda it was only 3c per litre cheaper anyway!) Not following my own rules'.

You'd think I would have learnt. Since then I've almost run out of petrol at least twice, sometimes because the expected petrol isn't there, but usually because I think I'll get it more cheaply somewhere up ahead. I've *almost* learnt. I swear never again—at least until next time!

OK, THE REAR VIEW IS RESTRICTED BUT EVEN SO ...

Naomi's and my next mishap occurs on Kangaroo Island—a dirt road again. We blame bad signage for this one (notorious in South Australia and even friends in Adelaide agree on this).

The native garden we are on our way to visit has a sign outside the gate, but it's small and not what you'd call obvious and we've seen no brown 'Tourist Attraction' indicator, nothing to warn us of its imminence. So we are past the gateway before we see it. If we hadn't been on a dirt road and travelling quite slowly we might still be looking for it.

332

Naomi is driving and she pulls up gently—all OK so far. But as she begins a three-point turn and I'm asking, 'Why don't you just reverse?' (don't you hate passenger-seat drivers) the back gets caught on the *very* hard edge of the road. At first we think we are bogged—I even get out the bits of carpet and put them under the wheels, but their spinning as Naomi tries to move us forward just drops the back even further and we are completely jammed. Around a curve—again—what is it with Ski2 and curves. But this time I have my reflective emergency triangles. As we are stuck well across the road I put one of them where oncoming traffic will be warned of a 'situation'—as the military say—up ahead.

An elderly couple stop. Smartly dressed, off to lunch somewhere and apologise that they cannot help. He says we should let air out of the tyres—helpful, but wrong. Then a charming young French couple pull up. He is very gung-ho and tries to help me jack up the back of the van. Unfortunately he will not take my word that where he has positioned the jack is not right and I have a slight bend in the bodywork to prove it. A positive is that I realise that I don't know the rear jack points—Tut! Tut! Jackie—and the diagram in the van manual is useless. We get out my loo-digging spade and he tries to dig the back out with great enthusiasm despite the terrain being solid rock. His companion tells me she is used to driving in snow and has many suggestions, all of which we try but to no avail. Ski2 must like it here, she has no desire to move other than settling even more firmly on the shoulder.

333

Our saviour arrives at last in the shape of a local with his four-wheel drive ute and a strong tow rope. Five minutes later we are picking up an assortment of very dirty tools, jacks and carpet and ready to visit the native garden. Shaken, hot and dirty. But the garden is wonderful—and calming.

As my email to friends says: 'Another dirt road lesson learned (I hope!)'.

THAT CARPET COMES INTO ITS OWN, AS DOES BUSH PHILOSOPHY

I've been carrying that get-out-of-a-boggy-situation carpet around for a couple of years—behind my seat along with my solar panel, my piece of pipe to extend the wheel-brace handle, my steering wheel lock and Ski2's table. The carpet has been used by another traveller who was having trouble getting out of a boggy dip, but not by me—yet. I suppose it's like insurance (though a lot cheaper): it's good to know you have it if you need it.

I'm at Winton in Queensland, close to Bladensburg National Park and I'm ready to spend another night in a park. Bladensburg isn't in my national parks' book but the details given by the tourist information office sound just what I need. I do the sensible thing and check with them and a couple of locals whether the unsealed access road is suitable for a conventional vehicle; I am assured that it is.

It's only about 30 kilometres to the camping ground via a circuit road into and through the park from just outside town, and the advice given has been right. The road is corrugated in places, with a few potholes, but taken

334

carefully it is perfectly manageable—and I'm looking forward to camping alongside the creek which I am assured has water in it.

All goes well until I turn into the camping area. Fifty metres in the track descends, only a short way but quite steeply, and as I start down I feel the wheels losing their grip. I am in sand—after clay slurry my greatest fear—and I can do nothing, the track is too narrow to turn so I have to keep going. A few metres on is another short descent, not as steep but the wheels lose traction again. Then I am into the camping area and it's as beautiful as expected—shady trees alongside a water-filled creek, level sites, one caravan and me with Ski2. Perfect. Except that I am now nervous about getting out in the morning.

Deep sand in a two-wheel drive vehicle is almost unmanageable. It requires a four-wheel drive and probably full-slip differential (the wheels working independently of each other), but I don't have any of those goodies. There's another rig there: a large four-wheel drive vehicle and a caravan. The van hasn't been unhitched but this vehicle *might* be my only way out through the sand.

At first I think the man sitting peacefully under a tree reading is camping by himself, and after popping Ski2's top and turning on the gas I disturb his solitude.

'Excuse me, sorry to bother you. Will you be here in the morning?'

'Yeees?' A questioning uncertainty in his voice.

'The track's sandy and I wondered if I need a hand with a tow or a push, whether you might be able to help.'

335

'We're staying, but I'm not unhitching the van.' Not unfriendly, but neither is it enthusiastic.

'That's OK. If I need any help it will probably only be a push while the wheels gets a grip. I've got carpet and I can let the tyres down but I'll feel better if I know there's someone here.'

'I suppose so,' is the grudging response.

Not a perfect result, but better than nothing. I walk up to the track with a stick to try and ascertain how deep the sand is. It's very deep, the hard surface well below what I imagine I'll need.

Walking back to the camping area I decide that I'll stay if my neighbour is willing to help if I get into trouble, otherwise I'll get out now. I approach him again.

'Sorry to be a nuisance, but I need to know if you'll give me a hand if I need it. I probably won't, but just in case. If not, I'll try to get out now and go back to Winton.'

At this his wife erupts from their caravan (my first sight of her). She says she's surprised at my cheek, that they don't want to unhitch their van and that my suggestion about going back to Winton is a good one. Strange reaction—usually travellers help each other—but who knows what might have caused this response. I'm not sure why I think going without their help now will be better than without their help in the morning, but I guess it's peace of mind I'm after.

336   I love the camping area—it really is peaceful and pretty—but I won't sleep easily in the uncertainty of the sand, or their company. So I pack up and leave. Gently, I drive up the inclines and the first is fine, but as I suspected I get bogged in the steeper one. Time for the carpets. I lay

them in front of the rear wheels, lightly accelerate and move on. No problem. As I'm picking up the carpets I hear shouts from behind, but ignore them. I drive the circuit through and out of the park, then back to Winton and the free camping behind the pub where a crowd of us share drinks and a cheap counter tea. Who needs unfriendly co-campers.

This isn't the end of the story.

I run into the campers again at the Longreach Caravan Park a few days later. The wife informs me that she told the ranger at Bladensburg that there was an 'English woman' who didn't know what she was doing and could be in trouble somewhere in the park.

I inform her that I am Australian *not* English, that I knew what I was doing, and that though I *had* got bogged I was able to get myself out. I had been cross with them because of their unwillingness to help but am well over my anger. Interestingly in a book I'm reading at the time I come across an American Indian saying that expresses my thoughts: 'Don't criticise your neighbour until you have walked ten miles in his moccasins'. Quite right.

AND OF COURSE
THERE ARE BATTERY MISFORTUNES

Ski2 has two batteries, both of which recharge as I drive but both will (of course) go flat without due care. A battery's age, its quality, how often and how flat you allow it to get, will affect its life. But it will die eventually. At the time of writing, I've flattened both Ski2's batteries—and I mean completely, irrecoverably, no half measures with me.

337

The first hardly warrants a mention: the old chestnut of leaving the lights on—I'm sure you've all done it but I'm telling you anyway! Penny from England shares my first long journey with Ski2 and we are driving up Green Mountain in Lamington National Park on a grey rainy day. The road is winding and narrow in places so lights are the go. We just want to get started on the walk when we arrive despite the rain absolutely sheeting down. In fact I have photos of us 20 metres up at the lookout in a fig tree, in our rain jackets and saturated. We walk, picnic in the rain, eventually returning to Ski2 hours later to find no sign of spark in her battery. There's no sign of lights either of course, and it's only when the RACQ serviceman connects Ski2 to his jump-start battery that I realise why the battery is flat.

But a two-hour wait for a serviceman is when a campervan comes into its own—we have tea-making facilities, games to play and books to read. Definitely not a hardship.

Easily fixed, and as long as a phone is available and you are not *too* far away from a service facility, or you have jumper leads and a sympathetic car driver close by, it will always be easy. (In fact, had Ski2 been a manual vehicle it would have been even simpler as we are at the top of a very long hill.) I now carry jumper leads with me at all times and have a back-up battery so I can jump-start myself if necessary—sounds slightly rude, doesn't it?

338

The second time I flatten a battery completely I am travelling alone. I'm an avid journal keeper and email writer so, before going to Cairns and The Tip in 2004 I source a second-hand laptop, an IBM Think Pad—not that it does a lot of thinking. I purchase a power cable to plug into a car-lighter socket to run the laptop and recharge its battery as I drive. As I rarely stay in places with power, I plug the laptop into the socket for the back-up battery because I have a solar panel to recharge it—when I remember to plug it in!

I am at The Boulders, a gorgeous free camping spot south of Cairns where, carried away by the creative environment, I forget about battery-flattening until the laptop beeps at me and says it is about to die (maybe it *is* thinking), so I shut it down. No harm to laptop—it just needs a long drive or 240 volts to recharge its battery—but Ski2's back-up battery is completely dead. Bad mistake with that type of battery, I subsequently learn. My plug-in fluoro light won't light, and the internal 12-volt lamps are very sad—no reading that night. By the time I reach Cairns the next day there is enough power for the internal lights but it won't hold a charge. Cactus as they say. But as Craig—my Ski2 Upkeep Angel—later says, I've had the battery for four years and let it flatten more than I should, so it's done well.

I've subsequently discovered that the back-up battery was only trickle charging and was probably never fully charged. I had a neat little gizmo that indicated—with green, red and amber lamps—whether the battery was fully charged, flat or somewhere in between (I think it was usually at the bottom of the latter). Now, along with a marine-strength, deep-cell battery I have better cables to recharge it properly, and a smarter gizmo that shows actual voltage and the amount of charge going into the battery (much more technical) and I'll really have to work at letting it get flat. But most important this battery won't mind if I do—Yay! If your eyes have glazed reading this techo stuff don't worry, just remember 'marine-strength' and 'deep-cell' and you can't go wrong.

In 2006 I'm sure I've destroyed the solar panel, the wonderful deep-cell battery and the gizmo all at one stroke. I'm camped at Ormiston Gorge in the West MacDonnell Ranges, one of my favourite places in the world. I've been without power for many days and have only driven short distances, and I'm going walking for the day so I plug in the solar panel. Even on overcast days some recharging happens and I'm interested in just how much. I don't have to clip the gizmo onto the battery I just plug it into a socket close to the one for the solar panel. I do, there's a large puff of smoke, a horrible smell of burning and melting plastic and all the gizmo lights expire.

I grab my fire extinguisher, lift up the seat and look behind the small metal plate that contains these two sockets. Luckily it's not actually on fire, but there's an awful mess of melted plastic and blackened wires. With fingers crossed and a doubting heart I turn on an internal light—it still works so at least I didn't flatten the battery, but now I have no way of recharging it.

What the hell—the worst that will happen is that I'll run out of light and not be able to read at night; I'll just have to sit around the campfire with other campers a little longer. I have a few more days planned in the West MacDonnells and refuse to cut them short—time enough to sort it out when I get back to Alice Springs. In fact one of the campers is from that city and recommends an auto electrician.

I have to spend a couple of days in Alice but I haven't done any major damage. I just shorted out the two sockets with the jack, and the electrician assures me it's easy done. He rewires where necessary and puts in a fuse that will just blow if I short it again.

And I have time in Alice to sort out a camera that I dropped when I tripped in Redbank Gorge west of Ormiston. I could feel paranoid about these two things happening at the same time, but I don't. Accidents happen, things get sorted out and I was never in danger—unless Ski2 had gone up in flames of course.

Having got to the end of these 'misadventures' it seems as if I've spent a lot of time dealing with things that go wrong, paying for extra peace of mind, fixing things which, through my negligence or just circumstance, need attention, and generally that it's all very depressing. Anything but! At time of penning these tales I have travelled almost 90,000 kilometres in Ski2 so that's not a bad average of kilometres per problem.

I love journeying with her and any mishap is fixable. Even better, I have a sense of achievement each time I deal with something that goes wrong. As I say somewhere else, I can add another notch to the belt of challenges met and strengths found.

Ski2 continues to go well; she and I are a successful team and luckily she forgives me my sins of omission. Generally I look after her, never speak unkindly, apologise profusely when I have been uncaring and *always* thank her for her dependability, loyalty and protection.

'It may, I think, be justly observed,
that few books disappoint their readers
more than the narrations of travellers.'

—Samuel Johnson

FIFTEEN

A TRAVELLING WRITER OR
A WRITING TRAVELLER?

People who read my stories ask how I remember events in such detail, especially years after they happened. I am an avid keeper of journals—handwritten and lengthy—scribbling details of places I go, people I meet, conversations enjoyed, good and bad experiences, the emotions felt, and the few facts I remember.

These journals often include memory-jogging scraps of paper—a theatre ticket, a library card, a café bill, a shopping list, and even a police report. Having journals stolen on two different occasions was devastating—far worse than the inconvenience of those plastic cards going! For some reason it didn't happen at the start of a journey, when my ageing brain might recall details, but after weeks when I could perhaps remember where I had been and what I was doing, but not moments or feelings. The journals are wonderfully evocative of what I was doing and how I felt when I wrote them.

When I first dip into one I cannot believe how much depth my words bring back: sadness and joy, smells and sounds, colours and textures—the handwriting is incredibly powerful. Before travelling to Cairns in Ski2 in 2004 I buy a second-hand laptop, thinking it will be easier than handwriting. I have arthritis and after a few minutes of concentrated writing my hand begins to hurt and my writing becomes illegible, even to me. But I find the computer-based journals soulless—the printed words on those pages cannot move me in the way my handwritten scribbles do.

But the pain in my hands becomes irrelevant or, more strangely, disappears once I realise that the handwritten journals and their scruffy pages—stained with tears, soup and coffee, even disgusting scraps of food—truly portray my experiences.

Often the journals are just exercise books with a scribbled note on the cover that says which 'Ski' journey it was and to where. And they look interesting—tatty pages with extra ones stuck in where I forgot to take it on an expedition; bulging with memory scraps, lists, recipes, and names and email addresses of people I've met. Often one exercise book isn't enough so I must find another, whether from a market in Chau Doc in Vietnam, a shop in Stavanger in Norway, or the newsagent at Agnes Water in Queensland.

HOW DOES A TRAVELLER BECOME A WRITER?

When I began travelling I had no idea that I'd eventually be putting my journeys into published form; inspiring people to seize the day, to follow a dream and do something they have always wanted to do. I was just going on a holiday to escape the reality of widowhood and an empty nest, and to explore a small part of this wonderful world in which we live.

I don't even remember why I'd put an exercise book in my backpack. I had been a computer consultant and quality assurance manager—the most non-creative pair of roles you can imagine. I have people skills, organisational skills, report-writing skills, and even good technical-writing skills. But writing creatively? I don't think so. (Although some people who have had dealings with consultants might suggest that everything they do is based on fantasy and

345

creativity!) Before I even leave Australia on my first journey I have hours to fill in at the airport, so I pull out that exercise book and describe my introduction to solo adventuring.

I'm on the airport bus when reality strikes: I'm actually retired and off journeying alone; and I feel excitement, apprehension and amazement at what I'm doing. It is also on the bus that I realise the next stage of my life is beginning and, as I later write in my first published book, 'needing a symbol of where I am now, I move my wedding ring to my right hand—and Ian is with me'. Eight years on and he, and the ring, are still with me.

When I start scribbling it's more than just the bare facts that I record—I've been on an emotional roller coaster, and never having been one to keep my feelings hidden they flow onto the paper.

By the start of 2005 I have been travelling and journal-keeping for about six years. I have accumulated thousands of kilometres in the air and on the ground; and thousands of handwritten lines in eight journals that range from a beautiful hard-cover book given to me by a friend to scraps of paper used when I have nothing left to write on.

The early journals are just words—thoughts, sadness-filled sentences, joyful jottings and possible plans. The brochures, maps, tickets and goodness knows what else come home with me in plastic bags. Some might be stuck into a memory book with photos, and maps might be kept for later use but the majority finish up in the recycle bin. Until I take scissors and sticky tape with me: and then brochures, train and theatre tickets, and café bills enhance my words.

But how did these journals become published tales? That laptop should have been a great way to write journals and the emails that my friends expect to receive as I travel, but I find I hate the electronic journals—and not just because the laptop flattens my battery! I give it to a friend and revert to wonderful handwritten books. But in a previous incarnation I had been a computer person and the keyboard, an extension of my brain, gets my itchy fingers going. It's time to take those paper journals and get them into some sort of order.

I'm home in September wanting to begin; to start with that first journal from the airport—sadness and all—before working through each of them until I reach the soulless electronic one. I want to give them some shape, improve the structure, but most importantly get them formalised and onto my 'proper' computer so that they can't fade and take my memories with them.

However, Ski2 and I are committed to going to the Flinders Ranges with Naomi for October and November so sadly I cannot start; itchy fingers notwithstanding. And worse, another damn journal will be generated. But I promise myself that on 1 January 2005 I will begin. I'll be disciplined and go back to work—Monday to Friday, nine to five.

I am and I do. But suddenly the transfer of my journals into electronic form grows into much more. I realise that my words are my life philosophy: always to be ready for another adventure; never sitting at home afraid to take on another challenge; ready to grasp life with both hands. Moreover these scruffy exercise books might help others and give them the courage to start something that they really want to do.

347

I also realise that my words are actually quite good. My disjointed sentences and messy prose scrubs up quite well. The vivid moments they recall—of things seen and done and feelings of sadness, loneliness, joy and excitement—are transformed from fading pages into published book.

I still have the journals and however 'safe' it might be to have them in electronic form, it's the handwriting and pasted memory-joggers I go to when I want to remember a whole picture and not just the outline. So you can understand why for me having a journal stolen is one of the worst things that can happen. It's not just the challenge of reconstructing events and emotional states; far worse is losing all those wonderful bits of paper, those irreplaceable memories.

Samuel Johnson, whose proposition at the start of this chapter I try to avoid, also wrote: 'Every writer of travels should consider that, like all other authors, he undertakes either to instruct or please, or to mingle pleasure with instruction'. I hope my writing brings as much pleasure to my readers as my journals do to me—I spent too many years writing instruction manuals to do that any more! The only 'instructions' I would give are to seize the day, take life in both hands, and unless something is likely to kill or maim you, never say 'No'.

ACKNOWLEDGMENTS

My thanks to Kay Scarlett, Sandra Davies and Colette Vella and the Murdoch team for their support (yet again), and their encouragement and help as we journeyed together towards another book. Also eternal gratitude to friends without whom developing my manuscript would be much harder: Monica Bois who first insisted I 'do something' with my writing and continues to nag (if I need it); Judy Turner, a natural-born proofreader; Judy Lashin with whom I share a glass of red as I read my opus aloud in search of the elusive bits that don't work; and Greg Sargent who keeps me sane when my computer or printer goes on strike.

First published in 2008 by Pier 9, an imprint of Murdoch Books Pty Limited

Murdoch Books Australia
Pier 8/9
23 Hickson Road
Millers Point NSW 2000
Phone: +61 (0) 2 8220 2000
Fax: +61 (0) 2 8220 2558
www.murdochbooks.com.au

Murdoch Books UK Limited
Erico House, 6th Floor
93–99 Upper Richmond Road
Putney, London SW15 2TG
Phone: +44 (0) 20 8785 5995
Fax: +44 (0) 20 8785 5985
www.murdochbooks.co.uk

Chief Executive: Juliet Rogers
Publishing Director: Kay Scarlett

Editor: Sandra Davies
Cover design: Alex Frampton
Cover photograph: Getty Images
Internal design: Jacqueline Richards
Production: Kita George

Text copyright © Jackie Hartnell 2008
Design copyright © Murdoch Books Pty Limited 2008

All rights reserved. No part of this publication may be reproduced, stored in a
retrieval system or transmitted in any form or by any means, electronic, mechanical
photocopying, recording or otherwise without prior permission of the publisher.

National Library of Australia Cataloguing-in-Publication Data

Hartnell, Jackie.
Still no fixed address.
ISBN 9781741960662 (pbk.).
1. Hartnell, Jackie – Travel. I. Title.
920.72

Printed by Midas Printing in 2008. PRINTED IN CHINA.

DISCLAIMER
Still No Fixed Address tells my tales as I remember them. When I describe shared
experiences they are my perceptions; others might remember them differently.